WHAT GOD EXPECTS FROM ORDINARY PEOPLE

Mere
Morality

Lewis B. Smedes

Grand Rapids, Michigan
WILLIAM B. EERDMANS PUBLISHING COMPANY

Copyright © 1983 by Wm. B. Eerdmans Publishing Co.
255 Jefferson Ave. SE, Grand Rapids, MI 49503

Reprinted 1996

Library of Congress Cataloging in Publication Data

Smedes, Lewis B.
  Mere Morality.

  1. Christian ethics—Popular works. I. Title.
BJ1261.S63 1983   241   82-21071
ISBN 0-8028-3571-6

CONTENTS

To
WES SMEDES
Caring Brother
Good Friend
Christian Person

INTRODUCTION

Let me explain what I mean by the title *Mere Morality*.

I take it for granted that most people believe there is such a thing as morality, that our lives have a moral component, that we make real moral choices.

We have a deep primitive sense that morality is woven into the fabric of our humanness. Morality is not a con game that makes losers out of those who play it seriously. It is not a false rumor planted in an insecure society to help the weak keep the powerful in check by playing on their conscience. Nor is morality just an impressive name for the strong feelings we have about some things, a word we use to add some clout to our complaints. Morality is a basic component of any human sort of life, a reality we feel surely even if we cannot define it clearly. We do have choices, and they are sometimes between real moral options. The choice we make can put us in the wrong with God and our ideal selves—or leave us in the right. And being in the right means being in harmony with God's design for our humanity.

Morality, then, emerges from what we are as human beings. To demoralize life is to dehumanize it. The call of morality is an invitation to the truly human life.

What do I mean by *mere* morality? It is not morality *plus* something else. What I am going to talk about in this book is not a special brand of morality for extraordinary folk. Mere morality does not make you a saint or a hero. All it makes for is humane living. Perhaps I can make this clearer by distinguishing "mere morality" from certain special features of Christian living.

1. *Mere morality is not the same as Christian devotion.* Those who follow Jesus are expected to be much more than moral. They are expected to honor Jesus Christ as Lord, to be members of a worshiping community, to bear their cross and to suffer with Christ. Mere morality does not obligate people to undertake these specifically Christian acts of devotion; it only requires what needs to be done if we are to be human.

2. *Mere morality is not heroic.* God may call some people to live unusually sacrificial lives—to give all their possessions to the poor, or to give up sex and children for a life of unencum-

bered service. Mere morality does not, for the most part, summon us to the peaks of heroic devotion; it deals with life on the plains. It does not ask whether we should give our body to be burned, but whether it is permissible to get a divorce, have an abortion, or tell a lie to help a friend. To be sure, this distinction is not absolute. The command of love calls all of us to the limits of morality and gently nudges us beyond. Still, morality is what God expects, not just of saints and heroes, but of all common folk.

3. *Mere morality is not for believers only.* It has to do with what God expects of all people, regardless of whether they believe in him. You do not escape God's demands by denying that he exists—any more than you stop being God's creature by denying his creation. He does not cancel his rules when you trade in your faith. He may, if worse comes to worst, leave you to stew in your own denial—as Paul tells us in Romans 1. But while he may leave you on your own to act as if there were no God to obligate you, he does not annul his own demands.

4. *Mere morality does not make anyone a Christian.* That happens only by grace. Such grace provides powerful motives for being moral. A notion of grace that allows a person to remain indifferent to morality is a cheap and un-Christian idea. But grace brings more than a new moral drive; it offers joy and peace and hope—gifts abounding far beyond morality. By comparison with grace and its gifts, all morality is mere morality. Grace is the ultimate; morality is what Bonhoeffer called the penultimate.

5. *Mere morality is not mysterious.* Any reasonable person can understand the sense of what God expects ordinary people to do in living their human lives together. God may use a special act of revelation to let his people clearly *know* the rudiments of morality. But what he reveals is not irrational or bizarre. If I try to explain the holy Trinity to my unbelieving friends, I'm likely to elicit a bewildered smile. But if I talk to them about the place of honesty in social life or the problem of private property, an intelligent dialogue is probable. They may not agree with everything the Bible says about morality, but they can understand it.

6. *Mere morality is not sectarian.* God's moral will is not Protestant or Catholic; it is human and ecumenical. I cannot get out of my own skin, of course. I am a white male, middle-class Protestant living in Southern California. Readers familiar with the history of Christian doctrine will find evidence in what follows that the tradition which has shaped my life and thought is Reformed, Calvinist, evangelical. But if anyone is seeking a special

"evangelical morality," this is not the place to look. What I have tried to do in writing this book is merely to think straight, out of a Christian perspective. If what I write cannot stand up under reasonable Christian inspection, it has no right to qualify as evangelical either. What God expects of ordinary people, he expects of them as his creatures and his children. It is, to use C. S. Lewis's famous expression, as a "mere Christian" that I have tried to understand God's will for what is merely moral and therefore merely human.

In saying this about the title, I have already said a lot about the point of view that shapes the contents of this book. I believe that God does reveal to us what he expects us to do, and that what he expects us to do is the sort of thing that people must do if they are going to live as human beings. Of course, much remains to be said about how we *know* it and how we *do* it.

*   *   *

I want to conclude this introduction by thanking some extraordinary people. I am uniquely grateful to Robert Ferguson, doctoral candidate at Fuller Seminary, for preparing the index and the questions for discussion. To Dr. Marguerite Shuster, thanks for encouraging me early on, in spite of all the rough edges in the draft she read for me. Thanks to Dr. Richard Mouw for reading the whole manuscript, saving me from several mistakes, and encouraging me nevertheless to get on with it. To Margo Houts, thanks for skilfully transforming my wretchedly messy manuscripts into beautiful copy on her marvelous word processing machine; and thanks to Karyl Lynn Burns, Linda Harter, and Michael Stribling for tending to my numerous revisions. Thanks, too, to my student Linda Smith who helped me especially with the chapter on property, and to my friend Mary Tregenza who helped me care more about the style of the book. Finally, thanks to my graduate assistant, Ted Dorman, for much helpful advice along the way.

I am more indebted than I can say—more, probably, than I even know—to my friend and editor, Marlin Van Elderen; his generous and intelligent work on my writing has, in this book and others, made me look better than I deserve.

So far I have mentioned only people who have had their hands on the manuscript for this book. I owe far more to many teachers from whom I have learned. Some are still teaching, others are at home with God; some taught me face-to-face, others taught me though we have never met. I thank them all; and

x   the others will indulge me if I mention by name only Henry Stob, who showed me by his example what it can be like to think clearly before the demands of reason and humbly before the face of God.

Finally, thanks to my family for sustaining me when I despaired of ever finishing this book; theirs is the last laugh.

Pasadena, California   LEWIS B. SMEDES

Mere
Morality

He is a little man in a long green coat and a cocked hat, standing with one leg on a steep roof, playing the fiddle. He is all of us, trying to make some meaningful music out of our lives but lacking a level place to stand on. "We are all fiddlers on the roof, trying to scratch out a pleasant little tune without falling down and breaking our necks." And how do we keep our balance? "I'll tell you," sings Tevye in the opening song of the musical inspired by Chagall's painting, "in one word, I'll tell you, tradition! Because of our tradition, everybody knows who he is and what God expects him to do."

To know in advance what God expects us to do—before a new wind threatens to blow us off the roof, before a new crisis shakes our foundations—would be a great gift! Is it possible? Are there signals from God—directions, norms, rules, commandments?

To people cut off from any moral or spiritual tradition, perhaps hankering for something to help them keep their balance on the slippery shingles of freedom, any claim to represent what God expects us to do may evoke recollections of a childhood faith forever lost. Still, freedom without direction and responsibility without rules get to be burdensome after a while, and we may be more ready than we have been for a while to ask whether there is a way to know the will of God. Is there any help for us fiddlers as we try to scratch out our individual tunes without falling off the roof?

We are talking about God's will for the stubborn and haunting presence in our lives that we call moral, the sense that keeps us wondering whether we are in the right or the wrong with our own conscience or with some standard that outranks even conscience. To ask what God expects us to do is to ask how we can know whether we are doing the *right* thing. This question flits about the edges of our minds even after we have earned a dollar or two, felt beautiful feelings, and created exciting relationships.

It is a truism today that we are in a crisis of morals. The crisis is not simply that people are doing wrong things; that has been going on since the Fall in Eden. The crisis is the loss of a shared understanding of what is right. Worse, it is a crisis of

2 doubt as to whether there even is a moral right or wrong at all. The most obvious and sensational evidence of the crisis is in sex and marriage, but it reaches almost every other arena of life as well. Can anyone know any more "who he is and what God expects him to do?"

The Jewish people of Anatevka knew what God expected of them because they knew their traditions. Christian believers today are not as certain that their ethnic or religious traditions serve as signposts to God's will. For some, this ambivalence may come from having neglected their own tradition. But they also recall how often Jesus opposed Jewish traditions. "Why don't your disciples follow the traditional rules?" the Pharisees asked him, certain that tradition told them what God expected of them. Jesus threw the challenge back. They had lost track of God's will: "You leave the commandments of God and hold fast the tradition of men" (Mark 7:8). Paul, though shaped by Jewish tradition, came to hate the rules and regulations of all traditions, and he cringed when Christian believers kowtowed to them: "Why do you submit to regulations. . . , human precepts and doctrines?"—in other words, tradition—he demanded (Col. 2:20, 22).

But if the New Testament makes us wary of tradition as the way to know what God expects us to do, how do we know and where do we look for God's will? Does the answer come in the wind, which "blows where it wills, and you hear the sound of it, but you do not know where it comes from or where it is going" (John 3:8)? Does God speak to each of us privately through the intimations of the spirit, heart to heart, mind to mind, divine Word direct to human soul? Must each of us go it alone while waiting for the voice of the Lord?

No, says the sage of Ecclesiastes, it is neither tradition nor private revelation which tells you how to find out what God expects you to do. I will give you the answer in one word: "Let us hear the conclusion of the whole matter: Fear God, and keep his *commandments*; for this is the whole duty of man" (Eccl. 12:13). The direct word from the commanding Lord answers the challenge of keeping one's balance while playing the fiddle on the steep slopes of this risky life. "Then shall I not fall and break my neck, when I have respect unto all thy commandments" (Ps. 119:6). If Tevye had been a biblical Hebrew instead of a modern Russian Jew, he too would have said: the commandments, the

Torah, the law of God! And Jesus would agree, for when a rich
young ruler asked him what he should do, Jesus did not say,
"Consult your tradition," but "You know the commandments"
(Mark 10:19; Luke 18:20).

To read through the first five books of the Old Testament
is almost to be washed away in a cascade of commands covering
an enormous variety of human situations which might arise within
the ancient community of Israel. There are commandments for
settling civil conflicts, regulating cultic customs, and guiding the
moral lives of the people who were brought together in a covenant they made with the Lord God at the foot of Mt. Sinai. The
religious and moral nucleus of these is the "decalogue," the Ten
Commandments.

We are told that God wrote the Ten Commandments with
his own finger on two tablets of stone at the top of the mountain.
A cloud covering the mountain marked it as a holy place, which
the people, encamped around it, were not to touch. God called
Moses to the top of the mountain. He went up and came down
several times; we cannot keep track of all his meetings with God
at the summit. But each time Moses came down, he brought
more commandments for the life of the covenant people. And
each time the people covenanted to live by them: "All that the
Lord has spoken we will do."

Among the many words Moses carried from God was the
code of the covenant for the myriad of ordinary affairs in Israelite
life. Its wording resembled the legal codes of other peoples in
the area—the Hittites and Assyrians, for example. There is perhaps one crucial difference in content. Property is of the essence
in other Mesopotamian legal codes; almost every loss, including
a human life, can be compensated by a property settlement. In
God's code human beings are of the essence. They alone are
God's image, and they cannot be replaced with material things.
The difference can be seen in the fact that capital punishment
is never required by Moses' law for a violation against property,
though it is for the violation of human beings.

After Moses' rage against the people's impatient lapse into
idolatry led him to shatter the first edition of the Ten Commandments, he went up into the mountain for the last time.
There he stayed with God for forty days, eating no bread and
drinking no water. During those days God gave him the foundational commandments, the ten words which became the sum

and substance of all that God expects his children to do. Moses returned to the people, his face so radiant with the reflection of God's presence that the people could not look at him. And they accepted the words as the way of life for a people of God.

Thus, a God no one can see and a multitude of recently liberated slaves enter into a covenant, a treaty between a Superior and a subordinate in which the inferior swears to do all that the Superior expects him to do. It is in this covenant setting that we still may find the small capsule of commands which we recognize as the substance of moral duty, not for Israel alone, but for all who belong to the human family.

The decalogue is recorded with slight variations in Exodus 20 and Deuteronomy 5. Many scholars believe that both versions have their origin in a simpler, shorter form that might have gone something like this:

> These are the words of Yahweh.
> I am the Lord who brought you from Egypt.
> You shall have no gods besides me.
> You shall not make yourself a graven image.
> You shall not take the name of Yahweh in vain.
> Remember the Sabbath day.
> Honor your father and mother.
> You shall not kill.
> You shall not commit adultery.
> You shall not steal.
> You shall not bear false witness.
> You shall not covet.

There is much we do not know about the story of the decalogue.[1] We do not know, for instance, exactly how it came to take the different forms we find in Deuteronomy 5 and Exodus 20. But we are certain that the covenant people originally received these commandments from Moses' hands at Mount Sinai. We know that they formed the heart of Hebrew life and worship ever after, the standard by which the life of the people was judged. The massive indictments that later prophets like Isaiah and Amos brought against the people centered on the failure to live up to what the decalogue required. And when Jesus came to fulfil the law, he fulfilled this law, the law of the Ten Commandments. When he set the law anew on its foundations of love, it was the decalogue that he restored to its place. All of Judaeo-Christian morality is lodged within a covenant

made by the Savior God, who wills that we should be just to 5
each other and love one another, and who gives his commandments to show us how.

Our task is to find out what the commandments for this
ancient covenant tell us about the will of God today. If God
gave us new commandments in each new situation, speaking
directly to each of us, we would not have to consult the ancient
words. As it is, we read his commandments as they were spoken
to other people—people with customs and a language strange
to ours, people who never wondered whether it is right or wrong
before God to remove an irreversibly brain-damaged person
from a respirator. So the question of this book will be: can the
ancient commandments tell us, in our time and our place, what
God expects us to do?

Before going on, I should specify some limits to the claims
we can make for the commandments. For one thing, I do not
mean that God speaks his moral will only through the "Thou
shalt's" and "Thou shalt not's" of the Bible. The Bible has many
styles and many methods for telling us what God expects us to
do.[2] Moreover, the Bible is not the only place that God speaks
his will. The community of faith may discern the will of God in
the silences and storms of its own life, and it may hear the voice
of God in the cries of the hungry children of our world.

But I am going to the commandments because, of all the
places where God's voice may be heard, they speak it most urgently and clearly. Where else does God confront people as
urgently as in his undebatable "Thou shalt?" Where does he pre-
empt people's freedom to do wrong as clearly as when he utters
his "Thou shalt not?" Never mind, for the moment, that he
spoke his "Thou shalt's" and "Thou shalt not's" long ago. The
fact is that he did speak them, and biblical faith holds that in
speaking them to others, he somehow spoke them to us. There
they are in print, the commandments of God—not the only way,
but the one way that no one can ignore. How can we take these
clear commands into the confusing dilemmas of contemporary
life and hear what God wants us to do there, at the borderline
of ignorance, where the wisest and best of persons dare not claim
to know what they ought to do?

Second, I do not mean to say that *all* the commandments in
the Bible tell us what God wants us to do. Anyone with a shred
of moral sensitivity will recognize that some commandments re-

6 corded in the Bible are not the voice of God telling us what we
ought to do. God is not telling today's parents to have their rebel
children executed (Deut. 21:18f.) or today's city fathers to kill
someone caught in adultery (Deut. 22:22). And we have
learned—insufferably late in time—that God is not still commanding slaves to obey their masters with all honor (1 Tim. 6:1).
Many today are not sure whether the Lord commands women
everywhere to subject themselves to their husbands (Eph. 5:24).
But can anyone doubt that, in saying "Thou shalt not kill" to the
Hebrew people, God said it to all people? The commandments
I will be talking about in this book are the ones which every
believer in his right moral mind will recognize as God's will for
all his children.[3]

Finally, I do not mean to suggest that all we need in order
to know God's will is a book of commandments, indexed to help
us find the one that applies. The divine commandments are not
the blueprint for a morally ordered life, with specifications for
every nook and cranny in it. We must not suppose that the Bible
gives regulations to fit every situation, and that if a rule does not
fit our situation, we can lop off the bothersome corners of reality
to make the situation fit our rule. A morality guided by biblical
commandments is not necessarily legalism.[4] The commandments
in the Bible give us more to go on than loving hunches and
benevolent intuitions, but they do not offer a detailed and up-
to-date road map.

Before we dig into what the commandments actually tell us,
however, we must do some spadework around the edges. What
sort of thing are these ancient commandments, that modern believers should listen to them as if God is still speaking through
them? Let me propose some descriptions of the biblical commandments which, if true, qualify them to be commands for us.

1. *The commandments fit life's design.* Behind all the trauma-
tizing questions thrust at us by the cultural revolutions of our
day lies the question of whether there is, in our spiritual environment, a creative Mind who wills human life to develop and
grow within certain patterns and toward a purposed goal. Are
there any divinely drawn configurations into which we are expected to fit our search for private happiness and public weal?
I am not talking about a kind of fate, as if each of us is born
with a moral script imprinted on our genes. I am asking about
a personal will which an intelligent Creator has for rational crea-

tures, a design to which he would have us adapt our choices but which we are free to ignore or deny if we choose. Is there a way in which we ought to walk?

Or is human life all open-ended, with no plan, no pattern, no pre-established ordering, a play without a plot? Are there no ways of structuring the truly human life? Are all human relationships so pliable that they can be kneaded into any shape, pushed in any direction? Must we always be improvising, contriving, adapting? Are we like a quarterback who has no game plan but to score points? Is the price of freedom the burden of having to watch every instant for the right signal? If so, the moral life is a wearisome round. But life without order is an option.

I believe that we do not have to choose between total order and perpetual innovation.[5] God wants it both ways. He sets us in broad channels, within which he expects us to develop our lives to fit the needs and visions of our time. He calls us to respect the boundaries, but he invites us to be free within them, for the channels do not cancel freedom. If we respect the order, we can unfold our human potential, develop our gifts, exercise the freedom of love, change our fashions, recreate old forms of family, marriage, and other human alliances, and respond to the challenges posed by our environment and technology in the full acceptance of our own responsibilities. If there is a design for life, first in the Creator's mind, then in ours, it may be the one thing we need to keep the human community from turning into a jungle of predatory plunderers.

I have no illusions about the extent of our ability to know the exact contours of God's order for life. We must certainly allow for unpredictable novelties and varieties in the cultural forms of human life. All I mean to say here is that if the ancient commandments are still commandments for us, there must be a stable, abiding order for life which they match.

2. *The commandments tell us all what God expects us to do.* When the Lord God commanded specific people in biblical times to do this or not to do that, he usually left no doubt about whom he was talking to or what he expected them to do. His word was direct, specific, and clear. The only question left over once the command was given was that of obedience: would the persons addressed do what they were commanded to do? In this sense, the commands are not like abiding laws laid down for all time and all places.

8   If God's ancient commands tell all people everywhere what he expects them to do, those commands must somehow embody an abiding law of human life. If the "Thou shalt" aimed at a very specific person in past time is also directed to human beings of all time, it must have told that one person to do what everyone ought to do. Something about that person's life-situation and very being must have made God's commandment just the right thing for him to do, not just as an ancient Hebrew but as a human being. Such ancient divine commands, says Karl Barth, demand nothing other than "what is demanded by the nature of the creature as God created it."[6]

At least some of the biblical commandments, therefore, are both direct commands and abiding laws. Perhaps an example can show how a specific command can carry a universal law. A father tells his son: "Tom, bring the car home by 11:00 tonight." Here is a command meant only for Tom, about one car, and on one night. There is no abiding law here. But at breakfast the next day, Tom's father says: "Tom, tell me the truth about why you didn't come home until 1:00 this morning." This second command is also personal, directed to Tom, about one car and one morning. But this command invokes an abiding law. Tom ought to tell the truth because, in human communication, truthfulness is a law of life.

It seems clear that the Ten Commandments convey duties for everyone, though they were aimed at specific persons and were to be obeyed simply because it was the Lord God who commanded. "Thou shalt" can be translated "Everyone ought." What must be obeyed because of God's authority ought also to be obeyed because what he commands matches what we are and what we are meant to be. The commander is the Creator; what he expects all of us to do fits what he created us to be. This is what I mean by an abiding moral law of life.[7]

But if some of the Bible's commands convey abiding laws, others certainly do not. God's dreadful word to Abraham does not carry an abiding law: "Take your son, your only son Isaac, whom you love, and go to the land of Moriah, and offer him there as a burnt offering upon one of the mountains" (Gen. 22:2). What God commanded Abraham to do at that moment is something any reasonable father would consider insane. No one is likely to believe that this command tells all fathers what to do with their sons.

Possibly this story carries the oblique message that every believer ought to be willing to go so far as to kill his own son if God commands it. Abraham enroute to Moriah is thus seen as an example of the radical obedience of faith. But then we have a model of radical faith, not a moral law telling us all what to do. Possibly the story illustrates *how* God sometimes commands us still, in the privacy of our inner hearts. Maybe we ought to keep listening for the divine command in the dead of night, as Samuel did, and say with him: "Speak, Lord, for thy servant hears" (1 Sam. 3:9). Or maybe we can hear him during crises of faith, as Peter did, when God called him from his religious prejudice against those who ate ceremonially unclean food: "Rise, Peter, kill and eat" (Acts 10:13). No one who believes in a living God would want to rule out the possibility, if our hearts and minds are open, of hearing his direct command to us, in our special situation, tonight.

Some theologians have insisted that God *normally* tells us what he wants us to do by way of direct, personal, and concrete address. We must not look for abiding laws in the biblical commands; we must listen for God's voice anew to us in our concrete situations. No one said this more forcefully than Barth:

> The command of God as it is given for us at each moment . . . wills us precisely the one thing and nothing else, and measures and judges us precisely by whether we do or do not do with the same precision the one thing that he so precisely wills.[8]

Emil Brunner stressed how unpredictable the commands might be: "We cannot know beforehand the content of the command. . . . [We] can only receive it afresh each time through the voice of the Spirit."[9] Dietrich Bonhoeffer expected anyone to be able to hear and understand it when it came: "If God's command is not clear, definite, and concrete to the last detail, then it is not God's commandment."[10] God's will, said Barth, is not known in the "guise of rules, principles, axioms, and general moral truth, but purely in the form of concrete, historical, unique, and singular orders, prohibitions, and directions."[11]

If we had to wait for God to speak afresh at every new moment of decision, the moral life would be awesomely exciting. If we were constantly open to the living voice of a God who is free to bring new messages for new situations, we would awaken every morning to life studded with divine surprises. Further-

10 more, waiting for God to speak might prevent our private grids of prejudice from filtering out God's will.[12] But the ticket to such an adventure with God is too expensive if it means we must trade abiding moral law for an ethic of personal command.

Two things persuade me that at least some of the ancient commandments embody abiding moral laws that we can consult as a source of God's will. First is the identity of the commander: the God who commanded is the same as the God who created. A purposeful Creator, planning a world of rational beings, would have some sort of design for their development as a human community. And if he wills that his people live by that design, would his commandments not embody that will? At least something of what he always intended for humanity must show through in what he commanded that specific group of people whom he called as the avant-garde of his new humanity. We must remember, of course, that the one who commanded the biblical people was the Redeemer. But the Redeemer is precisely the Lord who made us and calls us to become what he made us to be.

The second reason lies in the commands themselves: some of God's commands simply force us to see that they are for everyone on his earth. Who could suppose that "Thou shalt not kill" was a direct personal command to an ancient group of migrating Hebrews but not an abiding law for everyone on the planet? Barth himself, in spite of his theology of commandments, tackles the commandments of the decalogue brilliantly as general and abiding laws. And so we would expect, for these commandments simply cannot speak to the normal conscience at all if they do not speak as abiding laws.[13]

3. *The commandments tell us to do what we already know we should do.* When Moses announced God's moral expectations for the covenant community, he did not stun the crowd with novelties. No Israelite could have been the least bit surprised to hear that God was against stealing and lying. What Moses brought from Sinai endorsed a morality that was endemic to the human race, affirmed in conscience as much as it was violated in practice. People who know little and care less about what the Bible tells us to do tend nevertheless to know in spite of themselves what the Bible actually requires in the moral life. Paul assumed that, as far as morality was concerned, people who never heard of God's commands were somehow familiar with his will:

When Gentiles who have not the law do by nature what the law requires, they are a law to themselves, even though they do not have the law. They show that what the law requires is written on their hearts, while their conscience also bears witness and their conflicting thoughts accuse or perhaps excuse them on that day when, according to my gospel, God judges the secrets of men by Christ Jesus (Rom. 2:14-16).

As anyone who has read Paul's lament for reprobate humanity in Romans 1 knows, the apostle was not naive about the moral powers of fallen people, Gentiles or Jews. Still, even if they did poorly, they *knew* better.

The divine commandments, then, do not inject a secret and superior morality in the Jewish mind. Nor should this surprise us, if we remember that the commander is the Creator. C. S. Lewis makes the same point about Christian morality:

Did Christian ethics . . . enter the world as a novelty, a new peculiar set of demands, to which a man could be in the strict sense converted? . . . The convert accepted forgiveness of sins. But of sins against what law? Some new law promulgated by Christians? But that is nonsensical. It would be the mockery of a tyrant to forgive a man for doing what had never been forbidden until the very moment at which the forgiveness was announced. . . . Our faith is not pinned on a crank.[14]

Evangelical Christians have sometimes tried to find theological reasons in the doctrine of sin for denying any overlap between what the Bible requires and what a reasonable unbeliever knows he ought to do. They have argued, in the first place, that given the Bible's teaching about what sin does to our conscience, there must be a great gap between God's will and our *moral sense*. The human conscience has been cast over with an egotism so thick that it cannot recognize the altruistic demands of God; thus, even if our human nature had some access to God's moral law, we would suppress it before it got into our consciousness. Second, the Fall distorted *God's original design* in created life so badly that what we know as nature today has no contact with the original pattern of creation. Finally, even if natural reason can know some of the routine biblical moral norms, it cannot grasp them in their depth. Their roots are in a personal God whose amazing grace is totally alien to the natural moral sense. On this view, then, there is really no point to carrying on a dialogue

12   between the morality of common sense and the morality of the Bible.[15]

We should not, I think, reject our common moral sense so quickly. Despite what we learn from the doctrine of sin, we ought not to overlook the staying power of God the Creator within his fallen world. Though badly wounded, our moral sensibilities were not destroyed in the Fall; how else could God reasonably hold people responsible for disobedience? The divine commandments do not come to us as to total strangers but as to estranged friends of God. Calvin's word is a good caution: "If we regard the Spirit of God as the sole fountain of truth, we shall neither reject the truth itself nor despise it wherever it shall appear, unless we wish to dishonor the Spirit of God."[16]

I have no vested interest in celebrating the soundness of humanity's fallen mind. One can only marvel at our talent for rationalization, duplicity, self-deception, and sheer stupidity— and this says nothing yet about the weakness of our will.[17] Still, I think it is important to say that it is reasonable for God to expect what he does of people, and that it is the sort of thing reasonable people can understand. I do not want orthodox Christian pessimism about human nature to obscure the humaneness of God's law. To be sure, someone who denies the grace of Jesus Christ will not hear God's trumpet of morality within a symphony of mercy. If you do not experience God as Savior, you will not know that he gave his commandments as pointers to a truly human life within the love of Christ. But you *can* know the sheer moral content of the law. You *can* know that God says No to certain things, and you can know it because your own conscience says No to them. And when you do those things anyway, you can claim neither that God was unreasonable nor that you were ignorant.[18]

4. *The commandments are the way of life in Christ.* Having insisted that the Bible's basic commandments are guidelines for a basic human life-style, I must add that they are the commandments of the Lord of saving mercy. From the beginning at Sinai they were clearly identified as the will of the Redeemer for the survival of the redeemed community: "I am the Lord your God, who brought you out of the land of Egypt." The commandments came *after* liberation; they pointed to a life of freedom within the covenant. This is why the Psalmist is continually singing love songs to the law (cf. Ps. 119:97). But remember that the cove-

nant community was the first seedling of the renewed human family tree.

If we remember that the commandments to his special covenant community were God's guides for the human community, we can understand Jesus' attitude toward them, and Paul's as well. Jesus, to be sure, was not a moralist; he was a Savior. He did not come like Moses with a set of commands; he came with grace and truth (John 1:17). But he was not an enemy of Moses nor of his commandments, though he vigorously opposed a religious system that twisted them into prescriptions for gaining status with the Creator. As to the commandments themselves, he assured his listeners that not one of them would ever become invalid. "Think not that I have come to abolish the law and the prophets," he said. "I have come not to abolish them but to fulfil them" (Matt. 5:17).[19]

Having affirmed the commandments, however, Jesus demonstrated that their purpose was to point the way to a loving community. First, he showed that traditional rules clustering around the divine commands were invalid if they kept people from the humanizing intent of the law. With his disciples on a Sabbath afternoon's walk, he casually violated a Jewish rule for the holy day. Feeling a little hungry, the Master and his men picked and ate some grain growing along the way. Why not? It was pleasant to eat and the company was splendid. The Pharisees leaped to the attack. There are rules, you know, and harvesting grain is against the rules. Jesus was well aware of the traditional rules, but he ignored them because they did not serve the loving purpose of the divine commandment. "The Sabbath is made for man, not man for the Sabbath" (Mark 2:27). The commandments are signals of the life of constructive joy; they aim at our welfare and happiness.

The second thing Jesus saw in the law was this: the commandments depend on love. Love turns the negative "Don't's" into positive "Do's." Love turns the passive avoidance of evil into the active doing of good. Love translates the morality of "live and let live" into a morality of "love and help others live." Law without love tells us not to kill a stranger; law with love moves us to go out of our way to help a wounded enemy.

Paul felt the same way about the commandments as Jesus did. He hated a system which used the imperatives of unconditional love as techniques for manipulating divine approval. As

14 a device for nailing down God's favor, the law was an evil thing.
It was the demonic drive behind the worst of sins (1 Cor. 15:5),
the destroyer of souls (2 Cor. 3:6), a prison of the human spirit
(Gal. 3:22, 23), and the jailor who bound it there (Rom. 7:6).[20]
But set within grace, placed on the foundation of love, the commandments are good. Grace does not make them obsolete; it
gives them solid ground (Rom. 3:31). As for the Spirit of liberty,
he was given precisely to empower us to do what God expects
of us in his commandments (Rom. 8:4).

The God of morality is the gracious Savior; the lawgiver of
Sinai is the God who was in Christ reconciling the world to
himself. He who leads us through the wilderness by his command is the Father who made us and wants us only to be true
to our own being. He cares for us, loves us, and seeks us by
means of his commands; and he thereby offers us the best way
to keep our balance on the slippery shingles of human existence
while we scratch out our little tunes. We must agree with Karl
Barth that "the command of God is . . . the command of Jesus
Christ and therefore the law of the Gospel, the form of grace."[21]
But we should also listen to Barth when he recalls that the command of God is at the same time "the command of his Creator
and therefore . . . the command which is given with his life."[22]

Encircled by grace, the commandments point to the life grace
came to restore (Titus 2:11, 12). I say this only to establish the
mood and temper of what follows. We shall be looking at the
content of the commandments: what they tell us to do, what they
do not tell us, and how we can best understand and obey them
in the midst of life's conflicts and on life's borderlines. My point
of view is that the commandments are guides to grace-filled
living, invitations to the good life within the grace of God. They
are only guides, helping us find our way to the humanity we
almost lost, the true human life opened to us again by grace.
They cannot give us the steam to make it; only God's Spirit can
do that. But a guide along the way helps us.

*   *   *

This book is not about all of the biblical commandments; in
fact, it covers only a few basic commands which obviously contain the abiding moral will of God for the human family. In a
way, I am following the Heidelberg Catechism, which answers
the question "What is the Law of God?" simply by quoting the

Ten Commandments (Q. & A. 92). In so doing the catechism was itself following the common practice of catholic Christian liturgy. I am also imitating Paul who, when he speaks of the law of God, cites only the second half, the moral part of the decalogue, which deals with human relationships (Rom. 13:8-10). And I am affirming Calvin's conviction that God gave the decalogue for all people, including those indwelt by the Spirit of God, as "an instrument" to teach them "more thoroughly each day the nature of the Lord's will."[23]

The moral commandments of the decalogue are not barked at us by a capricious heavenly staff sergeant. As I view them, they match the configurations of life as God created it. Each commandment seems to cordon off a sector of life and pinpoint the moral nucleus of that sector. Family life is one sector of life in the human community; and "Honor your father and mother" signals respect to parents as the moral nucleus of that sector of life. Marriage is another sector; "thou shalt not commit adultery" identifies fidelity as its moral nucleus. Communication is a dynamic sector of life in the human community; "thou shalt not lie" points to truthfulness as the moral core of communication. If we think of any community as a network of these sectors, we can see that the commandments are survival guidelines for the human community.

These commandments make more specific the two fundamental commandments for the moral life—that we should do justice and act in love. Justice and love are absolute,[24] unconditional, unequivocal. They are global, universal, all-embracing commands. They pin us down at every corner, grip us at the center, allow us no qualifications or evasions. Justice and love cover every conceivable human situation. They are the be-all and end-all of the moral life.

The moral commands of the decalogue build on the commands of justice and love. In spelling out how justice is to be pursued within a specific sector of life, each command asks for respect of the person of a neighbor in his or her role within that sector. Respect is a sense for the other person's right to be who he is, to have what he properly has coming to him, and to be allowed to do what he is called to do. So, for instance, "thou shalt not steal" points to the respect we should have for a person's right to have what is properly his own. "Thou shalt not commit adultery" points to the respect we should have for a

16   person's right to be an exclusive partner within the sexual covenant we call marriage. In short, the commandment specifies what justice calls for within a given sector of life.

But the same commandments point to love as well. Love means caring for what a person needs in order to play a role as a member of the community. Hence, we let love transform the prohibitions into positive commandments. Love tells us that "thou shalt not kill" means we must care for our neighbor by doing all we can to foster and nourish the life of another person. "Thou shalt not lie" means we must care for our neighbor by doing all we can to protect our neighbor from lies about him. So while each commandment as it stands points to the minimal life of justice, it also calls us to the maximal life of love.

As we encounter each command in the following chapters, we will pursue three simple and basic questions: *What* does the commandment ask or forbid us to do? *Why* does the commandment ask or forbid us to do it? *How* should we obey the commandment in the complex and ambiguous situations of our lives?

What sorts of answers will we be looking for? For the most part we shall answer the first question by looking at the text of the command and other texts that help explain or elaborate it. We shall not limit ourselves to the ancient setting and the sheer letter of the text; we shall also have to ask about its positive implications for us in our own setting. Love's imagination will not let us read the negative commandments simply as "live and let live." So when we ask what the commandment requires, we will need to transform the prohibition into a positive command with a sweep as wide as human need.

The second question goes deeper. Note that asking *why* God should have forbidden this act or commanded that one is not the same as asking whether he should have commanded it, nor (like the serpent) whether he did in fact command it. The question *why* is a question of faith. Since we believe that the commander is the Creator, who asks his human creatures to be nothing but what they were created to be, we may also believe that obedience is a reasonable service (Rom. 12:2). The commandments fit life, but we want to see the match between what we are by creation and what God expects us to do. The question "why" does not put God on the spot; it can only open us to the ways that God's will wisely fits what we are. We will not always be sure. Sometimes we can only make some suggestions, which may or may not be helpful. Remember that we are trying to move from faith to understanding, trying to discover in life our "reasonable" service.

The third question, the one that asks how, arises when we take the commandment from Sinai's mountaintop to the streets of our city, from the ancient text to contemporary life. The commandment is simple; life is complex. Thomas Aquinas long ago observed that when we "descend into detail" we have to hedge the simple commands with "caution and qualification."[25] We will always work with caution, I trust, and yet dare to make the qualifications reality compels us to make.

We need not always ask "how" to obey a command. Most of our decisions can be made with God's will staring us in the face. In almost every human situation, our strong bias will be in favor of keeping the commandments in the most simple and literal way. And we will probably discover that the human needs present in that situation are best cared for by simple obedience. But the right decision is not always the one clearly at hand. Sometimes we need to "watch and pray" with the question of "how" painfully on our mind.

We ask "how?" in two different kinds of situations. One kind forces us to ask for the best way to fulfil the positive intent of the command. How can we most lovingly honor our aged parents—by inviting them to live in our own homes or by providing for their care in a nursing home? How can we best help the hungry survive a famine? How can we be most helpfully truthful to someone for whom the truth will be painful unto death? The "how" in these cases requires spiritual discernment of the human factors in their human setting to the end that the command may be, in actual life, fulfilled in love.

The question "how?" also confronts us in the sort of case in which obeying one command seems to force us to violate another. Situations in which doing what love commands requires us to do what a commandment forbids are familiar; we all know about lying to save a human life, stealing bread to feed a hungry child, or letting a sinner die so that a saint can live. But we want more than a compassionate tolerance of necessary evil; we want more than understanding enough to *excuse* disobedience for love's sake. Are there any guidelines for *righteous* commandment-breaking, any tests for *justified* lying, *justified* stealing, *justified* killing? Or *justified* adultery?

18   We want to know whether or when we may be sure that disobedience to a command is *right* before God—not only to excuse or forgive it, but to judge it as the right and good thing to do. So when we ask "how" we will be asking for some guidelines that will work, not just for me in my emergency, but for everyone in similar situations who wants to know whether God himself will say that it was *right* to break one of his commandments.

There will be testing and there will be doubting. We can probe the "how" only by keeping in touch with both the mountaintop of the simple command and the marketplace of complex reality. We need to take the command to the marketplace. But we must also take the facts of the marketplace—and the hospital and the parliament and the bedroom—to the command. The command gives us our moral bias. The facts must tell us whether our bias really bears on the case.

When Moses said, "Thou shalt not steal," he did not foresee the possibility of manipulating the price of common stock. When he said, "Thou shalt not kill," he did not envision the possibility that amniocentesis could tell a mother, three months or so after conception, that the baby she is carrying will likely die a horrible death within two years of its birth. So we must carry our facts—as we know them so partially—and our intelligence—as we use it so fallibly—back to the commandments, and ask *how*, in the light of all we know and think about the life situation before us, we can obey the commandment in a way that promotes what the commandment is all about: fairness and love to all the people whom our decision touches.

Struggles of mind and spirit lie ahead along this path. But the goal is always simple: "to know who we are and what God expects us to do," so that we can "scratch out our little tunes without falling down and breaking our necks."

QUESTIONS FOR DISCUSSION

1. What sort of moral guidance do we get from the larger biblical vision of human life and its meaning—apart from any specific moral rules? Can you think of examples?

2. How do we know whether or when an ancient biblical commandment contains an abiding moral law?

3. Do you agree that there is a general design for human life which matches the divine commandments for life?

4. Why—if you do—do you think moral laws are real, as opposed to being mere folkways of cultures?

5. What motivates some theologians to deny that God tells us what to do through moral laws?

6. Do you agree that the moral commandments of the Bible are valid for all people, unbelievers as well as believers?

7. Is it important to you whether non-believers as well as believers can understand and affirm biblical commandments?

8. If biblical morality matches creation's design, and if any reasonable person can grasp biblical morality, what keeps us from simply basing everything on natural law?

9. Do you think all moral commandments are absolute? How can we know which ones are absolute?

"What does the Lord require of you but to do justice...?"

(Micah 6:8)

Everyone in heaven and on earth wants justice. No man or woman, prince or peasant, saint or sinner has ever wanted injustice for himself or herself. Most people even want it for others. Someone who claims to care nothing for others is immediately marked off as a misfit in the human family. Justice, said Aristotle, is one star in the firmament more glorious than the evening and morning stars. And most everyone agrees.

But although everyone praises justice, no people has ever achieved it. Justice is still a hope. When the apostle spoke of "a new earth in which justice dwells" (2 Pet. 3:13) he depicted this as a good hope for a happy ending for God's human family.

God's own passion for justice shows itself throughout redemptive history. When he allied himself with Israel as an advance guard of covenant people, he made justice a prime condition in the covenant with them. At its birth, the fundamental character of the community was established: "Justice, and only justice you shall follow, that you may live and inherit the land which the Lord gives you" (Deut. 16:20). Ever afterward, the acid test of the community's obedience to their covenant with God was: is justice done among the people?

The covenant community repeatedly failed the test. The rich were unjust to the poor, the powerful were unjust to the weak, and no doubt the poor and weak were unjust to each other. Although they might try to cover up their foul unfairness with religious scrupulousness, the Lord was not hoodwinked:

> I hate, I despise your feasts,
> and I take no delight in your solemn assemblies. . . .
> Take away from me the noise of your songs;
> to the melody of your harps I will not listen.
> But let justice roll down like waters,
> and righteousness like an ever-flowing stream (Amos 5:21ff.).

22 To claim religious virtue while practicing injustice was to minic the man who brutalizes his wife every evening and claims virtue for staying home nights. Were the people fasting?

> Is this not the fast that I choose:
> to loose the bands of wickedness,
> to undo the thongs of the yoke,
> to let the oppressed go free. . . ? (Isa. 58:6).

Escape from national disaster was offered, but only on condition that justice live again: "If you truly execute justice one with another. . . , I will let you dwell in this place, in the land that I gave of old to your fathers for ever" (Jer. 7:5-7). As time went on and the poor cried in vain to the human powers, hope for justice from established systems turned to prayer for the coming of the Messiah.

> Give the king thy justice, O God,
> and thy righteousness to the royal son!
> May he judge thy people with righteousness,
> And thy poor with justice! (Ps. 72:1).

And the answer of promise was:

> He delivers the needy when he calls,
> the poor and him who has no helper (Ps. 72:12).

The justice of God would come in the advent of a child, whose birth would signal the coming of justice and peace:

> Of the increase of his government and of peace
> there will be no end,
> upon the throne of David, and over his kingdom,
> to establish it, and to uphold it
> with justice and righteousness (Isa. 9:7).

The Bible ends with the expectation of the justice God had commanded all along—the anticipation we cited earlier from 2 Peter: new heavens and a new earth in which justice dwells (2 Pet. 3:13).

These snippets from the biblical story are enough to warrant our belief that Micah's word is a fundamental answer to the question, "What does God expect us to do?"

> He has showed you, O man, what is good;
> and what does the Lord require of you

but to do justice, and to love kindness,   23
and to walk humbly with your God? (Micah 6:8).

As an obligation or as a promise, justice or righteousness appears
some 800 times on the pages of Holy Scripture. It is a primary
character component in the biblical model of the new creature
in Christ (Eph. 4:24; 1 Tim. 6:11; 1 Pet. 2:24). Is there any
doubt, then, that with the God who is love, justice is a foundation for whatever else he expects of the human family?

Justice is the premise of mere morality. Let us then take a
closer look at what this thing called justice really is. We will
cluster our thoughts around three simple questions: (1) What is
justice about? (2) Why do people have rights to justice? (3) How
can we do justice in a world of conflicts? In trying to answer
these questions, we will be comparing the biblical message of
justice with the ordinary sense of justice that any reasonable
person might have.

I. WHAT IS JUSTICE ABOUT?

Anyone who reads the Bible's call for justice already has a notion
of what justice is. Aristotle observed that we know what justice
is when we feel the wounds of injustice, and since every person
on earth has, at some painful moment, joined the primeval cho-
rus, "It's not fair!", we may assume that everyone has at least a
primitive sense for the sort of thing that justice is. But wise
people have sought to press beyond this intuition to elaborate
theories of justice. Do we take our cue from these? Does the
Bible's sense for justice reinforce our common sense? Or does
it exceed or complete or correct it?

Surely the Bible gives us a powerful motive for doing what
we knew all along was ours to do. Our task now is to examine
both senses of justice, compare them, and find out where the
Bible reaffirms and where it redirects our common sense of
justice.

A. THE COMMON SENSE OF JUSTICE

Justice is about human rights
Through every dream of justice flows one conviction: people
ought to get what they have a right to have.[1] But what do people
have when they have a *right* to something? When we talk about

24 rights, we are talking about what is due us, what is properly ours according to some undeniable standard. When we talk about what is ours by right, we mean something we need not say "thank you" for. If we have a right to something, it is morally wrong for anyone to take it away. For that reality of getting and keeping what is rightfully ours we use the word justice. When people in a society generally get what is theirs by right, we call that society just.

Justice, then, is all about rights. Thus, rights exist before justice does. The very idea of justice occurs to us only because we believe people already have rights. And the fact of justice, in real life, occurs only if people receive whatever is their right. A little girl has a right to enough to eat. This makes us *think about* justice, but justice exists in fact only when she gets food in her stomach. Rights are a reality invested in persons; justice is a situation in which people actually get their rights.[2]

Obviously, mere justice does not meet all human needs. We need love, we need joy, we need forgiveness. But people who make derogatory remarks about "*mere* justice" are usually those who already have more than what they have coming to them. The man who is unfairly imprisoned and the mother whose children go to bed hungry are not likely to talk of *mere* justice. When you are starving, a piece of bread is never "mere" bread.

Justice entails obligation

If one person has a right, someone else has a duty to honor it. If I have a right to stay alive, you have an obligation to keep your hands off my throat. If you have a right to your private place, I have a duty to stay away from it. If a stranger has a right to some food for his hungry child, someone has a duty to see that he gets it. Whenever someone has a right someone else is obligated to honor that right. If my right does not obligate anyone, it is only a piece of fiction.

In one way or another, we are all obligated by other peoples' rights simply because they share our humanity. I must honor everyone's right to life and everyone must honor mine. But some rights, such as those which come from private contracts, obligate only the people involved in a certain transaction. For instance, I am not obligated to pay my doctor the overdue bills of his other patients. We are also obligated by special relationships we have with certain people. My neighbor is not obligated to provide for my children in the same way that I am.

Thus, we are obligated by other people's rights according to our connection with them. I have mentioned only three such connections: our common humanness, our contractual commitments, and our special "fiduciary" relationships. But whatever the setting, if a person has a right to something, someone is obligated. When you press a claim to your rights, you need not apologize, you need not beg, and you need not feel beholden after your claim is honored.

Justice is impersonal

Only persons have rights. But justice is impersonal in that it does not depend on our personal attitudes toward individuals. We want justice from each other whether we are friends or foes, lovers or strangers. I owe my neighbor what he has coming to him, whether we often enjoy barbecues together in the backyard or scarcely say hello to each other on the way to work in the morning.

This impersonal quality of justice means that it can be measured and judged. A judge would be hard put to know just how I feel about my neighbor, but he can determine whether or not I have done my neighbor justice. Justice can be calculated, and this is a great advantage. A wife could quibble endlessly with her husband about whether he really loves her, and nobody could step in to arbitrate the debate. But if she claims that her husband has done her an injustice, an outsider could help decide how the scales are tilted.

Justice is social

Justice has to do with arranging things in human society so that individuals and groups respect each other's rights. There are different kinds of social relationships in which we press our claims to rights on each other. Sometimes, justice is small scale. For instance, I may make a contract with you to overhaul the engine to my car, for which I will pay you $1000 when the job is done. Such a contract gives each of us a right that we can press against the other. Justice is done when you have overhauled the engine and I have paid you the thousand dollars. We call this *contractual* justice.

But I as an individual also confront society as a whole and

26 press certain claims against it. Society owes me a fair share of the many goods that it distributes to its members. Some of these goods are simply there, like the country's natural resources, life, land, air, and water. Others are contracted for, like the money gathered and set aside for social security payments to the elderly. Others are intangible sorts of wealth, like opportunity for learning, power to determine my own life, and protection from people who might otherwise hurt me. Justice is done when all people get a fair share of these kinds of wealth. We give the name *distributive justice* to this situation.[3]

Society also presses claims against me, and I have a duty to honor society's rights. Just as I have a right to share in society's goods, society has a right to some of my goods. I owe a share of taxes, I have a prima facie obligation to serve in the armed forces, I must respect public property and obey laws. To withhold things like these from my society is to do an injustice, and society has the right to penalize me. It may take something away from me that matches the seriousness of my offense, but no more; and I may be punished only as severely as society punishes others who commit the same crime as I do. When society punishes me fairly we have *retributive* justice.

Justice, then, is done only in a social setting, and takes several different forms. But no matter what form it takes, justice always has to do with rights, my rights over against you, my rights over against society, and society's rights over against all of us.

Justice depends on just persons

In the long run, justice will be lacking when people are not just in their hearts. Plato spoke words of universal wisdom when he insisted that there can be a just society only where just persons live. A just person has an inner push toward justice; he is disposed to treat people fairly even if it costs him a profit. He wants to be fair to everyone, to people close to him and to strangers, to his partners and to his competitors. If he is rich, he wants to get justice for the poor; if he is poor, he demands no more than he really has a right to expect. Being just, for such a person, is a habit.

Although just persons will want to do the just thing, they may be mistaken about what the just thing is. There were many just people who wanted to be fair to their slaves; it never occurred to them that making people slaves was itself unjust. The

Founding Fathers of the United States *wanted* freedom for everyone; but they did not think that black Africans were included in that "everyone."

Still, justice in a society will eventually break down unless a high percentage of the people in the society are just. No one expects everybody to be just; and it is foolish to expect anyone to be perfectly just all the time. But where very few people can be depended on to want at least to be just, justice is hard put to survive. The reasons are clear. For one thing, a society could hardly be just if people routinely sought to take unfair advantage of each other in their private relationships. For another, just people are needed to press government to make things right when people suffer injustice. Ordinary people who want justice very much, for others as well as for themselves, will keep pressure on their fallible judges and corruptible leaders.

So much, then, for the common sense of justice. All I have said about justice in these last few pages could have been said— and has been said—by people who have never heard the Bible's cry for justice among the children of men; and I appeal only to the reader's common sense to judge whether it sounds right. It may be that the Bible supports common sense justice, or that the common sense of justice can only be supported by the biblical vision of the human situation. But the point here is that there is a common sense of justice that people have without the help of the Bible. Now we shall try to capture the Bible's sense of justice.

B. THE BIBLICAL SENSE OF JUSTICE

The prophets of the Old Testament walked the streets of Israel's cities, probed into Judah's courts, poked around in the marketplaces, and were outraged at what they saw. They saw injustice aplenty, and they roared their indignation at those who had money and power for raping the poor and oppressing the weak. They were not detached philosophers spinning out theories of justice; they were angry prophets attacking injustice as they saw it.[4] Yet when the prophets spoke for justice, they must have been moved by some vision of justice, of a people made whole and right in the kingdom of God. We can extract some fragments of that vision from what they called Israel and Judah to do. But what the Bible has to say about justice is more than the de-

28   nunciations of the prophets, and we shall begin not with the Old
Testament but with the gospel of Jesus Christ.

The gospel's sense of justice

God's justice gives more than ordinary justice gives. At the heart
of the gospel, God's kind of justice appears to be a total reversal
of ordinary justice. Certainly that is how it looked to the first-
century Jews, with their powerful sense of divine justness. For
according to the good news, God does *not* give people what they
have coming to them, but what they do not deserve. He gives
aliens the status of children and sinners the status of righteous
persons. To those who objected that the idea of a God who
played fast and loose with justice was blasphemy, Paul replied
that the God of grace did not slacken justice; indeed, God justified the ungodly precisely "to prove at the present time that
he is just" (Rom. 3:26). The gospel of grace was not a reckless
rumor that God no longer cared about justice; it was final proof
that he is just. But what sort of justice is this?

What Paul really discovered was a new *way* for people to
become just. God had freely given himself in Jesus Christ, who
stood in our place as prisoner in the dock and there received the
full measure of divine justice. The retributive side of justice was
thus settled in Jesus' death (Rom. 3:25). The next step was to
allow Jesus' righteousness to count as ours. This could happen
if Jesus were somehow part and parcel of one's own life—which
takes place when his Spirit comes into our life, so that Christ—
in a way—lives in us and becomes our deepest selves. "I live,
yet not I, but Christ lives in me" (Gal. 2:20). Hence, the believer
has a real righteousness, as it were, and God's justice is not
compromised when he justifies the ungodly (Rom. 3:22).

Still, Paul's proof of God's justice leaves us gasping. Ordinary
justice is being transformed by the most radical upset ever. A
prodigious benevolence and a powerful freedom invade ordinary
justice, so that the human race is not mired forever in divine
retribution. Love takes justice beyond common sense. When we
receive *this* justice, we are not left with a sense of having gotten
what was ours by right. A taste of divine justice moves us to
exult with Paul, "I thank God through our Lord Jesus Christ"—
a Hallelujah which mere justice seldom inspires.

God's justice may contradict ordinary justice. To illustrate God's
freedom with people in the kingdom, Jesus once told a story

about how a whimsical estate owner treated his day-laborers (Matt. 20:1-16). A man hired some farmhands early in the morning for a wage both agreed on—one denarius for the day's work. A few hours later he hired some more, then some more at noon, and some more at 3:00 p.m., and finally he even took on some men as late as 5:00 p.m. At dusk, when no one could work any longer, the employer paid each laborer one denarius. The men who had "borne the burden and heat" of the long day complained. Workers should get paid according to the work they have done, they argued. It is unfair that all should be paid the same amount. But the owner had two rejoinders: (1) those who began early and worked late took home exactly what they were owed according to their contract, and (2) the others were paid according to the owner's free and magnanimous decision. Grace for some does not undo mere justice for others.

Those who started early argued that everyone should get only what is coming to him. The owner argued that the sovereign employer decides what is coming to workers. He is fair as long as he meets his contracts and pays the minimum wage; beyond that, he is fair when he chooses to pay some people over and beyond the contract wage. So it is, Jesus teaches, with God. He is free to be generous when he chooses, and those who are treated according to strict standards of human justice have nothing to complain about. God's freedom in his kingdom is not less but more than mere justice.

The evangelical sense of God's justice revealed in Jesus' story seems to contradict our common sense of justice. Emil Brunner was correct in saying that the sense of justice in Jesus' story was not the kind of justice that must dominate the bargaining tables of industry. The two spheres, he exaggerates, "lie as far apart as heaven and hell."[5] In the human sphere we must work by reasonable calculations of what people have coming to them, not by the benevolent impulses of owners and employers. But the story does open the possibility of a freedom to create flexible and responsive ways to meet the needs of some people even though they have come late to the vineyard.

The prophets' sense of justice
The prophets promise more than ordinary justice. The Old Testament prophets called for ordinary justice on a common human scale. They wanted poor people to get their rights. Yet they had

30   a still larger vision for them than mere justice. True justice is
fulfilled, they believed, in righteousness. Justice and righteousness come in tandem, as in this much quoted word from Amos:

> Let justice roll down like waters,
> And righteousness like an ever-flowing stream (Amos 5:24).

Amos was not envisioning two different sorts of things, justice
and righteousness, rolling down the hillsides into the villages of
Israel. He probably saw justice as one ingredient of righteousness. When people received their due, justice was done; but this
was only one step toward righteousness.[6]

Righteousness goes beyond our ordinary sense of justice to
a humanity made whole. Justice exists where people's rights are
respected. Righteousness exists where people care for their
neighbors and befriend them, concerned not merely that they
get their due, but that their deepest personal needs are satisfied.
This large sense of righteousness is what Peter must have had
in view when he summed up the hope of a new earth as a place
"in which justice dwells" (2 Pet. 3:13). It lies behind Jesus' words
that our righteousness must exceed that of the scribes and Pharisees; it had to be bigger than mere justice, not smaller (Matt.
5:20).

The righteousness of God, in turn, is complete only with
shalom, the peace of God. *Shalom* is righteousness erupting in
joy, the vibrancy of health, the creativity of love, the lust of
living. In the biblical peace, people are both good and happy,
and so have the perfect combination of *shalom* with righteousness.

> And my covenant of *shalom* shall not be removed. . . .
> And great shall be the prosperity of your sons. . . .
> In righteousness you shall be established. . . .
> You shall be far from oppression. . . .
> For you shall go out in joy and be led forth in peace (Isa.
>   54:10, 13, 15; 55:12).

Here again we see justice and righteousness and peace, flowing
together in no precise arrangement, with peace finally including
all that is joyfully human in life. In the kingdom of God righteousness and peace have kissed each other (Ps. 85:10), for it is
the work of righteousness to bring peace (Isa. 32:17).

God's will for the human family is not satisfied when people
get their rights. It was not enough for the poor people of Israel

to get a fair hearing in the court of law or for hungry orphans   31
to get enough to eat. These are the inexpendable rudiments of
righteousness, and God's global promises for righteousness and
peace would be unthinkable without them. The prophets never
demand less than justice, but they promise more.[7] Nothing else
is enough without justice; but justice is not enough by itself.

The prophets' passion is for the poor

The prophets were for the rights of everyone, rich as well as poor,
but they do not worry about justice for the rich, who can take
care of themselves. Besides, they tend to be so blinded by their
selfishness that they cannot be trusted to honor the rights of
poor people. They choked the poor, lured them into borrowing
money they could not repay, and then hit them with debtor's
servitude, which was little better than slavery.

Not even the judges were of help to poor people. Although
they had been warned at the very beginning to play no favorites
with the rich (Deut. 1:16-18), and although God had promised
that if judges were fair "there will be no poor among you" (Deut.
15:4, 5), every prophet who strode in anger through Israel's fields
and streets discovered venal judges playing into the hands of the
crooked rich. The poor were "trampled into the earth." There
were too many judges

> who afflict the just,
> who take a bribe,
> and turn aside
> the needy in the gate (Amos 5:12).

So God became the champion of poor people and the judge of
the rich. No wonder that when prophets called for justice, they
meant justice for the poor and judgment on the rich (Jer. 22:3).

Justice for the poor is not an altered understanding of *what
justice is*; it only steers our passion toward those who need it
most. The prophets' passion for the poor was a zeal for justice,
not merely an emotional plea for charity. Elementary human
rights were being denied in Israel. The rich and powerful were
not merely skimping on alms; they were defaulting on a debt.
Maybe the prophets wanted the rich to invite the poor into their
homes, maybe they wanted the poor to be befriended and supported by the gentle arms of friends. Maybe friendliness; but *at
least* justice, *at least* the rights of the poor respected!

32   *The commandments as guides to justice*
It would be foolish to expect the Bible to tell us how much to
pay a migrant vineyard worker or what the vintner should charge
for a bottle of wine. Labor negotiators would look in vain to
Deuteronomy for a model contract between General Motors
and the United Automobile Workers. To be sure, concrete rules
for just settlements in the Old Testament community appear:
how much a neighbor should be paid for damages done by one
of your animals (Exod. 21:35), how to treat a slave if you blind
his eye with your fist (Exod. 21:26), how much compensation is
owed to a pregnant woman who has a miscarriage when she gets
involved in one of your fights (Exod. 21:22). Some strategies of
justice are no doubt embedded in these detailed rules, but none
of them tells a modern struggler what rights he has in a dispute
with his neighbor.

In the decalogue, however, we find a series of five basic
human rights laid down. Each commandment which forbids me
to injure you implies that you have a fundamental right not to
be injured by me or anyone else. Every "Thou shalt not" signals
a right. The commandments do not cover every human right, of
course, but they do embody certain very important ones. Two
of them express the rights a person has within the institutions
of the family and marriage. The Fifth Commandment asks respect for the right of parents to be the authoritative guide and
teacher of their children in matters of deepest importance. The
Seventh Commandment asks respect for a spouse's right to loyalty and trust within the covenant of marriage. Other commandments express individual rights within any and all relationships.
The Sixth Commandment declares that a person has a right to
his own life. The Eighth Commandment affirms that persons (or
institutions) have a right to keep the things they properly own.
The Ninth Commandment tells us that everyone has a right to
truthfulness, first with respect to himself and his good name, but
also with respect to anything at all.

The decalogue's digest of human rights summarizes what
most people know—by what Paul calls the law "written on
their hearts" (Rom. 2:14, 15)—to be their neighbors' rights. In
sum, the Bible does not challenge our common sense of justice.
Rather, it assumes the existence of rights and the moral necessity
of justice. But it goes beyond mere justice. The gospel opens
the way for a flexible response to need as well as rights. The

prophets focus our zeal on the rights of the poor. And, beyond justice, the Bible promises a re-creation of the human family in total righteousness and perfect peace.

II. WHY DO PEOPLE HAVE RIGHTS?

There are three ways of looking at human life that discourage us from even thinking about rights as a basic component of our life together.

A perennially seductive view of humanity is that justice is a myth created by weaklings to protect themselves from the strong. Human beings are really refined animals, not so much different from beasts in a jungle competing for prey. The weak, on this view, persuaded the strong to believe that in some sort of "eternal order" all of us have certain rights to things; and to this systemic handcuffing of the strong they gave the name "justice."[8] Thus, it is argued, if we really understand what human beings are, we will see that it is nonsense to talk of rights at all.

According to one modern view of justice, while people do have rights, they have them only because society grants them. Society does not recognize people's rights because they are people; society *creates* rights as a way of helping people get along together. People get their rights by way of an unwritten contract with society. Justice stems from society's sense of decency; it just doesn't seem right to most people that some should be given unfair advantages over others. Our sense of fairness tells us to distribute society's wealth fairly. The bottom line of the contract we all "sign" when we agree to live together in society reads: Be fair to each other.[9] Better, then, to talk of justice as fairness instead of justice as a state of affairs when people get their rights.

Christian believers are sometimes reluctant to talk about human rights out of a kind of modesty before God. In the first place, we are only God's creatures, and our very existence is a gift—or better, a loan. We are not owners of our lives, or of anything else for that matter; we are only stewards. Creatures in our humble status should not clamor for rights. Furthermore, we have all sinned and become enemies of God. We have been selfish and unfaithful stewards of the wealth of God's world; we now must not only thank him for the gift of life, but also plead for his mercy. Leave justice to the crowd—believers will live by grace alone.

34   How may a biblical believer reply to these three versions of the denial that people have rights simply because they are people? To do so, we must consider reasons for justice that are rooted in how human beings are set together in human community. We shall look at the kind of being our neighbor is, to see whether it makes sense to think of him as having rights.

1. *My neighbor has rights because he is there.* My neighbor exists, separate from me, rooted in God, standing in his own space, different from me. He is *there*. I am *here*, separate from him, rooted in God too, a being apart. He has a right to be there because God set him there. When he claims his own right to be, he only claims the right to be what God created him to be. So I must respect him, keep my distance, and let him be. I must not try to own him, control him, seduce him, manipulate him, or deny him his place. It does not matter at all whether I like his being there or whether he is attractive or useful to me. He is there and I must respect his right to be there, because it is where God wondrously set him. As Josef Pieper wrote: "To be just means to recognize the other as other; it means to give acknowledgment even where one cannot love."[10] God's creation of distinct beings endows each with a right to respect as God's creature.

2. *My neighbor has rights as a person.* My neighbor is not merely there; he is there as the image of God on earth. If I suppose that my neighbor is an intelligent network of physical particles, I may grant him rights as being distinct from me, but I will not have a very powerful *reason* for respecting his rights. If I take my neighbor to be only a predator competing with me in the human jungle, I may contract to grant him conditional rights as long as there is plenty for both of us to get what we want. But if I believe that my neighbor is a person who images God himself, I have to admit that he has undeniable rights that I must honor even though there is not enough to satisfy both of us at the same time.

As a person my neighbor does not have to carry a report card to prove that he performs well, or an identity card to certify his bloodline, or papers to show that he belongs to the church. No matter whether he is beautiful or ugly, wise or foolish, strong or weak. All he need be is a person born of a woman; if so, he has rights to be respected as an inviolable human self that is only a little lower than the angels (Ps. 8:5).

3. *My neighbor has rights because he has a calling.* "My basic right," observes Henry Stob, "is my right to do my duty."[11] Rights follow duty, not as a reward for duty well done, but as a right to do the duty that needs to be done. Sometimes we earn rights by doing our duty, but in a deeper sense we have rights *in order to* do our duty.

Every human being has the duty to be a caretaker. All of us are called to care for other people in fair and loving relationships. Besides, each of us has a special calling to develop and use the gifts we have to make life more human for others and to add to the glory of God. And all of us are caretakers of some small segment of God's world and its resources. Therefore, we all have a right to follow our calling, to play our role as caretakers for people and for the earth.

4. *My neighbor has rights as a member of a community.* If my neighbor is a person separate from me, he is also a person joined to me in the human community. His being a fellow member with me in the human family gives him rights and puts me in his debt. If we think of the body of Christ as a paradigm of human community, we can understand the New Testament as expressing this ground for a neighbor's rights. Hints of our rights within community come from various corners. Paul says that our neighbor has the right to the truth from us because we are members one of another, as members of a single body (Eph. 4:25). And Peter says that we are stewards of God's gifts, which we are obliged to share with each other (1 Pet. 4:10). The Ten Commandments are guidelines to survival as a human community. As individuals in community, we have two basic rights with respect to the community: (1) the right to be left alone by the community, lest it swallow up our individuality, and (2) the right to the support and help our community can give us, lest it abandon us in our aloneness. Both of these rights are ours because we are created to be individuals within community.

5. *My neighbor has rights because he is a special kind of person.* The fact that my neighbor exists as a person in God's image gives him rights equal with the rest of ours. But since he is also a particular and unique individual, he has rights which fit his special characteristics. Not only is my neighbor distinct from me, he is different from me, unique in his needs and merits. Therefore, he may have some special rights which differ from mine. An aged person has different rights from those of a child. The

36 rights of a disabled child are different from those of a healthy child. Criminals do not have all of the same rights as law-abiding citizens. We cannot say in advance what sorts of rights our individuality gives us, nor which of our individual qualities gives us a special right to anything. One of the arts of managing a just community is recognizing when individual differences do create differences of rights. But the fact that we do not all have all of the same rights is rooted in our differences from each other in needs and merits.

I have mentioned several reasons why it makes sense to say that people have rights. What role does faith play in recognizing rights? Most people who do not believe in God nevertheless believe in human rights. A list of human rights champions in the past century would probably include as many unbelievers as believers. But it is clear that the Christian believer has a unique and powerful *reason* for affirming human rights—the biblical faith that we are all created in the image of God. Without this premise, it is quite possible to exclude slaves from all human rights as Aristotle did, or blacks as the American Founding Fathers did, or Jews as Hitler did, or women as many men have done. Faith that every human being is a person, equal to all others in this fundamental respect, is the most basic reason for affirming that human beings have rights, and that therefore when we talk of justice, we are talking about an ineradicable human reality.

III. HOW TO SEEK JUSTICE
IN A WORLD OF CONFLICTS

The prophets tell us we ought to seek justice. The decalogue gives us a minimal outline of human rights. The gospel provides a motive of love for seeking justice for others. The Spirit of God enables us to be just people. But how do we seek justice in the face of conflicting claims, when the cries of one group cancel out the pleas of another? We cannot find Bible texts that direct us to a just wage for government workers, a just tax scale, a just way to improve the education of ghetto children, or a just way to distribute food to hungry people. Does the Bible in fact guide us in doing what it requires—justice in our real world? Our only way to answer this question is to test the broad rules for justice recommended by common sense. We do not have to claim that these are drawn directly from the Bible, but we must test each

of them in the light of biblical perspectives on human rights and
human needs.

A. EQUALITY

There is a strong egalitarian streak in the Bible. Every person
bears the image of God and is in that sense equal to any other
person, and from this equality of being equal rights would seem
to follow. God himself models egalitarian treatment when he
lets the sun shine and the rain fall on the just and unjust without
discrimination (Matt. 5:45). James taught Christians not to separate rich from poor people, but to treat them equally (James
2:1). Similarly, Paul's doctrine of the body of Christ encourages
such equal treatment, for it assumes that every member is of
equal value, no matter what his or her particular function in the
body (1 Cor. 12:22ff.). Add the prophets' passion for the marginal people of society, and you have a strong line of biblical
evidence for the egalitarian principle of justice.

But common sense tells us that treating everyone the same
is no guarantee of justice for all. A father who beats one of his
children does not give justice to the other three when he beats
them also. A kindly judge who lets every criminal go free treats
all alike, but he does not give any what he deserves. Jim Jones
forced all of his cult followers in Guyana to drink cyanide-laced
Kool-Aid and then joined them in death. He treated everyone
the same, but only by giving all what none deserved. Equality in
itself is hardly a sure route to justice.

But the equal treatment rule not only cannot guarantee justice for all; it will create unfairness. Some people need more
than other people do merely to get a little closer to equality with
them. All children need a nourishing breakfast, and it seems fair
for any society to see that every child gets one; but it also seems
fair that only sick and crippled children get free medicine and
leg braces. All young people ought to have an equal opportunity
to develop their minds and their skills; it also seems right to
treat crippled and deprived young people unequally in order to
give them an equal opportunity. To make a horse race fair, light
jockeys carry weights in their saddles. In society we are more
likely to be fair if we give handicapped people a head start and
put a little lead in rich people's saddles.

Since the Bible is biased in favor of equality, but sheer equality ends in injustice, the egalitarian rule might be: "Treat people

38   equally unless and until there is a justification for treating them unequally."[12] This would demand, for instance, that we show cause why a small minority of rich people in the world should stuff themselves while a majority go undernourished, or why six percent of the world's people should consume sixty percent of the world's energy.

The rule of equal treatment is not absolute, but it is perhaps the fundamental assumption we must make before considering rules for treating some people differently from others. The burden of proof always falls on those who treat persons unequally.

B. MERIT

One popular principle in discussions of justice is that people should be treated as they deserve to be treated. If you claim certain rights, you must qualify for them. You must earn them or inherit them or show in some way that you deserve them. Being a person is not enough; it is the *sort* of person you are or the sorts of things you do that give you rights to things.

Meritocracy also gets support from the Bible. The scriptural authors knew the difference between a person who deserves what he gets and one who does not. If you won't work, says Paul, don't expect to be fed (2 Thess. 3:10). Offices in the church are to be occupied only by people who have established some merit in the community by the quality of their lives (1 Tim. 3:1-10; 5:17). God himself will discriminate between persons according to the works done in the flesh (Heb. 9:27), and when he judges no one will be able to claim that he was treated worse than he deserved.

The Bible is realistic about our inequality, but it does not tell us what sorts of merits entitle us to claim special treatment. We can make a simple distinction between two kinds of merits. Some people claim to deserve things on grounds of their birth. Other people claim to have merits because of what they have achieved. How do these two types of merit—those given and those earned—stack up against the Bible's egalitarian strain?

1. *The merits people are given.* The claim that persons have rights because of accidents of genes or geography usually rests in self-interest. Aristotle, with his brilliant mind, was serenely confident that intelligence—a gift of birth—made a person more deserving than a stupid person, who merited only the status of a slave. Not long ago many Caucasians believed that whiteness

was a test of whether you deserved to be free. Many men believe that being born male confers on them certain prerogatives that women do not share. And most of us act as though our living in a country whose soil is rich and black means that we deserve to eat more than people who were born on white sand.

But this assumption that a person's birth determines his share of the world's good things is questioned by the biblical perspective on the human family. The earth is the inheritance and trust of one human family. Starving people are earth-dwellers first and Haitians or Cambodians second. They are essentially members of the same human family as we, and only incidentally members of a given national society. The heart of the matter is that God has made of one blood the peoples of his creation to dwell on the face of the earth (Acts 17:26). The arbitrary factor of birthplace is irrelevant to a person's share in the food that comes from the earth's fertile ground. The child at his mother's breast in the Sahel has no less right to food than a child whose parents live on Iowa's rich topsoil.

Justice does not kowtow to anyone who claims to deserve better treatment than others on the ground of being better born than they are. We may shrug our shoulders and grumble about the "good luck" of such people, but we do not believe they deserve the life of Riley. Indeed, we believe that justice calls us to bridge some of the gaps that differences in birth arbitrarily create between people. We may believe that it is a wise God who distributes the destinies of children so unequally; it is he who puts a silver spoon or a tin spoon or no spoon at all in a child's mouth. But we may not model human justice on divine predestination; in fact, justice is the human task of removing inequities people suffer merely because they were born poorly. The Bible urges us to bridge these gaps, not to make them normative.

There is a simple reason why the Bible does not allow us to stake our claim to rights on our birthplace or genetic stock. Where we were born and what we inherited are pure gifts of God. We did not earn them; we just happen to have them. It seems very odd to say that we deserve special rights because we were given special gifts.[13]

2. *The merits people earn.* Most people would agree that we have some rights only because we earn them. It would be a gray and uninteresting world if we all had the same things coming to

40   us regardless of what we had achieved. But having said this, we must make certain that we really have earned our right to things that other people do not have.

What sorts of achievements count for merit? The merit I earn must first of all be relevant to what I claim to have coming. A student's merit on a football field might be relevant to his claim on a share of the money his school gives out in athletic scholarships; it is surely irrelevant to his claim to a passing grade in Philosophy 201. The question that gnaws at our every effort to deal justly with people is: How do we decide what is relevant? We may pray for spiritual wisdom on this question, but the Bible offers little data.

Take a setting in which merit is the ordinary basis for distributing rewards—a business where wages are earned by jobs done. Joan is a vice president of First National Bank and her friend Nick is the custodian at one of its branches. Both do their jobs well. Joan's monthly paycheck is much larger than Nick's. She deserves more, we agree, because she has more merit, in the sense that her work contributes more than Nick's to the success of the bank. This difference between their contributions seems relevant to how much they are paid; therefore, Joan has a *right* to more money than Nick.

Now the scene shifts. Joan and Nick are waiting in line at the airport to buy tickets on the same flight. The plane is clearly going to be full. Nick is third in line, sure of a seat; Joan is fifteenth, not at all sure. So she walks up to Nick and tells him he should switch places with her in line because she is a vice president and has more responsibilities at the bank than he does. He answers: "The fact that you are vice president of a bank where I'm a janitor makes no difference *here*." The inequality of merit which allows Joan to earn more money than Nick is irrelevant in this setting. The relevant merit is Nick's having arrived at the ticket counter before she did.

Suppose further that Joan learns that one of the other vice presidents of First National Bank is being paid $5000 a year more than she is. She wonders why. She and Michael do the same work and are equally good at it. So she asks to see the bank president. He offers a couple reasons why Michael is paid more than Joan. He has been at the bank three years longer than she has. Furthermore, he has a master's degree in accounting, while Joan has only a bachelor's degree in fine arts.

As the conversation goes on, the president lets it slip that Joan really ought to consider herself fortunate, as a woman, to be vice president. Joan is furious, and threatens to publicize the bank's injustice to women. So the president injects still another merit factor: it is not so much Michael's maleness that accounts for his greater salary but his role as the breadwinner for a family of five. After all, he fumbles, Joan has a husband who is a well-paid advertising executive. Joan insists that Michael's family situation is irrelevant to his merits as a vice president. If the bank is determining salaries according to need, she argues, it should be paying Nick more than any of them, since he has an invalid wife and seven children.

If we project this simple scenario from a local bank on the infinite network of life situations, we get a sense of how difficult it is to achieve even imperfect justice based on merit. It seems reasonable for a person to claim some rights on the ground of merit. It is just as clear that in other situations, merit has no relevance. Most of us would agree that a 75-year-old man does not have to earn the right to be protected from assault and robbery. But we would also agree that he does have to earn the right to payments from the union pension fund. No one is wise enough to spell out ahead of time the sorts of things we deserve to have only because we earned them. Our common sense for what counts as merit shifts, and so does our sense for the things we need to earn by our merits.

If the Bible does not clearly specify *which* merits count as rights, it does hint at *how* my merits are balanced by my neighbor's needs. If we take the body of Christ as a model of what a human society is really meant to be, we get a hint of when our personal merit could give us a claim to a larger share of wealth than others have. In the body of Christ, we are all members of each other: what hurts one hurts the other, and what helps one helps the other. All need each other and all depend on each other (1 Cor. 12:14-26). From this picture of how we belong to one another, we could say that people can claim a right to a larger share for themselves only if they contribute a larger share to the total wealth—spiritual and material—of the body. My claim to an extra share because I have earned it is valid only if the extra that I get is balanced by an extra share for those whose handicaps prevent them from earning it. I justly enjoy an extra share only if my extra share does not leave less for my handi-

42 capped brothers and sisters. And I justly enjoy a large increase only if my increase also brings more to the handicapped.

In short, merit as a basis for rights must take into account the fact that some people are born with handicaps that they inherited from others, and that the handicapped people have a claim on the wealth of others. This very general guideline, which seems to match the image of humanity reborn as Christ's body, also matches, I think, the deepest moral intuitions of ordinary people.

C. NEED

The biblical concern for the poor and the weak members of society seems to support the Marxian principle, "from each according to his ability and to each according to his need." The prophets did not discriminate between deserving and undeserving poor, but simply pointed to the needs of the marginal members of Israel. God himself will respond to people according to their need: "For he delivers the needy when he calls, the poor and him who has no helper" (Ps. 72:12). There is indeed biblical support for the rule that, in human society, we should treat people according to their needs.

People's needs are of different kinds. We can distinguish first of all between "survival" needs and "flourish" needs. Who would disagree that every living person has a right to what is needed for survival? A baby born, through no choice of her own, into a poverty-stricken family has a right to nourishing food, a warm bed, and loving care. But as she grows, she also has a need to flourish as a whole human being. She needs education and books, music, access to dentists and doctors, and a chance to develop her gifts for creative work. Does she have a right to these bounties? Does the community owe her things that she needs in order to flourish?

A second distinction is between the right to have what we need and the right not to be prevented from earning what we need. Perhaps the best that most societies can promise is to protect every child from sinister forces that prevent him from doing what he can to flourish as the specific human being he is, to the limits of his own will and talent.

Third, we must see that needs differ according to the people who have them. The question of whose needs come first is as hard to answer as the question of which kinds of needs imply a right to have them satisfied. Some people need more or different things than others. Do the needs of children come before those of adults? Do the needs of sick children take precedence over those of healthy children? Are the needs of retarded children more important than those of precocious children? And what of the needs of productive adults over against the needs of retired people, or the needs of tomorrow's children versus those of today's? This brief catalog of mind-boggling questions is enough to prove that a benign decision to make needs the criterion for rights does not really change the basic question of what people have a right to.

By itself, none of our three criteria for distributing the goods of the human community—equality, merit, and need—is the right way. In its place, each of them is partly the right way.

*   *   *

To summarize, then, the Bible does not propound a unique theory of justice. It shares a common human sense of justice as a state of affairs in which people's basic rights are granted. It reveals the fundamental bases for people having rights at all. And it points us to a creative balance of the three common guidelines for getting justice in the human community.

We seek justice as fallible and selfish creatures. The Bible is not congenial to the assumption that we might create a perfect system of justice. It does not offer a blueprint of justice for all societies. But neither does it allow us to be comfortable with injustice. It drives us to try to achieve some fragments of justice within the changing scenes of fallen humanity in the moment of history we share together. What gives strength to the biblical command is the hope that in God's time Jesus Christ will bring perfect justice, as a basis for *shalom*, in the redeemed humanity of the new earth (2 Pet. 3:13).

QUESTIONS FOR DISCUSSION

1. In what way is the biblical vision of the kingdom of God like the ordinary notion of a just society?

2. Do you think that justice means more than "getting what one has coming," and, if so, what more does it mean?

3. Do you think that Brunner was right in saying that Jesus' par-

44 able about the laborers in the vineyard has nothing at all to do with ordinary human justice? Why?

4. Do you think that people's rights are given by society or do you think that society only recognizes rights people have? Do you think it is important to know the difference? Why?

5. Do you think that human rights come before human duty or that duty comes before rights? Why?

6. Do you think that the biblical message about justice is part of the good news of Christian faith? Why?

7. Do you think that believers have a specially strong reason for seeking justice? Why?

8. Do you think we have a right to flourish as human beings, as well as a right to survive? What are the limits of our rights?

9. Do you think that the Bible tells us anything about what we have coming to us in our society? If so, what does it tell us?

10. Do you think that justice is worth fighting for in a sinful human society even though we will never have perfect justice? Why?

11. Do you think that the Bible's concern for justice for the poor and the oppressed tells us what our duty is for today?

12. Do you agree that persons must be just if we are to have a just society? If so, do you agree that we must seek justice even though persons are not all just?

13. Do you agree with Frankena's principle for justice: "Treat people equally unless and until there is justification for treating them unequally"?

14. Do you agree that hungry people in Africa have a right to a share in the corn that grows in Iowa?

15. Do you agree that a man's family needs are irrelevant to whether he has a right to a larger salary than a single woman who does the same job with equal efficiency?

CARE FOR PEOPLE'S NEEDS 3

*"This is my commandment,
that you love one
another as I have loved you."*

(John 15:12)

Love is a power that rises from our soul's need; it is also a strength that flows from our soul's fulness. It drives me to seek another for my sake; it moves me to help another for his or her sake. Love seeks and love gives. Can love be one thing when it moves on two such different tracks?

We live by two separate powers, and we call them both love. We may set them apart by adding adjectives, as C. S. Lewis did, and name them "need-love" and "gift-love." Or we may use the Greek words, as theologians do, and call our two loves *eros* and *agape*—eros being the power that drives us to satisfy our own deepest needs and agape the power that moves us to satisfy the needs of another. Both of them are the strength of life. Without either of them, our humanity wrinkles and withers like dead fruit. But they are not the same.

The love we meet in Jesus Christ is agape, gift-love, the current that bears us to others for their sakes. This love is not our seeking, not even our seeking of God, but God's giving his very Son to help us (1 John 4:10). God's love becomes our love when he invades the center of our being, when God who is love "abides in us and his love is perfected within us" (1 John 4:12). He becomes our power of love to move toward persons who need us.

But love is a command as truly as it is a gift, a duty as much as a power. A lawyer asked Jesus for the most important of all divine commands, and Jesus said:

You shall love the Lord your God with all your heart,
and with all your soul, and with all your mind.
This is the great and first commandment.
And a second is like it,
You shall love your neighbor as yourself (Matt. 22:34ff.).[1]

45

46   Love as power may enable us to do what God expects of us, but it is the command of love that tells us what to do. Love is what all other duties are about. Love ultimately explains *why* we ought to do all things we ought to do.

We are tempted to think of love only as a good feeling. But if love is just a feeling, it will flutter through our affections and sedate our spirits, never catalyze our commitment. So we must ask: What sort of thing is the command of love and what does it ask us to do?

We shall bring the same three questions to the biblical command of love as to the commandments we shall consider in the remaining chapters: (1) *What* is biblical love and what does it demand? (2) *Why* does God expect us to love? Is it reasonable to love or is God asking us heroically to put our lives on the line? (3) *How* does love tell us what to do in the conflicts of real life?

I. CHRISTIAN LOVE AND HUMAN LOVE

We do not need the Bible to tell us to love. We come to the gospel with love already on our minds, if not in our hearts. How then does the Christian law of love relate to our common sense of love, the sense we all share because we share common human needs? We will begin by examining our common sense of love and go on to the Christian revelation of love, aiming always to focus on what God expects us to do.

A. THE COMMON SENSE OF LOVE

Love for our own sake
Natural love is the energy of human need. We are driven by a need for another to complete us and make us whole. Alone we cannot flourish; we cannot become what we need to be unless another comes to be part of us, close to us and within us. So we stretch ourselves, reaching beyond our own souls to someone who will join himself to us so that, in our union, each of us may become more whole. We climb a ladder of need, out of the isolation of our own ego, beyond our aloneness, into the life of another. The power that moves us to climb, to stretch, to reach out for another is the power of love.

To be sure, giving is also part of need-love. If there is no

giving, there will never be finding. So I give myself to another 47
so that she will let me find myself through her. The search for
self is of the essence of eros even when we give ourselves to our
loved one, for eros is conceived and born of a human need to
be whole.

When we love God, too, we seek him in order to find ourselves. We love him for our own sakes, for we cannot live without him. We seek him, for if we miss him we miss our joy, our
hope, our life.[2] We seek God for our own sakes, and this is why
we also seek him for what he is. There is no contradiction here.
We have reached the heart of love when we love him for the
wondrous beauty of his own being. As Francis Xavier put it:

> I love thee, Lord, yet not because I hope for heaven, nor yet
> since they, who love thee not, must thereby burn eternally. . . .
> Not with the hope of gaining aught; not seeking a reward; but as
> thyself has loved me, O ever-loving Lord.

I love him for his sake because it is in him, in what he is, not
what he gives, that I have highest hopes of finding my true self.

Love for the other's sake

We have been talking of eros, the love awakened by our feelings
of need, the love that drives us to another so that we can be
made full in him. Now we shall turn to benevolence, a rational
sort of gift-love. Thoughtful people have argued that all of us
ought to live in ways that are helpful to our neighbors. Many of
life's simple duties we accept because we are convinced that
other people will be helped if we do what we ought to do. If
you ask people why they *ought* not to lie or steal, they will tell
you that lying or stealing hurts people and that everybody will
be better off if we do not hurt our neighbors. This has led some
philosophers to conclude that benevolence is the bedrock of all
morality,[3] which is something like saying, as Jesus did, that all
the laws rest on love. In any case, benevolence is a rational law
which many unbelievers endorse.

Immanuel Kant claimed that the single duty which pins us
all down is to treat every person as an end, not as a means to
our own advantage. Kant's fundamental law of life was a law of
love requiring each of us to "promote, according to his means,
the happiness of others who are in need."[4] A despiser of the
Christian gospel, Kant nevertheless appears to make gift-love
the guiding star of human morality.[5]

48   Erich Fromm sees authentic human love as a giving of self
for the sake of the loved one. A lover who is acting naturally
"gives of himself, . . . of his life, . . . of that which is alive in him
. . .: he gives of his joy, of his interest, of his understanding, of
his knowledge, of his humor, of his sadness. . . . He does not
give in order to receive; giving is in itself exquisite joy."[6] Healthy
human love blends four gifts into one act of loving:
      Care: love as "the active concern for the life and growth of
that which we love."
      Responsibility: love as a "response to the needs . . . of another
human being."
      Respect: love as a feeling "with him or her . . . as he is, not
as I need him to be as an object for my use."
      Knowledge: love as "active penetration of the other person,
in which my desire to know is stilled by union."[7]
Herein is love, says Fromm, not that we seek ourselves alone,
but that we give ourselves rather totally for the needs of the
other person.
      Christian believers who know saving love in Jesus Christ
may have a hunch that Kant and Fromm were salvaging their
notions of love from their early Christian memories. Regardless
of the source, however, the point is that gift-love—as well as
need-love—is alive in the common sense of love.

B. JESUS: LOVE'S LIVING MODEL

Jesus' love for us is God's norm for our loving: "This is my
commandment, that you love one another as I have loved you"
(John 15:12). Rather than listing rules for the loving life, he
made his own life the authoritative model for our loving. So we
need ask only one simple question: How did Jesus love us?
      1. *Love moved Jesus to help people.* No doubt Jesus *felt* for
people, but his love came to life most clearly when he acted. He
came "to give his life as a ransom for many" (Matt. 10:28), to
take away our sins and bring us good from God, to liberate us
from the devil and make us free. And he did what he said he
had come to do. Wherever he went he was found helping people,
healing their diseases, forgiving their wrongs, teaching them God's
will, promising to make them completely whole. Helping was his
life-style—and his death-style, for he turned even his dying to
our good. Love is the power that moved Jesus to live and die as
the "man for others."

2. *Love moved Jesus to help all people.* Love made Jesus indiscriminate. He excluded none; indeed, he seemed to go out of his way to embrace the scandalous sinners who were repugnant to the righteous folk (Matt. 9:10; Mark 2:15; Luke 15:2). He moved beyond family ties to claim a motley crowd as his brothers and sisters (Matt. 12:48). He dismissed ethnic identity to embrace the despised Samaritans (John 4:39). Going beyond virtue, he forgave sinners (Luke 19:7). As God's perfection made him willing to let the rain fall on the just and unjust alike (Matt. 5:43), the same disregard for differences marked Jesus' life of love. Love made him the man for *all* others.

3. *Love moved Jesus to help all people for their sakes.* Jesus came "not to be served, but to serve and [thus] to give his life as a ransom for many." Is it possible, Dag Hammarskjöld once mused, that Jesus did it all, "yet for his own sake—in megalomania?"[8] What seems like sacrifice may have been an investment in future pleasure. Perhaps he was savoring the anticipation of the sweet taste of victory, and of the applause for his global coup. But Jesus' manner does not encourage us to ascribe such self-seeking erotic motives to him. His love seemed to drive him to us for our sakes, so that we could be saved. Of course, Jesus cherished the joys that followed final victory; the thought of them sustained him in his time of ultimate suffering (Heb. 12:2). But knowing he would enjoy the results does not mean that he paid the price only to win a crown for himself. We must believe that he suffered *for our sakes*. He was the man *for* all others, for their sake.

4. *Love moved Jesus to help all people for their sakes without regard for cost.* To provide the help we needed most, God had to give us himself. "For God so loved the world that he gave his only begotten Son . . ." (John 3:16). Love moved him toward us for our sakes; and our great distance from him meant love could set no limits. So, although Jesus "was in the form of God [he] emptied himself, taking the form of a servant . . . and being found in human form he humbled himself and became obedient unto death, even death on a cross" (Phil. 2:7, 8). Two moments in history signal the price of love: the moment of Jesus' birth and the moment of his death. In the light of these events, we must think of gift-love as a push toward ultimate sacrifice. Moved by love to help us for our sakes, he was committed to do whatever had to be done to help us. So he gave up his divine status

50   and became human; and in the act of total identification he was
crucified as a sinner. Love moved him to help without regard for
the price he would have to pay.

These four pencil strokes in the infinite portrait of divine
love suffice to remind us that the love which moved almighty
God into our need-zone was very different from the good feelings one has in the presence of an attractive person. The love
God acted out in Jesus was a spiritual energy that moved him
to overcome all obstacles so that he could get close to us, only
in order to help us.

C. CAN CHRISTIAN LOVE AND HUMAN LOVE LIVE TOGETHER?

Can Christian gift-love tolerate human self-love?

Forty years ago the Swedish theologian Anders Nygren wrote
a book about the great gap between Christian love and human
love, between agape and eros. Nygren's scholarly masterpiece
remains the centerpiece of any serious discussion about the
unique character of gift-love. For him, agape is utterly incom-
patible with eros. The two cannot coexist in the same human
heart. Eros is incurably self-centered, acquisitive, and demanding. It is evil when it wallows in concupiscence; it is even worse
when it soars toward God, for then it seeks to manipulate the
Almighty for our own selfish purposes.[9] Agape must have nothing to do with eros.

Was Nygren right? Does gift-love force us to turn against
our need-loves? I do not think so, any more than Christ asks us
to choose between his salvation and God's creation. Rather than
rejecting eros as an enemy, agape redeems eros and sets it free
to be a friend.

If we believe that eros can be a friend to Christian love, we
also affirm our love for ourselves. Jesus neither condemns nor
praises self-love, but his saying that we should love others as we
love ourselves leads us to suppose that self-love can be as good
as it is natural.

It seems to me that there are at least five good ways of loving
ourselves.

First, the search for one's own fulfilment is an appropriate
kind of self-love. Every living thing is kept alive with a vital
power to become what it was meant to be. A bush is restless

until it produces a rose. A woman is restless until she becomes
a whole self, at peace with her own being. Any person's wholeness comes in union with God; therefore a person's basic erotic
need is the need for God. So in loving God, we also love
ourselves.

A second way in which we love ourselves well is in our
longing for joy. A deep need for joy leads us to seek a feeling
of being one with the goodness of life. The Westminster Confession gives a theological slant to this; our true destiny, it says, is
to "glorify God and enjoy him forever." John Calvin said that
no one can know God without knowing himself;[10] it is equally
true that we cannot enjoy God without enjoying ourselves; we
cannot even want to enjoy him unless we want to enjoy ourselves. All those texts in the Bible that command us to rejoice
in the Lord are telling us to feel the goodness of our life. To
pretend to be too selfless to seek joy for oneself is hypocrisy,
Barth says.[11]

In the third place, a person loves himself well when he loves
himself as a member of the body of Christ. Only as one member
with others of a body, in which all are one as members of each
other, am I myself. I cannot love myself well unless I have love
for the body of which I am only a member. Nor can I love the
body without loving other members of it. As I affirm myself as
a hand, I affirm another as a head or a foot. In so doing I do not
love myself as an island, but as a part of a whole.

Fourth, self-love can be a means of loving others. You cannot
love anyone effectively if you hate yourself. Gift-love takes a
great deal of energy. We must not squander the energy we need
to care for others by failing to take care of ourselves. Furthermore, the gifts latent in you must be nurtured if you are to give
them for someone else's good. In this way, you love yourself as
a means of loving others; you seek to grow, not to become
something just for yourself, but to become an agent of agapic
love for others.

Finally, we may love ourselves well when we love sexually.
When a woman seeks a man, when she longs to be close to him,
their minds and bodies interpenetrating, she is loving herself, for
she is seeking herself in their union. She cannot desire him
unless she desires the self he gives back to her. In this way, she
desires him for what he is; she wants what he is, not merely what

52   he does, precisely because in him she seeks the fulfilment of
herself.

God's agape does not eliminate eros from the treasury of his
good created blessings. God's gift-love which came in Jesus was
meant not to destroy but to liberate his creation. It is not love
of self, but love of self alone, which is sinful. Indeed we ought
to love ourselves so that we can be loving agents of God's love.

The gift-love of Jesus flows in a direction opposite to eros,
but the two are compatible. The richness of love is accounted
for by this directional flow. We move by love toward our neighbor for his sake when God dwells in us. We can also move
toward our neighbor for our sake; and, in finding what we need
from him, we enrich his life in turn. We diminish him only when
we fail to respect him, turning him from a priceless person into
a mere instrument for our pleasure. Here justice plays a key
role, for it sustains respect for the other while eros seeks what
it needs from him.

Christian love and human benevolence

Agape is so much like benevolence that we must ask how they
differ. The gospel asks us to love our neighbor as Jesus loved
us, with a helping love. The rational principle of benevolence
asks us to live so as to increase our neighbor's good. What dis-
tinguishes the two?

1. *The law of Christian love has different roots from benevolence.*
Jesus' law of love is rooted in God. James Gustafson speaks of
the believer's "epistemological privilege": Christians are attuned
to the true "intentionality of the ultimate power."[12] That is, when
Christians accept the law of love, they know that gift-love is the
fundamental energy that binds the personal universe together.
They know that God is Love.

If you ask a non-believer why we all ought to help each
other, you are not likely to hear about obeying the God of love.
Unbelievers may feel that the roots of their benevolence go no
deeper than their own personal inclinations. A friend of mine
who professes to no particular religious faith lives out what I
would call a benevolent life-style. Some years ago he walked
away from a senior partnership in a large law firm to set up shop
alone in a vacant ghetto store, where he does legal work unpaid
for black and native Americans who are in trouble with the law.
If anyone were to ask him *why* he did this, he would say some-

thing like: "It seemed to be the only way to get this job done, and I just wanted to do it." It is enough for him to see a need and fill it. He feels no need for a law rooted in God.

But I think he was obeying a law—he did what he believed he *ought* to do.[13] Moreover, I suspect he believes that we all *ought* to help people who need help. And if we all ought to help others, there is a kind of law that obligates us. If the roots of this law are not in God, where are they?

Philosophers have disagreed about the roots of the law of benevolence. One view is that I ought to help my neighbor because he is a rational creature and as such is worthy of my respect. But he is also, sometimes, a *needy* rational creature, and since I respect him, I ought also to do what I can to help him.[14] Another view is that I ought to help my neighbor because everyone's life, including mine, will be better off if all of us (within reason) are helpful to each other. In either case, the law is rooted in humanity.

The Christian law of love is rooted in the heart of the universe, as is the natural will to love. Weak as it may be, every benevolent impulse, including the impulses of unbelievers, comes from the God of love. Calvin showed what ingrates we as believers would be if we did not thank the Spirit of God for every "natural instinct to foster and preserve society."[15] To set any benevolence in soil other than the Spirit of God is to rob the gracious Spirit of praise he deserves, for all love is rooted in God. Believers and unbelievers may disagree about the roots of love, but believers know that love itself grows only from the heart of God.

2. *The law of Christian love asks more than benevolence.* The cross is a sign that Christ's law of love asks more than the common sense of benevolence. Love, as we see it in Christ, knows no limits. It keeps pushing us beyond what good sense tells us we have to do. Have I written one check to help feed poor people? Love pushes me to write one more—and one more after that, until there is no more money in the account. Life, of course, does put limits on love. We cannot give the extra dollar if our account is overdrawn. We cannot give medicine to three wounded people if we have enough for only one. But love drives us beyond the limits of our resources, even if it cannot undo those limits.

Ordinary benevolence does have limits built into it. It does not lead to a cross; it only asks us (in Alan Donagan's words)

54   "to do what good one reasonably can" for other people's welfare. It is a cool form of care, cautious lest it go too far. Its general aim is to increase the good in the world without decreasing our own unreasonably. A "religious ideal of charity" may go "far beyond" the common call of ordinary benevolence, the philosopher concedes, but such heroics are not the duties of rational benevolence.[16] The law of Christian love asks for more.[17]

   3. *Christian love asks a more selfless motive than benevolence.* Christian love creates a very clear-cut motive—a desire only for the neighbor's good. Pure agapic love includes a pure will to help the neighbor so that he will be better off than he was before, not so that the lover can get something for himself from loving. In an expansive moment, Paul enjoined: "Let no one seek his own good, but the good of his neighbor" (1 Cor. 10:24). Here we have a pure will devoted to the neighbor in forgetfulness of our own needs.[18]

   Benevolence is more accommodating. It is less concerned about a pure motive than about a helpful concern. We need not seek our neighbor's interests purely for his sake: if we give a costly gift to our neighbor because we enjoy the thought of sacrificing something, we do not violate the principle of benevolence. All that matters is that we help people. Benevolence is thus a more reasonable principle than agape.[19]

How do love and justice work together?

The two absolute mandates that pervade all our human relationships are love and justice. How do these touch on each other? Does love tell us anything about the duties of justice or justice about the duties of love?

   Some would say that love and justice have nothing to do with each other. They speak different languages and work on different premises. Love is practiced person-to-person; justice is practiced through institutions like government and courts. Love is spontaneous and generous; justice carefully calculates the merits of competing claims. Love goes out to people regardless of their undeserving; justice deals only with what people merit. Love gives without counting costs; justice counts the cost to the penny. Love and justice are like oil and water; each has its place, but each loses its own usefulness if you try to mix them.[20]

   Quite the contrary, others would retort. Love and justice are the same: justice is the tough side of love. Or, to change the image, love is the motor, justice the rudder. Love has the vision, justice the direction. If there are two wounded men on the road to Jericho, justice is only love deciding which one to help first. And when we are asking what a decent wage should be or who should bear the brunt of the fight against inflation, justice is love's tough mind working out the painful compromise.[21]

The discussion of how love and justice are related tends to become a matter of definitions, and we find our attention straying from life to ideas. If we do focus on life, however, I think we sense that love and justice are two different dimensions of reality that belong together. There are several ways in which love and justice need each other, and if they are kept together they help us to know what God expects us to do.

1. *Love demands that we do justice.* Justice is love's minimum demand. Since the law of love commands us to help our neighbor, it requires us at least to help him get or keep what is coming to him. Although love does not tell us what our neighbors have a right to have, it does require that we support them in their right, whatever it is. Love always seeks at least justice because people are deeply hurt when they are denied their rights.

But love is never satisfied with justice. If people received only what was theirs by right and gave others only what they had coming to them, we would all be shorn of love's beautiful extravagance. No woman would ever pour expensive ointment on a Savior's head. Nobody would know what it was like to receive a gift and bless the giver. Love adds heart to the hands of justice. But we who love may never ignore the cool claims of justice in the name of love's warmer gifts. If love does not work for justice, it probably does nothing at all.

2. *Love enlarges the scope of justice.* Usually we do well first to care for people close to us. A father owes it to his own children to care for their survival before he tends to the claims of strangers' children. A city owes its own needy residents special care. If 30% of the heads of households in a poverty-stricken town in Appalachia have no jobs, is it reasonable to expect them to invite refugees from Cambodia or Haiti to settle in their town?[22] Love does not deny such special bonds of family and country, but it keeps our eyes open to the just claims of strangers as well. It nudges our concerns for justice beyond those who are close to us. It helps us see that hungry children far away are not getting

56   their rights to live and that we can best help our own children if we help other people's children too.

3. *Love enriches justice.* Love keeps pushing the common sense of justice beyond itself into the righteousness of the kingdom of God. The temptation to be satisfied too quickly with legal justice is a strong one: if others are getting what the laws of their society allow them, we too easily assume, justice is being done. But no society of sinful people achieves even the bare bones of a structure of justice through its legal system. Without generous love to move its people to a richer sense of justice, a society tends to be satisfied with the minimum.

The first way love enriches justice is by injecting mercy into law. Portia's word to Shylock reflects the spark of agape that still burns in the heart of everyone: "Earthly power doth then show likest God's when mercy seasons justice." Love enables us to push justice beyond legal codes to actual human needs, to accommodate the letter of the law to the special needs of real people.

Love also enriches justice by keeping the biblical vision of righteousness and *shalom* alive. Love wants more for people than what they have coming to them within a secular social order. Love envisions a community in which people care for one another and help each other find joy in life. Love seeks a society in which people flourish together as children of God. Under the sway of love's law, the believer will keep alive a vision of the City of God: "Behold the dwelling of God is with men. He will dwell with them, and they shall be his people . . . ; and he will wipe every tear from their eyes, and death shall be no more, neither shall there be mourning nor crying nor pain any more" (Rev. 21:3, 4).

4. *Love gets direction from justice.* There is seldom only one wounded man on the road to Jericho. And most Good Samaritans have a limited budget. Whenever we have resources for only one needy person and meet two, the calculations of justice must direct the work of love. If there are two wounded men, we need to ask which of them needs help most. Will one survive if he waits for the next Samaritan to come along? Is one more deserving than the other, more useful, more needed? Is one likely to die no matter what we do for him? These are not questions love is able to cope with; they call for the headwork of justice.

Justice also respects the responsibilities of the needy person. Justice says that a person who chooses to be poor should be allowed to have what he chooses. Nor will justice allow us—for love's sake—to assume responsibility for other people's mistakes. If my neighbor goes deeply into debt for luxuries he bought with his credit card, and then habitually expects me to pay his heating bill, justice holds back the hand of love. If my neighbor's business is on the verge of ruin because he is incompetent and lazy, justice may require love to let his business fail, and then help him find another line of work.

II. WHY DOES GOD EXPECT US TO LOVE OUR NEIGHBOR?

Why does God expect us to love people so selflessly? Niebuhr called agapic love sublime madness; is there method in this madness? Is agape reasonable?

I think we can claim that God's commandment is basically reasonable if we can give positive answers to two questions. (1) Is our neighbor intrinsically lovable? (2) Are we lovers by nature? If our neighbor has something in him worth our care and if caring agapically comes naturally to us, God is reasonable in commanding us to love our neighbor as Jesus loved us.[23]

A. ARE NEIGHBORS LOVABLE?

If our neighbors are lovable to God, they must be lovable to us. So we can ask: is there something about sinful people that God finds lovable? Anders Nygren contends that nothing in us can explain God's love to us; we are nobodies, empty and lost.[24] There is no reason for God to love us except the reasons of his loving heart.[25] God loves us and gives us value, but nothing about us explains why he should love us in the first place. The answer lies only in the love that flows freely, carelessly, unaccountably, spontaneously—and in that sense unreasonably—from God's heart.

To know God's forgiving love is to gain an insight into what is right about Nygren's theology. When love comes, the buttress of our pride is ripped away. Defenseless, we are held by love alone. Merton writes that love turns a man completely inside out, so that he no longer has a soul to defend, no longer an intimate heritage to protect against inroads and dilapidations. . . . The full maturity of the spiritual life cannot be reached until we pass through the dread, anguish, trouble, and fear that necessarily accompany the inner crisis of spiritual death in which we finally abandon our attachment to our exterior self and surrender completely to Christ.[26]

Inside the cold cave of our souls, love, when it holds us, is a miracle. Nothing can explain it except the loving will of God.

It is one thing to *experience* nothingness at the edge of night before the dawn of love. It is quite another to declare that human beings have no objective worth before the love of God. God probably would not die for tigers or trees; he set his saving love on his own fallen likeness. When Jesus loved prostitutes and publicans he must have seen them also as precious persons. God could never forget that even sinners are his created pearls of great price.[27]

God's symphony of love is played out in two keys, eros and agape. Had an angel dared ask God why he would go to such pains to save his rebel ingrates, God would *not* have answered, "I know they're worthless, but I'm caught in my own compulsive love." He might have reminded the angel that those ingrates were, after all, still only "a little lower than the angels" (Ps. 8). If our overwhelming sense of being forgiven leads us to sing of Jesus' death "for such a worm as I," we must nevertheless also understand that he died for creatures who create Ninth Symphonies, Sistine Chapels, and Roman republics—creatures all and obstinately sinful, but still creative images of God. The worth of sinful human beings makes it reasonable, even though not necessary, for God to love them in spite of their sin. The cross of Christ tells us that we were worth dying for just as it surely tells us we needed dying for.

It *is* reasonable to love our neighbor, because he is—in spite of everything—worth loving. He ought to be loved because he is lovable.[28] The hungry child whom I am moved to feed is precious beyond my calculation; can I ever forget his value? The nurse who washes the back of a dying leper is caring for someone worthy of her love. If you risk your life to pull a stranger from a burning car, you do not wonder whether the stranger is worth taking a chance for. If someone standing by says to you: "Don't bother, he's not worth it," you scream, "Of course he's worth it, you fool: he is a human being." But you would not have risked your neck to save the stranger's dog. There is a difference in value. In the indestructible nobility of every needy human soul is something that makes sense of the command: "Love your neighbor by helping him, for his sake, at any cost."

B. ARE WE AGAPIC LOVERS BY NATURE?

Agapic love is "the potential and perfection of every human being," as Niebuhr put it.[29] The law of love is therefore the law of life. Agape is what I was made for. To quote Merton again:

> There is in the human will an innate tendency, an inborn capacity for disinterested love. This power to love another for his own sake is one of the things that makes us like God. . . . It is a power which transcends and escapes the inevitability of self-love.[30]

Merton is right. Jesus calls us to be nothing else but human, and what he asks of us as disciples fits what we are as creatures. The costliest demands of discipleship are really invitations back to our true selves.[31] "Love is my identity. Selflessness is my true self. Love is my true character. Love is my name."[32]

Our theology of Jesus Christ confirms the humanity of divine love. For if Jesus is truly human, his love is truly human love. As the man for others, he tells us what it is like to be a person. He reached out his hand to heal people as if loving were the truly human way. In giving us a commandment to love each other as he loved us, he was inviting us to his own very human life-style.

Even within our fallen erotic adventures are agapic strains, perhaps weak, which hint that agape is naturally woven into our humanity. I cannot find my joy, my self, in the person I love unless I also give myself to her. If I am to gain the self I seek in her, there must be a touch of giving just for her sake. There is a desire inside me to tell her that she looks fine, to hurry to her side when she has the flu, to buy tickets for a concert she wants to attend just to give her some pleasure. And if our lot so falls, I will nurse her through all cancerous ills, to the end. And even if I know that I will get a dividend, I would swear that I was not doing it only for the payoff.

> Love seeketh not itself to please,
> Nor for itself hath any care
> But for another gives its ease,
> And builds a Heaven in Hell's despair.

60   Blake romanticized natural love into divine agape, but he did
see clearly that eros cannot be human without agapic insinuations.

Agape does not flow freely and easily from our sinful hearts.
Eros always tends to overreach, and our best love is twisted into
deceitful little demands for pleasure on our terms. We love, as
we live, by grace. What matters is that when, subdued by grace,
we love as Jesus loved, we are truly human again, loving as God
made us to love in the first place.

Realizing this, we can resist the false humility that says it is
only God who loves through us, as if we are at best like tubes
with divine love hardly touching us as it flows through them.[33]
We know better. When we do practice love, we know that it is
really ourselves who love, though we know it is Christ within us
who enables us (Gal. 2:20). God's love comes into our lives to
make them more, not less, human. God abides in us without
crowding out our humanity.

Someone may ask whether this really does justice to the
superhumanity demanded by the love of the extra mile? Is it no
more than human to pray for our enemies? Is it natural to do
good to those who persecute us? Surely there is a divine madness
about such prodigal love. My response is that the love of the
extra mile is no more new to humanity than the love of the cross
was new to God.

When we learn to love our enemies and to turn the other
cheek, we are learning to use human love in new ways to fit a
fallen situation. We must love enemies only because there are
enemies who need loving. In a sinful world we need to love with
self-giving extravagance only because sin messes up the human
situation very badly. But when creation is whole again, we will
love with the same sort of agapic energy and yet never need to
feed a hungry person or reclaim an enemy.

III. HOW DOES LOVE TELL US WHAT TO DO?

The love commandment asks us to help a neighbor, for the
neighbor's sake, at a greater cost than we may feel like paying.
The commandment is universal and absolute, and it is a law of
life—that is, it commands us to conform to what we are. But
what does it tell us to do when we meet a specific neighbor in

the crunch of cruel and conflicting circumstances? The law of life is as general as it is universal and as broad as it is absolute. Can we sharpen the focus?

Do the other biblical commandments tell us all we need to know of love's more specific duties? Once we know the commandments, do we really need the law of love to tell us what to do? The question brings to mind the conflict between the "old morality" and the "new morality."

The old morality believed that love does not tell us what to do. Our day-by-day directives come entirely from commandments or rules other than love. Love moves us to want to obey God's rules and helps us obey them gladly and with the proper motive. But love does not function as a law that tells us what to do. I think the old morality was wrong. Love does tell us what to do. It informs us as it enables us.

The new morality insisted that only the law of love tells us what we need to know. The other commandments are helpful hints, and if you use them as rules of thumb you will be in good company; but you must be willing to drop any of them whenever love tells you that your neighbor is better served by ignoring the rules. It is the human situation, not the divine commands, that gives concrete content to the general law of love. I think the new morality was wrong, too. The law of love is too general to replace the other biblical commandments.[34]

I propose that we look for cooperative links between love and the other commandments. Between love and the commandments there ought to be a "holy marriage" and mutual enrichment.[35] Neither the old nor the new morality seems to provide this. So let us see how a "holy marriage" of love and commands might make each of them more helpful to us.

A. RESPECT FOR THE NEIGHBOR

Paul said that love never hurts the neighbor (Rom. 13:10) and therefore fulfils the law. Behind the law of harmless love stands respect for the person of our neighbor. He is there, in his inviolable personhood, demanding by his very existence and his place in society that we respect him. The negative commands call us to stand back and let our neighbor be what he is and do what he is called to do. Following Paul's lead, then, we can read each commandment as a rule that tells us at least how we can avoid hurting our neighbor.

62   —Love respects a neighbor's right to his biological life.
—Love respects a neighbor's right to keep what is rightly his.
—Love respects a person's right to truthfulness.
—Love respects a spouse's right to fidelity in a covenanted relationship.
—Love respects a parent's right to the dignity and respect due to a parent of a child.

These are the least of love's demands: you could keep them by spending most of the day asleep. Yet if they were universally observed, the social order would be a utopia compared to our violent society. If we lived where no person needed to fear for his life, where no stranger ever was a threat to another's house and goods, where everyone could be trusted to tell the truth, where no one broke faith with the covenants holding marriages and families together, we would be living in a society that had at least the just foundations for a community of common respect.

B. NEGATIVE RULES AND AFFIRMATIVE PRINCIPLES

Love did not allow the Good Samaritan to "live and let live." Love translates the negative rules into affirmative laws. *Respect* becomes *care*.

"Thou shalt not kill" becomes: Do everything in your power to protect, nourish, and nurture your neighbor's life.

"Thou shalt not steal" becomes: Do all that you can to help people keep the property they rightfully have and to get the property they rightfully need.

"Thou shalt not bear false witness" becomes: Speak truthfully, act out the truth in your own life, and seek the truth on behalf of your neighbor.

"Thou shalt not commit adultery" becomes: Do all you can to nurture your marriage into a mutually enriching human relationship.

"Honor your father and mother" is already an affirmative rule, and love needs only to direct honor into personally helpful ways.

As love turns negatives into affirmatives, it pays the price of imprecision. We venture into uncharted regions with the commandments as a compass, not a map. It isn't difficult to understand what it means to refrain from stealing; but helping other people get enough property to survive as human beings is a loose-jointed mandate. Staying out of a neighbor's bed is simple;

creative fidelity to one's spouse in the boredom and agony of a bad marriage is complicated. In short, as love translates the law into affirmative directions, we are left with greater responsibility but less precision.

C. ARRANGING PRIORITIES

The compass needle of love always points in the direction of the neighbor who needs help. Helping my neighbor is of higher priority than whether I am personally tainted by telling a lie. Generally speaking, love tells me that my neighbor's life is more important than my property. If I can save my neighbor's life only by telling a lie, love would say, "Lie, by all means." If a mother could save her children by letting a rapist have his way, love would probably tell her to yield. Love, as a rule, indicates that "Thou shalt not kill" is usually more important than the other commandments, because the law of love is person-directed, and unless there is a person alive before us, we need not bother about his property, his marriage, or his good name.

"Here, therefore, let us stand fast: our life shall best conform to God's will and the prescription of the law when it is in every respect fruitful for our brethren."[36] This was Calvin's advice. It is the counsel of love.

D. COMMANDMENT-BREAKING

The law of love is too general to tell us when we ought to do what a commandment tells us not to do. We need more than love to know when to tell a lie or shoot a human being dead. We also need solid evidence that it is necessary to break one commandment in order to respect both the rights and needs of people involved. That is, we need a reasonable indication that breaking a commandment will serve the cause of justice as well as the law of love, and over the long run at that.

We are not asking whether the commandments may ever be broken. Most serious people agree that a person may sometimes by morally led to lie or steal. But is love enough to tell us when a commandment-breaking moment has come? I think not.

If John decides to tell his wife Mary a lie about his relationship with Phyllis, he needs more to justify his lie than a loving desire to make things easier for Mary. He needs a clear argument that lying to Mary will not hurt others—his children, himself, maybe Phyllis—just as much or more than it will help Mary. He

64   must show that "making things easier" for Mary now will not set
her up for much more pain later on. He has to have a convincing
answer to the probability that his lie will harm himself morally
even more than it helps Mary feel better. John needs to be
certain that lying to Mary does not erode the trust people need
to live humanly together. Finally, he needs to persuade himself
that *everyone* in his position should lie to his wife. The point is
that the justification for breaking a commandment requires a lot
more data than love itself can give us.

Can John demonstrate to his own conscience that lying to
Mary will make for justice? Mary, after all, has an undeniable
right to truthfulness from him, as his wife especially, but as his
neighbor too. Surely it is better for Mary to be given her rights
than to be denied them. So John has to prove that Mary's need
to be comfortable living with a lie counts for more than her
right to decide for herself what she wants to do with the truth.
Justice is as absolute as love is. If love can incline us to disobey
a commandment, justice needs to be consulted beforehand.

The conflicts of our world may force us to choose against
one divine commandment out of respect for another. Breaking
a commandment must be done in a way that upholds other commandments. The burden of proof is on the commandment-
breaker. He must demonstrate that his commandment-breaking
serves the moral absolutes of justice and love. Love may give us
the first indication that we ought to lie or steal or kill to help a
neighbor, but we will need more to go on than love.[37]

Sometimes we need more than love to avoid doing harm
when love by itself *seems* to be clear. As confusion and hysteria
swirled through Saigon when the Americans retreated from Vietnam, Christian hearts of love went out to babies who were left
behind as orphans. Love led magnanimous Americans to airlift
children out of the path of Communism to American families
waiting to adopt them. The law of love seemed clearly to compel
helping these helpless infant neighbors. Later, questions were
raised. Are we certain that all of these children were in fact
orphans? Was it fair to pluck them from their homeland, without
their choice, and transplant them into a foreign culture? If the
facts were all known, Americans may have kidnapped children
in the name of love. The hangover of doubt reminds us that we
need sound reason and adequate information as well as love.

E. BEYOND THE COMMANDMENTS   65

Moral commandments apply to the crucial moral nucleus of our actions. But most acts have no moral nucleus. Not everything is morally important. We are free to do what we please about some things. We may go to the theater or stay home and watch television. We may smoke a cigar or refuse to allow the stench of tobacco in our home. We may make love with our spouse three times a week or once a month. We may use our freedom to listen to rock instead of Bach, to drink wine instead of water. But what we do with our freedom may be morally wrong if it needlessly hurts our neighbor (1 Cor. 6:12). More, there may be a time and a place to say Yes to something and another time and place to say No to the same thing. How can we know whether and when to say Yes? Love says: enjoy your freedom, but never at your neighbor's expense.

With this law in our hearts, we may have gained what Paul called "the knowledge of his will in spiritual wisdom . . . to lead a life worthy of the Lord" (Col. 1:9, 10). Paul is talking about a spiritual sense for what is truly important, what really matters, for a situation in which the commandments have no word. We may be free to say Yes or No, as we please, to things that do not matter morally; we are never free to do what love tells us will hurt our neighbor.

Love does not give us a computer printout on the chances that using our freedom will hurt someone. When we are free to do as we please, love tells us not to be pleased by anything that hurts a neighbor needlessly. But we do not have 20-20 vision for what might hurt him. Love may help us distinguish between a neighbor's needs and prejudices. It may enable us to judge when a neighbor is really hurt by our act and when he is only enjoying self-righteous jealousy of our freedom. The law of love never tells us to cater to Pharisees' scruples, and its power for discernment may sensitize us to the difference between hurting a person and only pricking a prejudice.[38]

QUESTIONS FOR DISCUSSION

1. What can a person know about agapic love apart from Christian faith? How would he know?

2. Do you think that the law of love matches created human

66   nature and is therefore the duty of every man? Can the law of love be part of "mere morality," the morality demanded of ordinary people?

3. Do you think that self-love is consistent with giving-love?

4. If the law of love is rooted in God the Creator, is the same law obligatory for everyone, non-believers as well as believers?

5. Why does gift-love need a blend of erotic love to keep gift-love from being patronizing?

6. Do you think the law of love allows us to take care of "our own" before we care for strangers?

7. Do you think that anyone has ever lived by selfless love; do you think that you ever do; do you think Jesus was only serving others or do you think he was, in serving us, seeking a reward for himself?

8. How is Kant's view of benevolence different from the Christian view of agapic love?

9. Is it your true nature to love others and to help them only for their sakes?

10. Do you think that love can tell you whether it is right to disobey a command?

11. Do you think that some things we do have no intrinsic moral significance and that only love can tell us whether we should be free to do them?

RESPECT FOR AUTHORITY:

"Honor Thy Father and Mother"

The first of the moral commandments tells every child of human parents that his moral duty within the family is to honor those people who gave him a place in the land of the living. Whatever else he may feel about them, however deep his love or intense his anger, however rich his gratitude or bitter his resentment, he is called to respect those who, besides giving him existence, were given to be his prime teachers and guides. Honor is the unsentimental moral nucleus within the complex relationships between any child and his parents. From the day the child is born to the day the parents die—and even reaching beyond their grave as a relationship to an ineradicable memory—everything in the relationship changes except the moral duty of honor.

The rule of honor is probably as universal as any human duty. No child, young or old, ought ever to dishonor his parents. In every culture parents believe in their right to be treated with respect by their offspring. Plato probably registered a universal ethic when he said that on the scale of human decencies honor to parents is second only to piety toward God. But absolute as we admit it to be and universal as we imagine it to be, honor to parents is a duty that shifts and slips in our hands as we try to examine what it calls us, young or old children, to do.

As we noted earlier, we shall look at this commandment from three angles: first asking *what* it requires of us quite apart from our abilities to do this; then looking into the *why* of the commandment, to see what in our human situation makes it reasonable and right to affirm the commandment as our human calling; and finally trying to see *how* the commandment might be obeyed as it filters through some conflicts and complexities of real life.

I. WHAT THE COMMAND REQUIRES

There is a stubborn single-mindedness to the Fifth Commandment. To get a feel for the sharpness of its focus, we may notice

68   a couple of things that it does not say. First, the commandment
ignores the warm affection all parents want from their children.
It does not tell children to feel happy about their parents; it does
not tell us to like being with parents on camping trips or to relish
having them over for dinner; it does not encourage happy emotional relationships. All that it commands is *honor*.

Nor does the commandment tell parents to honor their children. The child's own right to respect is not in view. We may
agree that children deserve a sort of honor as precious human
beings, but this commandment is not about our worth as individuals. It is concerned with family structure and the role of
parents as teachers and leaders in the family.

The ancient word for honor was something like "weightiness" (Hebrew, *kabad*). To honor persons you had to respect
them as people who carried a great deal of weight in your life.
That is, you had to let them have influence, dignity, and above
all authority for you. *Kabad* smacks a little more of the military
academy than dinner at home on Mother's Day.

A child who honored his parents fit naturally into the ancient
Hebrew family. The Hebrew clan clustered around a patriarchal
center. The oldest living male was the hub around which the
family wheel turned; and the family included great-grandchil-
dren, grandchildren, children, along with an assortment of servants, slaves, and concubines. Children were neither a nuisance
nor an emotional luxury, but part of productive teams. They
helped keep back the ravages of nature and helped the family
make a go of the farm. And, above all, they were the next chapter
in God's romance with the human family, the link between God's
covenant of the past and his salvation in the future.

A child in turn was rewarded by getting his selfhood from
his family. He was not merely an individual named Pete or Tom,
but a scion identified by his parent's name, Lev-son-of-Ashur.
Moreover, children were accustomed to living with an autocrat
of a father, whom they saw as clan ruler, warrior, high priest,
and judge, as well as father. We can understand why young Hebrews did not resent the Fifth Commandment as a bridle on
their galloping individuality. And remember that the sons who
heard the commandment were often themselves men who had
become warriors, rulers, priests, and fathers.

But if we can see that honoring parents came more or less

naturally for Hebrew children, this does not tell us what a Hebrew child was expected to do by way of honoring parents. The writers of the Old Testament could spot outrageous acts of dishonor more easily than they could define honor. When they did indict flagrant violations of a parents' honor, they recommended no mercy: "Whoever strikes his father or his mother shall be put to death. . . . Whoever curses his father or his mother shall be put to death" (Exod. 21:15, 17). We hardly need to be told, of course, that it is dishonor to curse or cuff your parents. But what is worth noticing is that this was not just a private family affair; it was a social offense calling for community response.

> If a man has a stubborn and rebellious son, who will not obey the voice of his father or the voice of his mother . . . they shall say to the elders of his city: "This our son is stubborn and rebellious; he is a glutton and a drunkard." Then all the men of the city shall stone him to death (Deut. 21:18–21).

No wonder, then, that when a child ignores the "weightiness" of a parent, "all Israel shall hear, and fear" (Deut. 21:21). Dishonor a parent, and you remove a pillar from the foundations of Israel's society.

But what did this deference and respect for parents come down to? Honor was a willingness at least to listen to the voice of one's father or mother, those whom God gives to be our teachers and guides. For Israel, the family was the school where a person learned who he was and what God expected him to do.

> And these words which I command you this day shall be upon your heart; and you shall teach them diligently to your children, and shall talk of them when you sit in your house, and when you walk by the way, and when you lie down, and when you rise (Deut. 6:6f.).

In and through the family the good word was passed along to all generations of the human race; and in the family the father was the designated spokesman: the Lord had "established a testimony in Jacob, and appointed a law in Israel, which he commanded our fathers to teach to their children" (Ps. 78:5).

The father's authorized role was family storyteller; the child's authentic role was to be a listener. He showed his respect for the father by listening with a mind bent toward believing and obeying. In the long run the father's honor rested with the integrity of his office as spokesman for God in the family, the teller of God's story and the teacher of God's law. And the honor a child gave him was wrapped up primarily in his respect for his father's office.

A child honored his parents long after their roles were reversed. When the parents grew weak and the child grew strong, when the child became the parents' caretaker, when the parents' economic value was small and the child's was great (Lev. 27:7), the child remained a child called to honor his parents. The parents were to be kept at center stage in family affairs. They were never to be begrudged space, never asked to leave home: "He who does violence to his father and chases away his mother is a son who causes shame and brings reproach" (Prov. 19:26). The power of parents might wane and their active authority diminish, but they always stood for God before the child, and they never lost their dignity as caretakers and teachers.

Israel's family life is a profile of how the divine commandment infiltrated ancient Jewish ways. From it we can extract something of what the Lord meant for families across the borders of time and culture. What we distil is an unsentimental notion of honor, not the platitudes of the typical Mother's Day card, but moral commitment to filial respect and long-term loyalty.

Paul's uncomplicated word to Christian children carried on the Hebrew expectation: "Obey your parents in everything, for this pleases the Lord" (Col. 3:20). Or do it just because "this is right" (Eph. 6:1). Here is a sober way to honor one's parents. A hug or a kiss on the cheek is very pleasant, but nothing suits honor better than doing what your father tells you to do. Paul's word is, of course, meant for young children, not the child-adults who need to find ways of honor beyond obedience. Obedience is not the be-all and end-all of honor, but honor for parents, like honor to God, begins with obedience and lacking it comes to nothing (James 1:26).

The scattered biblical data give us some hints of what honoring a parent meant. A child was early led to understand that he was brought into life and was to find his own identity as a member of a family, not as a mere individual. He knew that he was not an equal in the family alliance, but was expected to defer to his parents as go-betweens between himself and God, mediators of his own past and pointers to his future. He accepted them as his teachers and guides, as well as his trusted protectors and nourishers. When he listened with respect and learned what he was taught, he honored his parents.

It is not hard to see why the commandment speaks of honor rather than love. Love is a natural impulse born of our intense desire to be close to someone we need. The commandment simply assumes that children will love their parents. Love is a natural impulse; honor is a moral choice. These two drives push children in opposite directions, and in doing so create most of the tension and vitality in their relationships with parents. Honor separates them; love draws them together. Honor keeps a distance, maintains a certain reserve; love pulls them close, creates a certain intimacy. When she honors her parents, a daughter stands back a bit, keeps her place, lets the parent keep to himself, with his own mystery. When she loves her parents, a child shares all, invades their sacred places, and enters her parents' private heart. Honor respects the gap between them; love bridges it. Honor is an act of the will that defers and stands back; love is an impulse of the heart that leans on a mother's breast at one stage and gently tucks a feeble mother to bed at another.

Honor and love need each other. Without love honor is frigid, strained, forced, infected with resentment, a hollow shell of polite anger. Without honor love lacks structure and is eventually destructive. Between parents and child, love without honor stands family life on its head, confuses the primal relationship of the human race. Honor is the moral fiber that holds the family together so that all the warm and loving, cold and hateful feelings between parent and child can be enjoyed and endured in a structure of loyalty and respect.

II. WHY SHOULD CHILDREN HONOR THEIR PARENTS?

What is there about parents that makes it imperative for children to treat them with honor? We are not asking what a parent needs to do to *earn* the right to honor; parents have a presumptive right to honor simply because they have conceived and cared for a child. The child's duty assumes the parents' right—but why?[1]

Let us first eliminate a few plausible but wrongheaded reasons for making honor a child's duty. First is the mystique of

72 blood. The Judaeo-Christian sense of filial duty does not stand or fall with the aboriginal rite of passage, the experience of birth. Some people may feel a sense of awe toward the older persons who channeled life's blood into them, bonding them to family, past and future. But what stands behind the duty of honor is not blood mystique but moral choice, not a sense of awe but a will for family order.

Nor is the duty of honor a consequence of the sinfulness of the child. Children are no more sinful than parents are, and it is no more risky to let a child be free than it is to give a parent authority. Families would exist in a perfect world, and no doubt parents would be in charge even of perfect infants. The duty of honor, like most primary obligations, is rooted, not in a child's sinful nature, but in a divine design for human family.

In the third place, we do not owe our parents honor out of gratitude for what they have done for us. Most of us probably do feel a great deal of gratitude to our parents, though many others store up bills of resentment for the grievous faults committed by parents. Where gratitude abounds, it is a powerful motive for obeying the command; but it cannot be the basic reason God uttered the command in the first place. The reason for the command must lie in the fabric of the family, in the role parents are called to play in the growth and nurture of children.

If there is a single reason why parents have a right to their children's respect, I suggest it is *authority*. Within the small society called a family, in which joyful and painful human intimacies are experienced in the fundamental human relationship, one of the strong fibers that holds the alliance together is the authority of the parent. Authority is not a popular facet of family life today, and countless homes have deliberately abandoned it, mistaking authority for a kind of tyranny which all who respect the rights of children should overthrow. Nevertheless, I am going to argue that parental authority, rightly understood, is the one quality all parents have which corresponds to the honor that children are asked to give them. Authority, moreover, is the backbone of family life. So important is it to the strength of the human community that the Lord God—in one of the five primal commandments for human life—called us all to honor our parents for their calling to nurture and guide us, the children set in their care.

A. AUTHORITY IN CRISIS 73

Fear of authority

Among those who claim to be experts on effective parenting today, authority is generally in bad graces. Such aversion to authority plays on our fears of being manipulated into someone else's control. We are especially afraid of the oppression of the young; we fear parental tyrants who force children to do "good" while holding them in bondage. So, writes sociologist Christopher Lasch, authority appears to many today "as something altogether alien, something contemptible, sometimes truly terrible."[2]

Authority has become hopelessly confused with authoritarianism, though in truth they are utterly opposed to each other. Back in the 1930s a group of illustrious psychologists and sociologists published a book in Paris on *Authority and Family*; from it was derived a later English version called *The Authoritarian Personality*.[3] These two books have had a powerful impact on the serious study of the family. Their first thesis is that some persons have a desperate need to seem strong because they fear that they are weak; if they cannot control their world they are afraid of drowning in their own weakness. These are the authoritarian types. The second thesis is that when authoritarian people become parents they create authoritarian children who either become petty tyrants themselves or kowtow easily to tyrants who promise to keep their world under control.

Erich Fromm, one of these original writers, leaves room for no doubt about how he sees the authoritarian person: a child reared in an authoritarian family is likely to become a person of "strict super-ego, guilt feelings, [a] docile lover of parental authority, desire for and pleasure at dominating weaker people."[4] A coward and a bully at heart, the authoritarian person is ready to follow the cult heroes and saviors of the world and at the same time ready to be a tyrant himself wherever he finds weaker people, like the little children in his or her own home.[5] If authority is the same as authoritarianism, the one thing parents must do is to give up the pretense of authority. Who wants his child to become an authoritarian monster?

What we must get clear, however, is that authoritarianism and authority are related as sickness is to health. Authoritarianism is a pathological caricature of authority. Authoritarianism

74   is sick compensation for weakness; authority is a healthy expression of strength. Authoritarian people stifle freedom; authority requires freedom to make it work. Authoritarianism works only when people surrender their own wills; authority works only when people give free and critical consent.

Fear of authority is, in our time, actually a fear of authoritarianism, a confusion that cries for cure.

Loss of authority

But contemporary fear of authoritarianism does not fully explain why parents have lost their authority. Life itself has changed. The ongoing migration into cities crowds families into such close quarters that only a few can embrace anyone besides the parents and children. The movement of women out of the home into the office has drained the parental team of sheer energy to exercise authority. The psychologizing of life has heightened parents' awareness of their own emotional needs: what they often want in their passage years is a last chance to maximize their own experiences and to "get with" their own feelings while they can still enjoy them. Their devotion to getting more out of life for themselves tends to drain them of the emotional energy they need daily to exert authority to guide their children.

While parents turn feverishly inward to their neglected psyches, their children's lives are complicated by revolutions in sexual styles, popular use of drugs, bombardment by the media with violence and sex, unrestricted mobility, and resignation of authority in the classroom. Being an authority with their children in this bewildering circus is almost too much for parents who want somehow to seize what is left of life for themselves. The temptation is to refer children to the experts outside of the family.

The Carnegie Council on the Family took a long look at the crisis of the modern family and decided we should call it quits on the family as a human center for moral and spiritual nurture. Instead, we are told, we should settle for letting the family be a haven for emotional warmth. In a report written by Kenneth Kenniston, called *All Our Children*, the council suggests that the old-fashioned, self-sufficient family, in which parents could be relied upon to teach their children the important things of life, is a myth. In our complex world, parents are simply not competent to prepare their children for taking a poised place in society. "No longer able to do it all themselves, parents today are in some ways like the executives in a large firm—responsible for the smooth coordination of the many people and processes that must work together to produce the final product."[6] Parents shuffle children around from authority to authority and from expert to expert; their own chief business with the children is to provide emotional support. They have no authority of their own.

The one thing the Carnegie Report does not do is encourage parents themselves to recapture a moral sense of their own calling as authorities in their own families. Stanley Hauerwas is right, I think, in saying that the Report "reflects a profound fear and distrust of ourselves and our ability to have and raise children."[7]

Parents cannot give up authority, however, without robbing their children—and eventually society—of strengths neither can do without. The first thing a child loses in a home without authority is a strong sense of his own identity. We become strong individuals when we spend our childhood in a strong family. The child with a clear sense of place in a family is likely to develop a clear sense of who and what he is outside of it. The fact that suicide is now the second most common cause of adolescent deaths in the U.S. cannot be wholly unrelated to the loss of authority in the American home. Genuine authority, based in parents' belief in their calling, is probably the must reliable source from which a child can derive a sense of belonging to a family circle held together by loyalty and love. To know who one is and to whom one belongs is to have a sturdy support against the despair and joylessness of those who cannot find their real selves amid the fantasies of their minds.[8]

Second, it is only reasonable to suppose that loss of authority within the family will affect a child's ability to live with authority in society. Parents who give strong and purposeful leadership teach their children to live with and recognize true authority. If a child develops personally in an atmosphere where trust, loyalty, and honor are expected of him, he is well on his way toward responsible life in a society whose health depends on mutual trust, strong loyalties, and a critical caution with regard to all claims of authority. Permissive parents rob society of people who can distinguish genuine authority from its counterfeits.

Boszormenyi-Nagy and Spark, in a profound study of the invisible fibers that hold the family together, observe aptly that

76   "our society might ultimately be burdened by resentful and justifiably disloyal citizens as long as children are mass produced by
parents who do not intend or are emotionally unable to care for
them."[9] Never having lived with real authorities, young people
are not ready to move into a world in which pretenders to authority compete for control of the human spirit. "Weak families,"
observes Peter Berger, "produce uprooted individuals, unsure
of their direction and therefore searching for some authority,"[10]
and, we might add, finding it in authoritarian substitutes all too
ready not only to lead but control.

The character of a family changes radically when parents
abdicate as authorities. Instead of a community in which loyalty
holds people together in committed trust, it becomes a random
bunch of individuals competing for the affection and services of
the individuals who happened to have arranged for their arrival
on earth, a hit-or-miss arrangement of schedules and appoint-
ments, a crisis-prone conglomerate of people who sometimes
hate and sometimes love each other but who have to get along
because they all need a hearth and board. Into this kind of accidental alliance of individuals the biblical commandment comes
as a promise of ordered love.

B. WHAT AUTHORITY IS

To understand parental authority, we have to look at authority
itself. Parental authority is a species of a mysterious reality we
meet in every viable community.[11] We feel its support—and its
seductions—everywhere. Every time we are stopped in traffic
by the police, every time we take an expert's word for it, every
time we see a conductor move a great orchestra infallibly through
a symphony, every time we submit our life to the promises and
claims of the Word of God, we experience authority. *What* we
experience is someone's assumption that he or she has the power
and the right to lead us and tell us what to do or what to think.

Authority seems to be a blend of power and legitimacy, of
might and right. It is a legitimate power to prevail over other
people's wills. Sheer power without legitimacy is not *real* authority; the Nazis had power but not legitimacy in occupied
France, and hence no authority. But if you claim *legitimacy* without having power, you cannot count on your authority. Juan
Carlos claimed to be the legitimate king of Spain for many years,

but as long as Franco kept him out of power, he had no functioning authority.

What gives any person the right to use power of any kind over another person? From a biblical viewpoint, all authority comes from God. The Creator ordains that human society be kept humanely ordered by vesting some offices with the right to control—to a limited extent—the behavior of certain people. But we must bring this belief about the ultimate source of authority into the dynamics of real life, for human authority works in human ways. We must ask how all human authority is *mediated* through human agencies and how we *recognize* authority when we see it.

The German sociologist Max Weber identified three ways in which people get authority. The first is *tradition*. When people influence other people in the name of laws and customs which their society has believed in for all their history, they do so with authority. They gain authority as others feel their oneness with their own deepest reverence for the past which makes them what they are today. The second is *legality*. When people occupy positions of power according to the established rules of the group, they are given authority to govern people. The third is *spiritual*. When inspired persons call people to a new and better way of life, they are recognized as bearers of divine and righteous power to move people. In that sense they have spiritual authority.[12]

A person, then, must be *given* authority, not seize it as one seizes power. At one level authority comes to someone *before* exercising power; and he or she expects people to recognize it. At another level, however, it is the people affected by authority who determine whether or not someone has it. People must believe and affirm that a person has authority; otherwise, in a very real way, they deprive him of power and, thereby, of effective authority.

We see, then, a dynamic dialogue between a person who claims authority—on the ground that he has been given the right—and those who believe him and by believing enable him to possess authority. A government, no matter how legitimate in point of law, loses authority when the people no longer believe it has the power or the right to govern. A scientist's methods may be sound and her findings verified, but she does not have authority in her field until her peers credit her with it. Her intrinsic right is not enough; she needs to be believed in. So, to

78   be an authority we need investment, not only from God or tradition or the legal system or our own expertise, but also from the people over whom we seek to prevail, or whom we seek to lead, teach, or otherwise influence.

Jesus illustrates the dynamic of personal authority. He had legitimate power to change people's souls, to redirect their lives, to lead them into a new world. No legal apparatus invested him with authority; he wore no badge and never traveled in the company of a military escort. Yet he claimed supreme authority. "All authority," he said, is "given to me" (Matt. 28:18), and the people were astounded at his assumption of such authority (Matt. 7:29).

Yet while Jesus came with authority by virtue of who he was, his legitimacy had to be believed. No one doubted that he had power. But some said his power was illegitimate—of the devil (Matt. 9:34)—and that he therefore had no authority, no right to lead people and influence their wills. Sometimes at least, he lost his power when people refused to believe the legitimacy of his claims. He could not do many miracles in Nazareth because the people did not *believe* that he had authority (Mark 6:5). In some way that we cannot quite grasp, he needed the faith of people in order to exercise authority.[13]

What convinced people of Jesus' authority? People heard and saw and felt something *in* Jesus that made them believe he was a legitimate power. No doubt they sensed that he represented the spiritual tradition of messianic hope which was the essence of who they were as a people. But they conceded his right to prevail as a power in their lives also because they saw the very clear healing, helping, saving purpose in his power. He used power over them to heal, never to demand. He cured their diseases and asked nothing from them. He claimed to be Lord, yet used his lordship to liberate them. He claimed to be Master, yet he nurtured people into freedom. In short, his authority was the authority of a *servant*. In Paul's words, he emptied himself of the unilateral authority he had simply by virtue of his divinity, and became a servant (Phil. 2:1-5). Here was his secret. He was believable in his magnificent claim because he used power to serve people without enslaving them.

Richard Sennett concludes his splendid work on authority by saying: "To ask that power be nurturing and restrained is unreal—or that, at least, is the version of reality our history has inculcated in us."[14] Yet, he adds, we must "imagine" that servant authority is real; we must keep the myth of a servant-authority alive as an ideal. The gospel offers Jesus as that real ideal of the authority who uses power in order to serve. His power nurtures us; and, nurtured, we credit him with authority.

From Jesus we can draw a few tentative guidelines for thinking about the authority parents have to lead and teach and direct their children.

1. Authority is a union of legitimacy and power; the right to use power to influence people, even to prevail over them, gives a person what we call authority.

2. A person's authority must be believed by the people he hopes to lead; no one can function as an authority unless people are willing to trust him.

3. Persons have genuine authority only when they use power over people to nurture people into responsible freedom.

What we see, then, is that authority is a reality which exists only in a relationship where the authority-bearer and the authority-follower are active. People have no real authority unless they are trusted and believed; and no one deserves to be trusted unless he or she helps people be free.

C. PARENTAL AUTHORITY

Derived from the family

Why does an adult who happens to conceive and channel a human being into the world have the right to shape and form that child's life? Is it because the mother and father are smarter and wiser than a child? Hardly, since other adults are smarter and wiser than the parent and they could teach the child even more efficiently. Is it because the child owes parents obedience in return for the lavish sum they spend on his or her care? Hardly, the right to expect a return on your investment does not give you authority to influence another person at the core of his life. No, if parents have authority, it comes from their special roles within that troubled community of care we call a family. So we should ask what a family is.

A family is a group of people bound together in a covenant of care for one another. Though blood is a family's natural bond, it does not create a family. The sheer fact that people live together under one roof does not create a family, contrary to the U.S. Census Bureau's definition of a family as "two or more

80   persons related by blood, adoption, or marriage and residing together." In a moral sense, what binds people together as a family is the covenant of loyalty to one another from birth to death.

When two people bring a child into the world, they are called to be its caretakers. This calling, though parents may never give it a thought, is the first ingredient of a family. Parents are invested with the calling by virtue of accepting the child as their own, and they turn their little circle into a family when they covenant in their hearts to fulfil that calling.

The child, in turn, gradually learns to trust the parents to be his caretakers. This trust adds the second ingredient to a family. The child begins to trust that the adults hovering over him will be there to feed him, to let him touch human flesh, to give warmth against the cold, and above all to keep him from falling into the terrible dangers a small child fears.[15] The trust grows as the parents begin to give more than physical and emotional security. Gradually they tell the child what they believe to be true and right about life and its meaning. Again, the child trusts the parent to take care of him.[16]

But why should there be families at all? Why should societies be made up of these countless clusters of loyalty-bound communities? Conventional liberal wisdom has it that families are here to provide emotional support in a world that does not much care about us. The family is a "haven in a heartless world," a refuge from a society in which everybody is out to beat us to the glittering prizes. In the family, we have a place where we can be coddled, cuddled, and comforted in intimacy. In a way, families are therapy centers for harried spirits.

The Judaeo-Christian perspective, however, sees the circle of covenanted care as the right setting for the nurture of children into commitment to what is right and true about life. Parents are parents mainly to take care of the child's initiation into faith and morals. And the two go together. Morality has to do with what is truly important and right about life, and what is important about life depends on what is true about God. So, the heart of family is the parents' calling to pass on the moral and spiritual reality of life to their children. The covenant of caretaking, then, creates the family. In this context alone we can understand how a parent has authority and why the child has an obligation to honor the parent.

A family is not a spillover from our romantic passions, nor a product of society's requirement that parents provide their offspring with bed and board, nor a little circle of people deriving emotional support from living together, nor a social contrivance for keeping our broods in control, one which could become obsolete if a social planner were to find a better one. In a Judaeo-Christian sense, family is rooted in the Creator's design for the ongoing nurture of children who bring faith and moral value into the next generation. To undermine, neglect, or replace it is to wreck the core community that makes all other community possible.[17]

Focused on faith and morality

Unique to a person's authority as a parent is being a teacher of what is right and true about life. Naturally, a parent has other sorts of authority too. A mother may require her children to do chores, for example, but her clout in the kitchen is not basically different from a mess sergeant's clout in the mess hall. A mother acts in her special role as mother when she is, in the thousand ways available to her, helping her children know what is worth living for and what is worth dying for.

The mother may be wrong, of course. She may use her authority to teach her children unorthodox notions about God and misinformed ideas of morality. But she does not lose her authority if she lacks orthodoxy or profundity; parental authority is rooted in a calling to teach one's children what one believes to be true and right, not in expertise.

Better that a child grow up with some mistaken notions about what matters much than to grow up with the notion that nothing much matters. Besides, who is expert on God and morality? As Stanley Hauerwas points out: "In matters moral there are no 'experts'; and therefore all parents are charged with forming their children's lives according to what they know best."[18] What we teach our children is what we most truly believe. What costs a parent authority is not the chance of being wrong in his or her beliefs, but the failure to believe anything. Even worse, a parent may lose authority simply because he does not dare tell a child what he believes to be true and right. Hauerwas's indignation is well placed: "What must be said and said clearly, is that the refusal to ask a child to believe as we believe, to live as we

82   live, to act as we act, is a betrayal that derives from moral cowardice."[19]

What I have been claiming for parental authority calls into question a modern liberal premise about family life. Conventional wisdom tells us that we should respect children's sovereign rights to make up their own minds about matters religious and moral. In the liberal credo, everyone in the family is an individual with equal authority on these matters. Since nobody is an expert on belief, a father has no right to foist his beliefs on his children. Authority has to rest on proven expertise; if a mother lacks it, she should defer to an expert who has it. Only an authoritarian parent would send children into the world with a bias about morals and a prejudice toward any faith. The role of parents is to keep their children in a moral and religious vacuum until they are ready to decide for themselves. The only really important thing a parent may teach about these matters is that they are not important enough for a parent fervently to care that the child continue in the faith and morality of the family.

From the perspective of biblical morality, liberalism's family philosophy is a disaster. For the one reason the Bible gives for seeing the family as the basic component of the human community is that the family is the appropriate setting for a child to learn the core values of life and the meaning and purpose of existence.

There is a curious twist to the working of authority in a family. True authority, I have tried to say, is exercised—and in a way created—in dialogue. You cannot exercise authority unless the people you want to influence believe in you. This is as true of parental authority as of any other. A parent needs to exercise authority in order to awaken the child's belief in it. Belief for a child takes the form of trust. Where the simplest, least educated, and least skilled parent believes in his own authority as a parent, the child learns to trust him. The courage to tell my daughter what I believe helps make me credible in her eyes. A child does not lose trust when a mother makes a mistake, or when a father exposes his ignorance on a point of theology or ethics. A child loses trust when he senses that his father and mother do not really believe what they say they believe.

Aimed at the child's freedom
The goal of parental authority is freedom. Parents' authority aims

at releasing the child from their authority. This does not mean that parents lead their children toward freedom from authority, but that they use parental authority to help the child develop a responsible freedom that will enable him to live with—and be critical of—all other human authority.

The authority pattern of the family teaches a child how to live freely and critically within the authority structures of society. Living with parents who believe in their own authority and understand its purpose, children learn what authority is really for. Thus they learn how to size up anyone who claims to be an authority. Any society has powerful people who claim the right to influence and control others. Cultists, on the fringes of society, religious and secular alike, deploy mesmerizing gifts to seduce people who never have had a life experience with genuinely caring authority into giving up their freedom for the sake of security.[20]

Every parent who claims the right to respect for his authority must keep this in mind; parental authority aims at critical freedom under all authority.

Limited by the child's rights

We cannot discuss parents' authority without also talking about children's rights. The contemporary concern for the rights of children is not just faddish sentimentality. When the prophets summoned Israel to seek justice for the orphans and other weaker citizens, they were speaking for children's rights. And when Jesus added his terrible indictment against anyone who caused a child to sin, he declared the divine right of all children to be free from adult abuse (Matt. 18:6).

Children's rights no more undermine parental authority than the civil rights of an individual cancel out the authority of government. In both cases, rights only limit authority and keep it in bounds. But the rights of children are limited as well. For this reason we must speak as concretely as possible about them. A list of children's rights within the family should probably include the following:

1. *The right to life.* Every person's right to life is a moral armor for the child against a selfish decision by parents to let handicapped babies die or even to cause their deaths.

2. *The right to care.* No child chooses to be born. Brought

84 helpless into existence by two adults, he has a claim on them for responsible care during the time of his dependence on them.

3. *The right to safety from abuse.* No parent can guarantee a child safety from all the ills to which the flesh is heir. But parents can covenant to keep their own hands from abusing the children in their care. No parent can ever justify battering a son or daughter—with hands or mouth—on the ground of having authority over his own children.

4. *The right to fairness.* In a family of more than one child, each one has a right to fairness. Parents must distribute their gifts to all children fairly. A child may not have a right to birthday presents, for example, but if one child gets them, the other children have a right to the same sorts of favors. The right to emotional fairness is just as important; the ugly duckling has a right to as much affection as the beautiful swan. No child can reasonably expect perfect fairness from any mortal parents, but every child has the right at least to a parent's intention to be fair.

5. *The right to unconditional acceptance.* A child has a right to be affirmed, accepted, and loved unconditionally by the parents who decided the child should exist. No parent has the authority to say or imply that a child is too evil or ugly or dull or lazy to accept. Parental authority never gives anyone a right to reject his child.

Thus far we have been speaking of children's moral rights within the family. It may be, however, if parents are guilty of gross violations, that the state's coercive authority may have to invade the normally sovereign sphere of the family to protect the legal rights of the child.[21] Parents obviously do not have absolute authority over their children. But we must face the consequences for the family if we grant the state *carte blanche* to override parental authority. Do we have any evidence for thinking that judges, lawyers, bureaucrats, and social workers are likely in the long run to be more reliable protectors of children's welfare than fallible parents? And even if parents egregiously violate their children's rights at times, what would happen to society at large if this foundational mini-society, the family, were completely to forfeit its sovereignty to the state?

*　　　*　　　*

Was it really necessary to dig so deeply into the notion of parental authority to get a grip on a child's duty to honor his or her parents? I think so. Honor is an unsentimental thing brushing close to the heart of morality, a little moral finger pointing to the structure of creation's most delicate order, the family. For a child to learn to honor his or her parents is to learn to respect the human incarnation of moral authority. Parents have a calling, not just to feed their offspring or protect them from the hardships of a human jungle, but to share with them their deepest beliefs about God and his will for the human family. The only quality parents share which entitles them at all to children's honor is a calling to teach their children what is true and what is right about God and his world. They have a right to teach, to influence, to guide, and to persuade their children about what they, the parents, believe about the core matters of life. Their embodiment of this right makes them worthy of respect. If they forfeit their calling, by default, fear, or laziness, their loss of honor is their own fault.

III. HOW TO HONOR PARENTS IN THE CONFLICTS OF LIFE

Are there universal guidelines telling all the children of the world how to honor their parents? There may be signs and symbols of honor that every normal parent hopes to see, in any culture or any age. The child listens when the parent speaks, opens his mind when the parent teaches, yields when the parent urges, follows when the parent leads, keeps a distance when the parent pulls away. But every child must write his own lyrics to these melodies. In every culture—in every family, for that matter—children and parents develop their own styles of honor. We should not suppose that a clear-cut set of tests exists by which we can evaluate the quality of honor today's children give their parents.

In any case, my interest here is not in the cultural varieties of filial respect, but in the changing forms of honor we owe our parents as our relationship with them changes. Parents gradually get weaker and children gradually get stronger; parents gradually relinquish authority and children gradually move into freedom. As we said, healthy parental authority aims precisely at the child's ultimate liberation from it. But one thing does not change. The parent is always the person who once stood for God in the child's life and therefore had an authority that no one ever can have

86   again. No matter how fully free the child may be, he is never free from the moral obligation of honor to that person. In fact, it is only when we are free from their authority that we can freely honor parents as those who once had that authority.

The way to freedom from parental authority is a fitful struggle filled with alternating currents of pain and joy. Every child passes through certain rituals that mark subtle stages on the way: the first day of school, the beginning of menstruation, the first date, a summer away from home, the first experience of sex, the first paying job, graduation from high school—all these are moments that signal a move toward freedom from parents. Some children are traumatically shoved into premature freedom: a mother dies, a father is an alcoholic, parents are divorced, an older brother is killed. The variations on the struggle are endless. But one process is inevitable: the parent is losing power and the child is gaining it. Along the way, new styles of honor need to be created by the child and accepted by the parent.

Honor is impossible when a child does not grow into freedom, but remains under the control of the parent. A weak parent may still keep control of a powerful child. The key to the parent's power lies inside the memory of the child. Once there, it works even though the child becomes an adult and the parent is senile or dead. One child may do everything right, all in sad pursuit of the impossible virtue that her parent forced her to strive for and be miserable without. Another may rebel against everything his parent believed and wanted for him. He may be driven to drink too much, brutalize his wife, deny God, only because he is still resisting his parents' control. He does not so much choose to do destructive things as to react against the control he cannot escape. People may talk about what honor the first child brings to her parent, and in the latter case they may talk of the shame. In reality neither is honoring his parent.

Enroute to freedom, and within freedom, we experience conflicts of many kinds. Our moral responsibility is to find the right way to honor our parent within the reality of our conflict. In the rest of this chapter we will look at examples of honor within conflict. They represent three stages in our relationship with our parents through which many of us pass, and each stage opens up possibilities for its own sort of conflict.

The first stage is a borderline, when a child stands at the edge of maturity, but is still dependent on his parents and in deep conflict with them. A second stage comes when child and parents are equals—both are at their prime, and in conflict with each other. Finally, there is the last stage, in which the roles are reversed and the child becomes the caretaker of his parent. Here the conflict is subtle and desperate; how does an aging child honor his aged parents and yet fulfil his duty to his own children and to himself?

A. WHEN FAITHS CONFLICT: THE ADOLESCENT CONVERT

Ted Bevans is a senior in high school, the son of orthodox Jewish parents. He was converted to the Christian faith during the summer before his senior year. At school he has become the leader in a group of Christian students who meet regularly for Bible study. He believes that his relationship to Christ completes everything his parents taught him to believe, and that for this reason he is not in conflict with their faith. To his parents, however, his conversion is a betrayal and a dishonor. They hope that Ted will "grow out" of his Christian phase, but they take no chances. They tell him that he must stop seeing his Christian friends at school, quit the church group he had joined, and to say nothing at all about his conversion when at the synagogue. In short, Ted's parents tell him to obey the Fifth Commandment, putting honor to parents above his own will.

Ted's Christian friends believe that his faith may be at stake and that loyalty to Christ should come ahead of loyalty to parents. They think he should obey his Lord, as Peter obeyed God above the political authorities (Acts 5:29).

Ted seems to face a conflict between his duty to his parents and his duty to his own convictions. Ted's parents were his authorities in what is true and important. He now believes they were wrong in one crucial respect, a point that pierces to the heart of his life. He is at the edge of maturity, with one foot on the side of boyhood and the other on the side of adulthood. He is old enough to know and honor his conscience, young enough

88   to be under his parents' authority. What ought he to do, and
how can he do it in a way that honors his parents?

Aside from all of the psychological factors in this conflict,
we find ourselves pushed in differing directions by two important moral concerns. We enter every family situation with a bias
toward obedience to parents. We also believe that the conscience
of an 18-year-old is as sacred as that of anyone else. What is
more, we sense that where one's faith is involved we have a
special kind of issue. Does the Bible give us direction beyond
the commandment?

Christ loosened the ties of honor we owe our parents. Conscious of the effects his coming might have on family circles, he
said he came "to set a man against his father, and a daughter
against her mother" (Matt. 10:35). Did he mean to invite adolescent rebellion in his name? Jesus certainly did not untie children from the Fifth Commandment, but he did make clear that,
in the crunch, he came before parents. "He who loves father or
mother more than me is not worthy of me" (Matt. 10:37).

True, at 12 Jesus himself left his parents dangling in fear for
a while when he stayed behind to discourse with the learned
rabbis. But even here the real point is that afterward he went
home with them and was "obedient to them" (Mark 7:6f.). He
opened the door to special situations in which the First Commandment—"Thou shalt have no other gods before me"—would
take priority over the Fifth, situations in which we feel a conflict
between commitment to God and loyalty to our family. Exceptional moments may come when the Lord requires us to disobey
our parents, moments that turn normal human relationships up-
side down and the coming of the kingdom shakes the foundation
of the family. When it comes to an either/or, either for Christ
or against him, the decision must fall on the side of Jesus, even
against our parents.[22]

No one believed in the structures of authority more firmly
than John Calvin. Yet at the end of a vigorous endorsement of
the Fifth Commandment, he expresses some second thoughts:

> But we also ought in passing to note that we are bidden to obey
> our parents only "in the Lord" (Eph. 6:1). . . . Hence if they spur
> us to transgress the law, we have a perfect right to regard them,
> not as parents, but as strangers who are trying to lead us away
> from obedience to our true father.[23]

Even if Calvin overstates the case and makes the alternatives terribly cruel, the point is clear: when our parents use their authority to lead us away from "obedience to our true father," we must disobey them. Is this the way for Ted Bevans to go?

Ted's parents do not mean to "spur him to transgress the law." Mrs. Bevans is a pious Jewish mother who wants her son to follow the way of Yahweh in the traditions of the family, and Mr. Bevans is a faithful son of the orthodox faith, for whom it is the worst of all transgressions for a son to become a Christian. These are people who take their parental authority with the gravity of a modern Moses. If any parents merit honor from an adolescent son, Mr. and Mrs. Bevans do. But Jesus came between them.

In conflicts between parental authority and maturing conscience, the law of love calls for compromise. Parents must know that their authority has limits—and one limit is loving concern for the conscience of their children. And they need to remember that they are fallible, shortsighted, and selfish creatures, far from being gods. So, as the son grows into a man, the daughter into a woman, the parents must let the bonds of loyalty hang loose. And, on the other hand, love urges adolescent children to act in ways that are most helpful to their parents, to wait for them to come to terms with their own disappointment and anger. And while they wait, each can respect the other's convictions even while they are in conflict with them. Thus, for a while, parental authority should be muted for the sake of Ted's conscience and Ted's conscience should be sensitized to his parents' right to honor because of their authority.

But suppose Ted Bevans cannot wait long. Nor can he compromise much. He must, he feels, follow the path of his new faith. And this path leads him, for now, to associations with fellow Christians against his parents' will. He feels he must disobey. The question is: can he honor his parents in the process of disobedience?

He can, and love must show him how. He must make it clear that he is not a rebel bent on disavowing his father and mother. He can bow to their will in everything but this one thing that touches his soul. He can continue his Jewish allegiances, be an avid learner at the synagogue, give his heart to the celebration of the Jewish festivals, and in every way be a Jewish boy in the tradition of his family, a loyal son honoring

90   his father and mother as much as any parent could hope to be honored. He disobeys, selectively to be sure, and at the heart of the Jewish matter; but, in truth, seen from the vantage of faith, Ted's parents are honored and not shamed.

Conversions to Christianity are not the only way to spark a conflict of faith between child and parent. Presbyterian young people become Moonies and Catholic adolescents become disciples of Hare Krishna. What ought they to do if their parents require them to dissociate themselves from the rituals and programs of their faith? To the adolescent, the cult is an entree to a new life. It seems as much a matter of faith and conscience as Christian conversion does to Christians. Do they not have the same duty to their faith and their conscience as an adolescent convert to Christianity has?

Does Christian faith take priority over the Fifth Commandment because it is the true faith or because it, like other faiths, touches the child's conscience? If it is only the Christian conscience that justifies disobeying parents, then it is right for parents to force their children to leave cultic groups, even kidnapping them if necessary. If Christian commitment respects the conscience simply because it touches a person's deepest being, Christians must allow all conscientious adolescents the same freedom to disobey that they would want Ted Bevans to have. And it seems to me that this is right. From what Paul teaches about conscience (Rom. 14:7-12; I Cor. 8:12), we gather that he at least believed that conscience was inviolable, right or wrong. And so, with the same risk, even with fear and trembling, we contend that late adolescents who have come to believe with all their hearts what their parents despise must be free to find ways of honoring their parents while rejecting their wishes on the vital nerve of the faith.

We are talking, of course, about a free choice. If the parent has sound reason to believe that the cult has taken his child captive by using psychic techniques to manipulate him into conversion, the parent is justified in fighting back. For then he is not in conflict with his child's conscience but with the forces of evil who have taken his child prisoner.

B. WHEN LIFE-STYLES CONFLICT: THE ADULT CHILD

Tim Timmer is a success. He has more education, more money, and more prestige than his parents dreamed of having for themselves. He also has a life-style his parents never imagined having. Tim's parents believe that he has deserted the biblical version of the Christian life. Their church, where Tim got his religious moorings, was a "Bible-believing, Bible-preaching" group where people were taught Sunday to Sunday the precise meaning of the biblical texts. No wine bottle was ever found in the elder Timmers' cupboards, no spirits were ever poured at their table. Smoking was taboo long before the rest of the world learned that cigarettes had anything to do with lung cancer. Sex, condoned within the marriage bond, was never encouraged and certainly never celebrated. The important thing in life was to be a living testimony for the Lord, and the clearest witness was given by the worldly practices from which you conspicuously abstained.

Now in the third year of his second marriage, Tim has become an Episcopalian. He is more impressed with the social impact of the church than with saving people's souls. He no longer cares much whether Christ will return before or after a millennium; he cares a lot about racism and world hunger and nuclear arms. Though he has never taken up smoking, his wife goes through a pack a day, and the stale stench overwhelms his parents' nostrils every time they come for a visit. He enjoys a cocktail at lunch and now pours wine even when his parents come for dinner; he has decided to be "spiritually" honest with them.

Tim can sense his parents' judgment on his rejection of what they taught him to believe was important and true. Besides, he is burdened by the debt of gratitude he owes them, which he can never repay because they refuse to be paid. They gave, and they give even now, in spite of their judgments, but they will take nothing in return. So his debt piles high—and he cannot unload. How can this mature person, free from parental authority, give honor to his parents while he rejects so much of what they want for him?

There is obviously more than one way for Tim to be morally creative with his conflict. But let me suggest some conditions that need to be met if he is going to honor his parents now that he is his parents' equal and chooses a life-style they condemn, yet wants to treat them with genuine honor.

First is *freedom from parental judgment*. It is hard to honor parents when we are not free from our need of their approval. A child has a natural need for unconditional acceptance from his parents, but parents often have a tragic lack of power to give it. The parent wants the child to excel in all goodness and never lets him feel he is good enough to be unconditionally loved. The child gets the feeling that he will never be completely accepted because he will never be completely approved. Try as he will, he cannot get what his heart cries for: a love of which he can be absolutely sure. He carries his need far beyond the nursery into his adult life, and keeps it in his soul even when his parents are dead and gone.

The parent is the angry God, into whose hands it is a fearful thing to fall. And since he cannot get free from his parent's conditional love, he cries in his heart as Paul did: "Wretched man that I am! Who will deliver me?" (Rom. 7:24). He becomes angry at this parent-god. Some of his honest flaunting of his new life-style in front of them is a way of punishing them for leaving him out on the limb of conditional love. And he cannot be free to honor his parents until he is free from his hunger for their approval.

The avenue to freedom from this deep need for parental approval is via an experience of the freedom of grace. If Tim can experience a God whose love is unconditional, he may exorcise his need for his parents' approval. For if he feels accepted and loved *unconditionally* in his ultimate relationship, he can be freed from his need to win approval from his parents. Free from fear of their judgment, he can find a way of genuinely honoring his parents even if his way is not their way. He must be free to displease them in order to be free to honor them.

The second condition is the power to see *the difference between enjoyment and honor*. Enjoying our parents makes honor easier to give, but enjoyment is something quite other than honor. What one honors in his parents is their peculiarly awesome role in his life. They authored him, they authorized his very being, and were his authority for many years of learning. Honor calls for respect for what our parents were—and are. It can do without pleasant feelings, it can be managed even if we do not relish long visits with our "loved ones." Our parents do not have to be our favorite companions; they need to be honored as those who once were called to be God-with-us.

The third condition is recognition of *a parent's need to see himself or herself in the child*. A parent gets his identity from his child as surely as a child gets her identity from her parents.

Probably, Tim's parents fret about his ways not only because
they disapprove, but also because they cannot see themselves
reflected in his life. They need to know that he carries their lives
into the future, and they need to recognize themselves in that
son, now so different from the boy they shaped. For this reason,
honoring parents in conflict may require us to reassure the parent that the identity is still intact. To do this, parent and child
need to talk, and in the talk the sameness that binds the two
must be searched out.

The fourth condition is *respect for parents' own mystery*. To
honor parents, a child needs to let them be what they are, a
mystery not yet fully revealed. A mature child easily supposes
that the parent has emptied himself out, leaving no personal
mystery unrevealed, burned out, with nothing interesting inside
him any more. This stereotype dishonors parents by forcing
them into our own image of what a parent must become. To
keep our reserve is to honor a parent's sense that he is a mystery,
that his whole story has not been told; and this is to honor the
person whose job it was to be our stand-in for God.

The route to honor will have to be improvised. Along the
way, Tim will need to use familiar symbols of honor, as a kind
of sacrament—the place of honor at dinner, the prayer of thanks
said by the father, the titles of "mother" and "father" never dis-
placed by first name, opinions asked for and sincerely listened
to. Beyond the symbols, however, each child needs the power
of love to find his own way of respect for the parent who is now
an equal. There is no absolute model; love must be creative even
when affection is dry.

C. WHEN DUTIES CONFLICT: THE AGING CHILD AND THE AGED PARENT

Frank Stover has died, leaving his 84-year-old widow Mae alone
and frightened about her future. Although Mae is showing some
signs of her age, and is slightly crippled from a hip accident some
years ago, she can still get around the house smartly with a cane.
She dreads the thought of living in a nursing home, the only one
in town being a well-run but drab place supported by the Pres-
byterians. Her son Fred feels that, as a Christian, he is duty-
bound to honor his mother by inviting her to live with his family.
Fred is a paint salesman, away from home at least two and some-

94   times three days a week, bringing enough money home to live in middle-class comfort. He is 54, and suffered a heart attack two years ago. His wife Bernice broods nervously about Fred's heart condition. Now she fears that he might die and leave her a widow with his widowed mother. Besides, there are two children still home. Dirk, 18, is mentally retarded and will probably stay at home indefinitely. Mary Jo is 20 and works at the local branch of United Bank. Dirk wants his grandmother in the house; Mary Jo thinks it would be unfair to her mother.

A strong moral sense compels Fred to think God expects him to take his mother into his home; in any case, he is sure he will not forgive himself if he forces her to live in an institution. And since he never quite amounted to what his mother expected of him, this would be a way of making up for his failure. Bernice could get some help around the house if she needed it, and she would just have to compromise—as he would do if her mother needed a home.

Bernice's moral sense pushes her in another direction. She feels that Fred would be morally wrong to saddle her with the care of his mother while he is gone a good part of the week. If the Bible tells Fred to honor his mother, it also tells him to love his wife.

There is certainly no moral rule requiring all children to share their homes with aged parents. The three-layer family is unrealistic for the condominium generation, certainly in a culture that almost expects both parents to work outside the house and children to leave home by the age of twenty. The Hebrew patriarch of Old Testament times had a small army of daughters-in-law, maidservants, and grandchildren to tend to his needs; it would be insane to make that style of care for the aged a model for today. Not only is the modern family cramped for space and short on nursing hands, it is usually not psychically up to coping with senile and immobile old people. Honoring parents may often be done within the professional care of a good institution.

It is clear that Fred Stover equates honoring a mother with taking care of her at his home. He has turned a rule he picked up somewhere in his tradition into a moral principle. But the law of love tells him he ought to weigh the effects of his decision on the lives of everyone in his family. To be sure, having a mother-in-law within her home could be a chance for Bernice to discover yet untapped resources of love; it might also tax her decreasing energies to the cracking point. Living in an institution could be humiliating and offensive to Mae; it could also be the discovery of a new independence and new friends. Each option brings its possibilities and its risks. Fred will have to make his decision, not on the basis of a single principle, but on the basis of reasonable calculations of what would be most helpful for everyone in the family.

King Darius of Persia once asked some of his subjects about the proper way to honor parents when they die. First he called in some Greeks, whose custom it was to burn their fathers' bodies. "What reward would you take for *eating* the bodies of your dead fathers?" Horrified, they cried: "We would not eat the bodies of our fathers for all the money in the world." So he called in certain Indians, whose custom it was to eat the bodies of their fathers. He asked them: "What reward would you take for *burning* the bodies of your dead fathers?" Their answer: "We would not burn the bodies of our dead fathers for all the money in the world." The historian Herodotus mused on this deep dispute about how to honor deceased parents and decided: "Custom is the king o'er all."

Is custom also king when it comes to honoring aged parents? Or can the law of love help us find fair ways for the honorable care of parents who are past the age of caring for others?

The question of honor will not be settled by where Fred's mother lives, but by the role she plays in the family wherever she eats and sleeps. He could take her into his house but shut her out from the love of his family. He could keep her within the loving care of the family even though she has an institutional address. If Fred and Bernice keep in frequent and leisurely touch with her, if their children take time for listening to her stories, and if all of them take seriously her opinions and complaints and joys, they may be honoring her as much as they can. The crucial issue will be whether Fred and his family can get the message through to Mae that she is profoundly respected for the mission she had in the life of her son. The question is not whether she is wholly pleased, but whether she knows she is being treated with total respect.

The conflict of duties Fred and Bernice face is of a type that is epidemic. Demographers project that there will be 30,000,000 Americans over the age of 65 when this century ends—ten times as many as in 1900. About half of these will be over 75. Many

96 if not most of these older people will have children whose duty it is to honor their father and mother. Countless children will face the question of how to honor their aged father or mother while they themselves move into the irresistible twilight.

*   *   *

The Fifth Commandment does not remove uncertainty for people who try to live up to it. There is no single way to honor parents; there are a thousand ways to dishonor them. Within the conflicts of faith, life-style, and duty, honor will have to be improvised out of the creative resources of imagination and discernment. Each family will have to find its way to live honorably with its old generation. And each society must find ways to make it possible for all to keep their parents in honorable circumstances. For the people that loses its will to honor its aged eventually loses its humanity.[24]

QUESTIONS FOR DISCUSSION

1. How do you think a modern family can balance parental authority with the rights of children?

2. Authority seems to be given to people by the very ones over whom it is exercised. Can a parent ever lose his or her authority because the child no longer trusts the parent? How important *is* trust in a family?

3. Do you believe that the human race was created with a design for authority so that, within certain circles, it is natural for some people to exercise authority over others?

4. Do you agree that a family, at heart, is a covenant of mutual care and trust? Or is it a group where children just happen to be weaker than the parents, and so need them to survive until they can make it on their own?

5. How would you advise Ted Bevans to act so as to obey the intention of the Fifth Commandment? How would you advise his parents to act? Would you feel differently if Ted's parents were Christian and Ted decided to join the Hare Krishna cult? Is there a creative way for Ted to honor his parents even if he does not obey them in this one thing?

6. Do you think the five conditions for honor mentioned in the Tim Timmer case are helpful for people like Tim: Suppose Tim were

the conservative one in this story and his parents were liberal humanists; would your advice to Tim change?

7. Is there a moral rule that clearly tells Fred Stover what he should do about his mother? If there is no abiding rule, what factors ought he to consider? Suppose Dirk was not mentally retarded? Suppose his mother were senile? And suppose Fred were very healthy? Might it still be morally proper for Fred to insist that his mother move into a rest home? What convinces you?

8. When might a parent forfeit authority over his or her child? Who has the right to decide when a parent has lost authority? As a general rule, would you tend to tolerate abuses for the sake of maintaining family authority? Or would you step in early to protect children even if doing so eroded parental authority?

RESPECT FOR HUMAN LIFE 5

"Thou Shalt Not Kill"

The Lord God declares his devotion to the earthly life of his human creatures by commanding us not to destroy it. Most people still believe what the command tells them, that every person is a gift of God, to himself and for his neighbor, a gift not to be abused by murdering hands. But there is a deep irony to our assent to the Sixth Commandment. For we are members of a race that habitually slaughters its own children. We honor those who kill, as long as they kill our enemies. We allow children far away to die of hunger while our own children gorge themselves. We prepare for nuclear holocaust, as if it were our human destiny to perform one ultimate ritual of atomic genocide. And yet we still nod a yes to the sound of the trumpet blaring the message from ancient Sinai: "Thou shall not kill." We affirm the word and yet we know it is an alien message in our world.

In its austere generality this commandment spreads a protective moral shield around every person's life. To God, human beings are dear, be they friend or enemy, productive or dependent, elect or reprobate. No quality or lack of it can disqualify anyone from taking shelter under the moral command of respect for human life.

Yet, we must look carefully at this commandment and the life it means for us to respect if we want a clue to what God expects from us in the conflicts of this life. After all, "Thou shalt not kill" was spoken on a planet where things are badly out of kilter, where some people mean others much harm, and where it seems sometimes as though the only way to rescue life is to destroy the lives of enemies who kill. And the Sixth Commandment speaks to us of life's sacredness while we care for the shrunken bodies of persons who, in terminal exhaustion, call with feeble passion for death. The ambiguities in the human family, the loose ends and tragic contradictions, compel us to linger over this commandment awhile to find out whether this simplest and strongest prohibition against killing really means that no human being may ever preside over the death of another.

What did the ancient Hebrews hear this word from the God

100 of life say? What did it tell them? What does it tell us now? Is it an affirmation of life against all assaults on it? Or is it a narrow legal indictment of private, cold-blooded murder? We must ask also why God should have given the command. What is there about even the least of human beings that makes their lives so precious? After all, do we not all burn out sooner than later, like a blade of tender grass in a drought? In the third place, we must ask about modern kinds of killing that many civilized human beings seem all too ready to live with—suicide, capital punishment, abortion, and the decision of mercy to let people die.

I. WHAT DOES THE SIXTH COMMANDMENT TELL US TO DO?

A. KILLING AND MURDER

It is sometimes suggested that this commandment should be rendered in English as "Thou shalt not murder"—a prohibition, then, only of private killings which society cannot tolerate, not a word against killing in general.

Indeed, "murder" is not an unreasonable way to translate the Hebrew verb in the command; but it is not the only way. The verb is *rasah*, which the Hebrews usually used when a private citizen killed a personal enemy. The Hebrews had other words that covered the whole gamut of taking life—community stonings, private stabbings, and most every other act of mayhem. The commandment could have used one of these other words to make an inclusive indictment against taking human life. As a matter of fact, however, *rasah* is used at least once for capital punishment (Num. 35:30) and also for accidental manslaughter (Deut. 4:41-43; Josh. 20:3). From a textual point of view, we do not have a clear case for limiting the commandment to private killings, or murder.[1]

The average citizen in ancient Israel probably thought that God was referring only to the private killings we call murder. Israel itself had a ritual for killing people by throwing stones on them—for offenses which would provoke little more than a frown in most modern societies. And who has not heard of Israel's holy massacres against the inhabitants of Canaan? Since God thus seemed to encourage the government of Israel to kill, modern readers often assume that his command against killing was aimed only at vicious violence among private citizens.

If the command meant to prohibit only private murder, God would not be much concerned with the protection of human beings from slaughter. His concern would be only with the blood-shedding arrogance of the individual criminal, while the state would have a blank check for human blood. But is it likely that God would allow open season on the state's enemies? Nobody wants police to shoot shoplifters, executioners to test their equipment on political opponents, or nations to make war to avenge an insult. The killing of human beings shakes the moral structure of life to its foundation, whether the killer is an officer of the state or a psychopathic thug. If the state kills a human being, the burden of proof is on its head. Not even the holy wars of Israel could be justified simply on the ground that a pious man was the anointed head of state. Governments like individuals are set under the command of God: Thou shalt not kill. And, because governments have so much more power than individuals, the word against killing must be directed to them even more urgently.

Limit this commandment to "murder" and it becomes a pale tautology. "Murder," after all, means any killing that society considers immoral, so the commandment would come down to the truism that "immoral killing is immoral." Nor can we paraphrase the commandment, "Thou shat not kill illegally." Who could believe that legality is the test of God's will for human life? It was legal for Hitler to kill six million Jews and illegal for a German citizen to kill Hitler. We must assume, it seems to me, that God's manifesto of respect for his creaturely human beings is an endorsement of every person's right to exist before his Lord and with his neighbor. The text allows it; common sense requires it.

The story of the Old Testament is full of people who deserved to die. The enemy, God's enemy above all, lost his right to live. "So perish all thine enemies," rhapsodizes Deborah the judge, recalling the spike Jael pounded into Sisera's head (Judg. 5:31). Philistines, Assyrians, Egyptians—all of them enemies of the Lord and his people—forfeited the sacred protection of life. Fellow Hebrews, too—adulterers, homosexuals, abusers of parents, along with killers—were morally killable. Not everyone was protected by the Sixth Commandment.

People whose lives were marked for killing were, however, exceptions to the rule. Even in the early stages of Israel's moral history, people forfeited their right to life only by some specific and grievous offense. They could be killed only *in spite of* their humanity. The list of capital offenses may have been long, but it was nevertheless a list of exceptions to the primeval rule that everyone who bore God's image in his soul had a right to live (Gen. 9:6). The burden of proof, by implication, was on the Lord for allowing the killing. The historians of Israel were content, at least, to leave with God the justification for its own slaughters of the children of men.

B. KILLING ANIMALS

The acrid stench of burnt flesh in the temple air suggested that the Sixth Commandment was indifferent to animal life. To a casual observer, the precincts of the holy place smelled like an ordinary slaughter house. If killing was common in sacred places, do we not have a strong signal of divine disregard for the value of animal life? Or is there another message in the bleating of the slaughtered lamb?

Animals were sacrificed, to be sure, but a sacrifice was a costly price for human sin. It was not a trivial exchange, but a tragic drama. Set askew by sin, the world could not be put right without a ritual of life-giving. That God accepted the death of an animal to atone for human sin was a signal, not of his cruelty, but of how highly he esteemed the life of an animal.

Animals, after all, were God's possessions; the cattle on the thousand hills are his, and he cares for them. "The earth is full of thy creatures. . . . These all look to thee, to give them their food in due season" (Ps. 104:24, 27). No wonder that the sight of Nineveh's cattle helped move the Almighty to spare that violent city (Jonah 3:11). He allowed humans to eat meat, but only by a specific ordinance, as if animal slaughter for human consumption should never be taken for granted (Gen. 9:3). And when an animal killed a person, it was treated as a moral offender (Gen. 9:5). The animals of the world are, like human beings, embraced in the reconciliation of the word. They are part of the "all things" that are to be reconciled (cf. Col. 1:20). The wolf and the lamb will snuggle in warm intimacy to share *shalom* in the city of God (Isa. 11:6ff.; 65:25). For now, it may be, as Karl Barth says, that the screams of butchered beasts are minor sounds in the groans and travails of an unredeemed creation (Rom. 8:17), a signal that life is terribly at odds with itself.

If we cannot demonstrate that the Sixth Commandment protects animal life, can we at least assume that it calls us to great care with animal life? If we are forbidden to destroy the earthly, animal life of a human person, are we not called to reconsider our easy slaughter of beasts? Can we justify turning butchery into a major industry? Can we justify breeding cattle by the millions only to kill them out of lust for red meat? And is mass slaughter of grainfed cows not more dubious if it decreases the amount of protein available to hungry people around the world? An imaginative hearing of the Sixth Commandment may place a question mark behind our moral right to a life-style whose centerpiece is the beef steak.

C. SUPPORTING LIFE

The letter of this commandment asks us only to "live and let live," hardly a summons to heroic moral sacrifice. True, if everyone merely kept his hands off his neighbor's throat, life in our ravaged world would at least have a chance. But fulfilled in love this commandment requires much more. We have not read its real demands unless we hear in it God's will for us to do all we can to protect our neighbor's human life and help it flourish. If we read the commandment as Jesus did, it becomes the law of life that gives flesh and blood to love.[2]

As the law of life, the commandment sends every person toward any neighbor in the human community who needs help to keep life going. It compels us to get food to hungry children— by all means available to us. It requires us to find free medical care for elderly people who cannot afford to buy it. It demands that we assist, not hinder, the development of the unborn toward fuller human existence. Wherever a person needs a hand to help him keep body and soul together, the moral law compels us to reach out with ours.

The law of love moves us to other people simply because they are there, living human beings whose only claim on us is their need for our help to stay alive. They are God's creatures whom he wants to exist along with us, who prize life as much as we do, but who stake a claim on us no matter what benefit or burden their life will add to ours. Never mind that there are so many of them that you need to choose which ones will stay alive because of your help. Never mind the end that always comes to your energy, time, and money. You will have to figure

104   out a way to choose between your neighbors. The point here is only that love will not let us listen to the commandment against killing except as a call for helping our neighbor live. The law is positive and limitless. Pushed by its compelling majesty into the vicinity of neighbors who need us, we will have to pray for discernment, gather the facts, calculate the odds, and then answer our neighbor's right to life while others in this homicidal world ignore him.

II. WHY IS IT WRONG TO KILL?

Most people do not need a special revelation to persuade them that it is wrong to kill another person. As Paul puts it (Rom. 2:14f.), the law of respect for human life is written on their "hearts." It is an intuition—a reason of the heart stronger than most reasons of the mind. Materialists who think that a human being is an exquisitely refined network of physical molecules nevertheless admit that we need very special reasons to justify the killing of any human being. Even a Mafia hit man persuades himself that he is only a kind of "social worker" whose vocation is to eliminate the unworthy. But it is not as if ordinary people are likely to shoot each other in the streets over the price of a theater ticket unless they share a biblical view of the meaning of life.

It may, on the other hand, be true that in times of great testing, one's attitude toward killing a human being will be settled by his fundamental beliefs about what a human life is in terms of its ultimate relationship. So we do well to look more closely at the reasons supporting the divine command.

Faith assumes that what God asks *of* us is also good *for* us, precisely because what he asks matches his original design for our lives. Faith also nudges us to look for signals of that design. If there is a design that determines duty, we ought to be able to see at least some hints of it. A few facets of the human life we all share, which we see in the total biblical picture of humanness, make it clear why God would lay it down as a primal obligation for every human being: Thou shalt not kill.

A. THE SACREDNESS OF PERSONS

Why should human creatures be the one species on earth God declares morally unkillable? The simplest reason is that human beings are persons, and their sacredness as persons puts them off limits to killers. But sacredness is a difficult quality to define. Perhaps it is most easily described by pointing to what it does to people: it inspires *reverence*. Sacredness is a holy specialness that signals people to stand off. Karl Barth had a fine eye for this sort of awe and respect:

> Respect is man's astonishment, humility, and awe . . . at majesty, dignity, holiness, a mystery which compels him to withdraw, and keep his distance, to handle it modestly, circumspectly, and carefully.

When you feel this reverence-like respect while facing another human being, you have found his or her sacred personhood, the quality that makes him or her unkillable.

I think I would rather speak of the sacredness of persons than of the sanctity of life. Not that I do not feel the power of Albert Schweitzer's "reverence for life"; and I know that some of the best arguments against taking any human life are based on the sanctity of life. Who does not tremble now and then at the awful mystery of that vital drive within, which pushes people beyond their limits to love, to grow, and now and then to feel the springs of joy within? How can one never feel reverence for the force of life inside of oneself, threatening in its flimsy unpredictability but reassuring in its vibrant persistency? But Barth warns us against letting this abstract energy or *élan vital* get a tyrannical moral hold on us. Better, for believers anyway, to remember that while God breathes the breath of life into all things living, it is persons whom he loves as his children.

We should then speak of persons—of thinking, feeling, believing creatures—who are indeed alive, but who are always something more than and different from the life they embody. Sacredness belongs to individual creatures who have names, like John Perkins or Doris Dekker. Human life therefore is not to be killed only in the sense that it surfaces through a particular person. As a moral principle, being "pro-person" seems preferable to being merely "pro-life."

What is it, then, that sets a person so absolutely apart from the other marvelous creatures for whom we care? Why may it sometimes be right to shoot a noble thoroughbred or chop down a majestic redwood tree but never to lay killing hands on a dancing child or a crippled athlete?

We could, I suppose, say that the proper study of mankind's value is man himself. And we could then sing Shakespearean doxologies to the noble work of art a woman is, splendid in her faculties, exquisite in intellect, delicate in the ways of loving. We could count the ways in which she excels all creatures and say that, in sum, she alone is worthy of being declared forever unkillable. But if we are honest, we must counter Shakespeare's eulogy on humankind with a Dostoevskian plunge into the darkness of man's soul and acknowledge the legion of demons that compete for control of his ambivalent will.

If we rest our case for the sacredness of persons on our diagnosis of human character, we could be persuaded of our own divinity and our own depravity. A little lower than the angels, we are only a cubit higher than the demons; and we have no clear signal that of all creatures on earth the one who sings of love and plans for war is the only inviolable, untouchable, unkillable creature among them.

We must see every person as someone who lives each moment in relationship with God. We need to see the religious connection if we want to recognize the essence of human sacredness. The concrete person, beautiful or ugly, productive or idle, smart or stupid, is the one whom God made, whom God loves, whose life is in God's hands, and for whom his Son died on the cross. This is the person who walks humbly on the earth as the image and likeness of the Creator who made him. We do not have to agree about what particular feature marks him as God's image—intellect, creativity, or maybe sexuality. In any case, he is, with all his gifts and in spite of all his sins, the sacred person among all other valuable living creatures.

Looking at persons with a believing eye, we may see the advantage of thinking of the *sacredness* rather than of the *value* of persons—at least in this setting. Of course persons have enormous value; God prizes them above all the earth. We mentioned this when we argued earlier that God's love knows the lovableness of his loved ones. But now we are talking about why a mere human being has no right to take the life of another person. If we calculate value at this point, we are tempted to make comparisons. Some people are more valuable to society than others; they make better toys or better tools. Others are not much to look at and not much fun to have about, and they drain our energy and cash besides. And who knows whether a horse who wins the Triple Crown might not be more valuable than a pimp who keeps a stable of prostitutes? If we rate our neighbors on a sliding scale of usefulness, we may lose our hold on the deepest reason for their right to live. Better, then, to respect every person as a sacred being whose presence in life provides the basic reason for saying: Thou shalt not kill.[3]

When I focus on the sacredness of persons, rather than on the value of life, I can respond more fruitfully to questions of life and death in the dilemmas that confront us in this broken world. The "value of life" traps us into an abstract absolutism that cannot match the obscurities of reality. If I am aware of every person's sacred inviolability, however, I am still compelled to walk into every situation where a human life is in the crucible with a directive that life be prolonged and nourished where possible. At the same time, I have to face the specific question of whether or not a sacred person is actually present in the life that is in my hands.

To accept the sacredness of persons as the reason for the command against murderous meddling is also to be aware that we need, within the Christian community, a consensus about how to recognize a person when we see him or her. If we are caring for a live body through whose lungs we are forcing oxygen and through whose veins we are pumping warm blood, we may be sustaining life without a person. And we cannot believe there is a divine mandate to force bodies to stay alive with our marvelous machines. If we are caring for someone on the edge of personal life, without a future of any personal relationship, without a hope of ever being a person in actual living ways, we are probably not mandated to say to that marginal person: "You may die when we get good and ready to let you die." Or, again, when we are confronted with a fetal life whose future is going to be both monstrously difficult and tragically brief, the sheer existence of life need not determine the morality of abortion. I am not making a pro-abortion statement here. I am only saying that it is more compelling, helpful, and relevant to recognize not value of life but sacredness of personhood as the reason it is wrong to kill a human being.

B. THE AUTHORITY OF GOD

Again and again the Bible pictures our lives as nestled in the creative hands of a sovereign Lord. He knits together our inward

108   parts in our mother's womb (Ps. 139:13). He keeps us alive moment by moment, breathing life into us, so that when he holds his breath, we die (Ps. 104:29). He sweeps us away as we forget our dreams of last night, and this is our death (Ps. 90:5). When we survive accidents, it is because "our God is a God of salvation and to God, the Lord, belongs escape from death" (Ps. 68:20). He is above us, around us, under us, and in us: "in him we live and move and have our being" (Acts 17:28). He has sovereign right to determine our end because he in fact is the one who gives life and takes it away: man's "days are determined, and the number of his months is with thee, and thou hast appointed his bounds that he cannot pass" (Job 14:5).

God alone has the right to take life away, because he is the one who authors it in the first place. To end another person's life is to violate this basic premise. If there is a right time for any person to die, God alone may decide what it is. So it should be, for he is sovereign. The basis for the Sixth Commandment lies not so much in the sacredness of human beings as in God's creative authority.

God's unique authority to determine the ending of human life is a strong theological reason for our duty to respect and not to destroy it. But for the most part God shares his authority with us when he makes us caretakers for one another. He lets us decide whether a human being shall appear on earth by giving us discretion over conception. He gives us the right to stave death off, if we can, with medicines and machines. At both ends of life's line, he lets us collaborate. Does he also give us responsibility for death in those awesome moments when we have the power to let someone die? Does God share his authority with us to the extent that we have not only the power but the right to decide that we need not put our life-coercing contrivances in the way of his death? Divine authority over human life is a powerful reason not to kill. But his magnanimous way of sharing authority indicates that we may sometimes be responsible to act in ways that determine death itself.

C. THE COMMUNITY OF CARE-TAKING

"Am I my brother's keeper?" asked Cain when he murdered Abel. The silence of God was an eloquent Yes. Cain had violated his role as brother and caretaker. In this context the phrase "right to life" is appropriate. We belong to a community of God-like persons, which flourishes only as long as each of us trusts the other to care for his life as a neighbor. Killing destroys community as much as it destroys an individual. Calvin saw the communal reason for the commandment: the Lord, he said, has "bound mankind together by a certain unity," and it is out of this bonding that the obligation comes to man "to concern himself with the safety of all."[4] Because our life is gained only in community, our neighbor has no right to assault it but has an obligation to protect and nourish it, for we are, as Paul put it, "members one of another" (Eph. 4:25).

D. THE GIVENNESS OF LIFE

In moments of joy, when we are glad to be alive, we experience life as a gift. Now and then we feel the reality of being held up in life by a power beyond our control and we feel gratitude, which is the essence of joy. This is something different from the right to life. When we sense life as a gift, we do not so much feel a right to protection against assault as we feel a gratitude for what is given. It is simply a feeling of one's creatureliness, the anxiety of hovering over the cliff of nonbeing followed by the joy of being lifted by divine power into new heights of being. It is the feeling of being given life instead of having had to earn it.

There are paradoxes in the notion of life as a gift. Life is a gift we had to accept; none of us was in a position to choose not to be born. And it is strange even to think of our own lives as a gift to ourselves. But anyone who has deeply felt dependence on God knows that, while paradoxical, it is not nonsense: every person's life is God's gift to himself or herself. "What is given is not ours to dispose of as if we created it, not ours ... to mutilate, wantonly destroy, and to deprive others of. Rather, if life is given in grace ... we are to care for it and share it graciously."[5]

The gift of life can also turn very sour. This is the second paradox. Life is always a gift; but it can become an almost unbearable burden. A person may be more than ready to let God have his gift back again; indeed, he may give it to him with respectful resignation. Others, whose job it is to care for such a person, may feel bound to force him to bear the gift of life beyond the time when nature calls for release. Are we scorning the gift of life when we let nature release the person who has to

110   bear it? To feel life as a gift is a power to rejoice in it and nourish it. But when we sense that life is a terrible burden, do others have the duty to force us to bear it beyond the span that nature itself dictates?

*   *   *

In the biblical world the Sixth Commandment is rooted in the reality of what persons are in relationship to God and to each other. God's creative love gives them a sacredness. In their relationship with God, they are meant to accept his sovereignty over their lives. In their relationship to one another, they are meant to care for their neighbor's life, to honor the right he has to respect, and to protect his life within the human fellowship. And as possessors of the "grace of life" they are expected to rejoice in this precious gift, which is their birthright as creatures.

For the believer, these theological reasons for the commandment provide a powerful motive for obedient response to it. For believers hear the solemn summons of the Sixth Commandment as a call to the law of their own being. Not that biblical believers alone will contend strongly for other people's right to life; and if good reasons do not always inspire a great commitment, inferior reasons may inspire a heroic one. But when believers do show profound respect for life, they do so with profound reason.

III. HOW TO RESPECT LIFE
IN DIALOGUE WITH DEATH

The Sixth Commandment expresses a law of life that obligates us both to let people live and help them to live. By itself, however, it does not illumine life's dark places nor resolve its ambiguities. These we must enter ourselves, to try to discern how the commandment applies. Society today is sharply divided over how to respect human life in several sensitive situations. Are individuals morally free to decide to end their own lives when living becomes intolerable? Is abortion murder or only a sad choice? Ought we to kill those who have killed human beings; should capital punishment be outlawed or regularized? Is it sometimes right to discard life-supporting medical machines to let people die?

In probing these ambiguous situations to determine how the commandment applies to them, we will try to follow the facts

and the argument where they lead us. We enter each situation
with this presumption: if a human being is involved, we are not
permitted to kill him and we are obligated to preserve him. But
we will allow each situation to raise the question: *Is* a human
being involved and, if so, are we permitted to kill him anyway,
as an exception to the rule? The purpose will always be to ask:
what does God, in the light of his commandment, expect us to
do in this situation?

A. SUICIDE
On the face of it, the Sixth Commandment makes no distinction
between killing ourselves and killing a neighbor. My own life is
as precious as that of any other. It is God's gift to me, just as
my neighbor's life is God's gift to him. To assault myself is to
violate what God commands me to respect. It seems as simple.
as this: suicide is murder.

But suicide is a deep human paradox. It is, on the one hand,
a sign of human power, the ultimate power to determine one's
own final destiny. On the other hand, it is the ultimate sign of
human weakness and failure. This inner contradiction in suicide
obliges us to be careful in passing moral judgment on it and
explain why serious people have conflicting attitudes about the
morality of suicide.

Moral attitudes toward suicide
There are three basic attitudes toward the morality of suicide:
that it is a sin, a moral wrong forbidden by God; that it is a
legitimate option for any person to take if he or she chooses;
and that it is a tragedy, to be prevented if possible, lamented but
not morally judged. Let us look at each attitude more carefully.

1. *Suicide condemned as a moral wrong.* The early Christian
community decided that suicide was a sin. The Synod of Arles
(A.D. 553) condemned it; and later synods decreed that no
prayers should be said for a person who died by his own hands.
Potter's field, the gateway to hell, was the only proper place to
bury the damned corpse of a suicide.

The reasons for this certainty that suicide was a sin are not
hard to find. Thomas Aquinas offered three: (a) Suicide is a sin
against one's own nature. It is the nature of every living thing
to want life; and to destroy our own life is to act in a most
unnatural way. (2) It is a sin against one's community. To cause

112   our death is to deprive our family and friends of the support, care, communion, and love they need from us. (3) It is a sin against God. God alone has the right to take our life, as he alone has the power and goodness to give it.[6]

Summary judgments like these strike me not so much as wrong or too severe, but too quick, too abstract, too simple. They sound like answers to questions not heard out, judgments of things not carefully enough investigated. In short, a compassionate understanding of the paradox of suicide is lacking here.[7]

2. *Suicide justified as a responsible option*. Some people have revived the ancient Stoic notion that any responsible person has the moral right to end his life whenever death seems a reasonable alternative to the cruel circumstances of one's life. Medical science keeps people alive by drugs or machines when they may prefer to die. Some of us just grow older than we want to live, especially if old age is tied to dependency and disability. Sometimes accidents or strokes slice away the one part of our life that made it worth living. Suicide, then, is a choice to cut off the meaningless tail-end that remains. In short, the conditions of life may make the choice of death a reasonable one. While others may believe the suicidal person ought to live, they have no right to prevent him from dying. It is his right to make his choice, and the choice may be a good one.

The Judeo-Christian ethic rejects this. The Sixth Commandment prevents us at the very least from making suicide morally neutral. Yet, it does not rule out the possibility that taking one's life might be morally permissible given certain conditions.

3. *Suicide excused as tragedy*. With a bit of compassionate insight, we may excuse a person who commits suicide as a victim of forces beyond his control rather than as a free agent choosing death above life. People may be victims of enormous loss, terrible sadness, total despair. For someone else to render a moral judgment against their suicide, then, may be inhumane and naive.

Sigmund Freud said that we have two conflicting forces within us, the power of *eros*, which drives us to love and life, and the power of *thanatos*, which drives us to despair and death. If Freud was right, it is no moral wrong if the power of *thanatos* happens to be stronger in a person than the power of *eros*. If, as Carl Jung put it, we are all children of both light and darkness, with a few of us destined to be overcome by darkness, suicide is only a tragedy, not a moral choice.

But even if people are not destined by their own natures to
be suicidal, some are caught in such horrible hopelessness that
they are driven to seek escape in the arms of death. If suicide
is a tragic wrong more like cancer than murder, perhaps we do
better to hold back judgment, prevent it when we can, and weep
when we cannot.

Moral motives for suicide

Just as we take different moral attitudes toward suicide, people
take their own lives under different moral conditions. No matter
what the motive, a person choosing death against life is making
a choice that ought not to be made, but we must recognize that
not all suicides are the same, morally speaking. Looked at from
a moral perspective, people take their own lives out of differing
motives and in differing moral powers. Unless we appreciate the
differences *within* the people who commit suicide, we have no
right to evaluate their action. Let me suggest four distinct moral
kinds of suicide, based on the motives and the conditions of the
suicide's soul.

1. *The suicide of arrogance.* In fiction, at least, a person will
sometimes assault the forbidden citadel of divine freedom by
putting a bullet through his own head. People break human
barriers to seize a right that belongs only to God, a right that
would be ours only if there were no God. This is the suicide
of arrogance. Kirrilov in Dostoevski's *The Possessed* was arrogant
when he said: "I am killing myself to show my defiance and
terrible new freedom. . . . If there is no God, then I am god.
. . . I'm bound to shoot myself because the highest point of my
self-will is to kill my own self."[8] Without God, Ivan Karamazov
cried, everything is permitted. Without God, Raskolnikov believed that some superior persons were morally free to kill inferior ones. For Kirrilov, a world without God made it necessary
for some people to act like gods by killing themselves.

Bonhoeffer may have been right that every suicide has a
touch of this self-justifying arrogance about it.[9] A person committing suicide may be arrogantly rejecting love, rejecting forgiveness, rejecting light and hope and joy. But the person who
commits suicide in sheer arrogance is more a fictional titan than
a real person at the end of his tether. Most people who commit
suicide see themselves not as storming heaven but as sliding into
the abyss.

114   2. *The benevolent suicide.* It is possible to take one's life for so benevolent a purpose that the word "suicide" does not really fit: "sacrifice" is perhaps a better term. One does not choose to die in order to die; one chooses to die as a means to help another live. We say he *gives* his life, he does not take it.

This sort of will to inflict death on oneself we praise. Not only is it right; it is good. "Greater love has no man than this," said Jesus, "that he lay down his life for a friend." And no one who has read *A Tale of Two Cities* can forget Sidney Carton, walking to the guillotine for the sake of his beloved, protesting, "It is a far better thing I do than I have ever done before."

But just as it seems heartless to condemn all suicide, it seems sentimental to praise all self-sacrifice. It depends on the trade-off, one would think. It is hard to say what the balance has to be. But a life for a life ought at least to be an even trade. Nobody is going to write a poem to honor a man who dies for his German Shepherd or a redwood tree. And what about a great and good person for a scoundrel—a Paul for a Caligula, a St. Francis for a Stalin—or, let us say, a Jesus for "such a worm as I?" In the case of Jesus, of course, all our calculations are thrown off by his great love. Yet even here God must somehow have counted the prize *worth* the price he paid.

We must also ask whether a sacrifice is really necessary. During Scott's expedition to the South Pole, a certain Captain Oates and a few others went off afoot and on sleds, on a side trip into the cold wastes. Oates fell sick. Certain that he would not make it back to the depot, and that if his colleagues waited for him they would not make it back alive, he walked out one night alone, into the polar cold, to certain death. We can surely credit him with loving concern for his neighbors. But whether he did right depends not just on his good intent but also on his good sense. Was he reasonably sure the group could not have made it back if they waited awhile, or if they carried him? Perhaps not. In any case, a sacrificial motive is not enough to give moral *carte blanche* to self-sacrifice.

People may take their lives so that the lives of other people will be made easier. Their purpose is not to save someone's life but only to prevent suffering. Grace had multiple sclerosis. She had entered a debilitating stage of her disease, during which she would become totally dependent on her husband who, with five children in the house, had burdens enough. While she was still able, she found some poison and took it. Grace had a sacrificial motive and achieved a sure result: she really wanted to help her family and, on her terms, she was effective.

But it seems hard to justify Grace's sacrifice. For one thing, the good she achieved for others may not in fact balance out the loss she caused by destroying her life. Did she, in the long run, really make life better for her husband and children? Who can tell how much good they lost from life when they lost the burden of caring for someone they loved?

In short, the sheer fact of giving one's life for other people is not enough to justify the sacrifice. Even if the motive is generous, the end may not justify the means. We need some safeguards. As a general rule, if we justify self-sacrifice we must have reason to believe (1) that what we sacrifice our life for is at least as important as our life. Even then, (2) the sacrifice must be *necessary*; it must be the only way there is to serve the life of the other person. And (3) it must be *effective*; we must have very good odds that giving our life will actually serve the other's life. Even the supreme sacrifice of "greater love" must be an exception to the law of life.

3. *The suicide of escape.* Compared to our pain and losses in life, death may seem a gentle alternative. Suicide may be the only certain refuge from loss, from pain, from shame. For the strong, suicide may seem the ultimate cowardice, but many of us hearing of a suicidal escape from pain may say: "There but for the grace of God go I."

Is escape by suicide ever justified? What sort of loss might warrant it? John is a sculptor. He has invested his life in his art. Struck by a car, he would have died but for a surgeon's miracle which, however, left him paralyzed from the neck down. Sculpting gone, he feels that life is gone. The medical marvel has doomed him to conscious death. He demands to be left alone, unattended, so that he can let the curtain fall on a life-drama already finished. John chooses death as an escape from a meaningless life.

Other people seek escape from sheer pain. Unrelieved, irreversible, unremitting pain is more than some can bear. For others it may be the threat of future pain; to be told that bone cancer will bring a steady increase in horrible pain is to be given reason to hope for early death and, for some, to cause one's own death.

Sometimes it is shame from which people escape in suicide. Shame haunts both the failure and the perfectionist with the condemning innuendo of worthlessness. It may be secret shame, known and felt only inside a good person's soul, or public dishonor. In cultures with no place for forgiveness and new beginnings, hara-kiri is a proper exit, especially for a man who fails on the battlefield. But even the Bible has surprising tolerance for the suicide of escape from dishonor. Saul, faced with defeat, fell on his sword to keep his body out of the hands of the ungodly Philistines, "lest these uncircumcised come and thrust me through and make sport of me" (1 Sam. 31:4). They sang for him in Judah: "Thy glory, O Israel, is slain on the high places" (2 Sam. 1:19).

Known fully only to the person who suffers them, burdens may become too much to bear. Not everyone receives a sufficient grace. We must often withhold judgment, at least count on divine forgiving grace. Still, though we suspend judgment and count on mercy, we have not removed escape through suicide from the realm of moral concerns. The presumption of the law of life is always against suicide; even as an escape from life's cruel slings and arrows.

4. *The suicide of despair*. Despair is the state of a soul shorn of hope and stripped of joy. In despair, we lose the drive that moves us out of ourselves toward the others whose love sustains us. We have lost any feeling of gratitude that life, our life, is good. We have lost faith in God and his future. Beyond loving, beyond healing, beyond saving, beyond God, our soul is an abyss, dark, empty, and cold.

In despair, a person does not make a heroic decision for death. By the time he puts his finger on the trigger, life seems already flown. He has only yielded to the vacuum of his own nothingness. He feels no power of life; instead, he falls helplessly into the jaws of what looks like beneficent death.

What makes the suicide of despair especially sad is that it is usually the act of sensitively good people. There are people who are sensitive to all the suffering of the world—the cries of battered children, the pain of refugees, the outrage of the oppressed. And somehow they feel responsible and accountable for all the wrongs of this evil age. Worse, they feel unworthy themselves, full of foul sin, falling far short of divine perfection.

Complacent people may go blithely on their comfortable way; these burdened souls die of despair.

What point is there in talking of blame for their tragic act? Is it not a better moral response to recognize the signals of despair in people around us, to bring, if we can, some love to a loveless person, some reason for hope to a hopeless mind, and some possibilities of joy to a life whose cup has been drained dry?[10] Here, the primary moral response is not to condemn suicide as a moral wrong, but to save despairing persons from the threat of their joyless souls.

The moral question raised by the suicide of despair is: what is the moral alternative to despair? For the alternative to despair is also the alternative to the suicide of despair. And what can the opposite of despair be but joy? Since suicide may be only the final curtain drawn on a long drama of despair, we must think of the conflict, not merely as biological death attacking biological life, but as a conflict between the mind of despair and the mind of joy. We must, then, talk of the ethic of joy.

Joy: the alternative to suicide

No Christian believer can doubt that joy is his calling in life, his very end and purpose. Why else would the Bible constantly tell us to rejoice in the Lord? Why else would it promise us joy, perfectly and fully, in the kingdom of God? Where life is experienced in joy, despair is excluded. So is suicide. Therefore, joy is of the essence of obedience to the Sixth Commandment.

Karl Barth is one of the few theologians who treats joy seriously:

> In every real man, the will for life is also the will for joy. . . . He strives for different things with the . . . very definite . . . intention of securing joy for himself. . . . It is hypocrisy to hide this from oneself. And the hypocrisy will be at the expense of the ethical truth that he should will to enjoy himself just as he should will to eat, drink, sleep, be healthy, work, stand for what is right, and live in fellowship with God and his neighbor. A person who tries to debar himself from joy is certainly not an obedient person.[11]

What is joy? Joy is the experience of gratitude, of being glad for life in the presence of the Giver of life. Joy is also the will to give back to another something of what one is or has for the sheer desire of sharing the gift. Joy is a blend of gratitude and

118 giving. This truth was brought home to me one night after hearing Isaac Stern play Brahms' violin concerto in D Minor. We all received his gift and we blessed him for it by our applause. He bowed and accepted our gift of praise. He left the stage, and then returned again to our ovation. We stood. Some of us called "Bravo, Bravo!" I was in ecstasy, and I suddenly became aware that I had more joy in the applause than in the concert itself. And I knew why: I had felt the goodness of Stern's gift and was giving freely of my gift in return. And I knew that this experience was a paradigm of human joy in a life given by a loving Creator.

When gratitude and giving are merged in any human moment, we have a sign of the coming of Jesus. For he told us that his reason for coming and speaking in our world was to share his joy with us (John 17:13). We have joy only in fragments, to be sure, and we need to savor the moments when our hearts are opened to the goodness of life, no matter what the occasion. It may be in a rush of God's Spirit through our being while we pray. It may be in the loving embrace of another person, the good fellowship of friends, the discovery of a new insight into a piece of art, the shimmering beauty of a sunset over the ocean. No matter, whenever we feel within that life is good and return the gift of thanks, joy has entered into life.

What then is our problem? The problem, said Kierkegaard, is that we spend our lives building mansions for ourselves but choose to live in a dog house. We lock ourselves in an iron cage, as in John Bunyan's allegory of despair, an iron cage in a dark room, with no escape, and into which we feel that God himself has locked us. Barth writes,

> We can close ourselves to joy. We can harden ourselves against it. We can be caught in the rut of life in movement. We can try to be merely busy and therefore slothful in the expectation of fulfillments. We can regard life as such a solemn matter that there is no desire for celebration. We can look on an icy seriousness as the highest duty and virtue.[12]

But we must not let it happen, for to refuse joy is to violate both the will of God and the possibility of life.[13]

B. CAPITAL PUNISHMENT

Once we have heard the Lord God's "Thou shalt not kill" we must confront capital punishment with a powerful prejudice

against it. This starting point must be very clear. We do not
begin with the conviction that violating this commandment is so
evil that one ought to be killed for doing so; we begin with the
conviction that the commandment forbids killing anyone, even
those who kill others.[14] A criminal, even a murderer, is still a
human person, still the image of God. His life remains God's
gift, and no mere man may presume he has a right to take it away
from him. Thus our question is whether, in the light of the
commandment against it, capital punishment may be permitted
as an *exception* to the rule.

Redemptive love intensifies the bias of the commandment.
The intention of love is to redeem the guilty; therefore, love
will not let us close the door forever on the possibility of another
person's redemption. The Lord is "not willing that any should
perish, but that all should come to repentance" (2 Pet. 3:10).
His desire that the guilty be saved only supports his demand
that mere human beings keep destructive hands off each other's
life. Love "hopes all things"—even for the worst of criminals.
The commandment forbids us to kill; love moves us to honor
the commandment, even in the face of horrible guilt, because
love compels us to allow time for salvation.

Nevertheless, the believing community has traditionally gone
along cozily when the state has hanged, drowned, beheaded, or
otherwise done away with lawbreakers.[15] It raised little protest
when heretics were burned, pickpockets hanged, rebels beheaded. Indeed, resistance to capital punishment began only in
modern times, and then the first objections to it came not from
Christian but humanist voices.

Is capital punishment required by the Bible?

In a few places the Bible seems not only to allow but to demand
that murderers be punished with death. The Old Testament civil
rules called for death to such wrongdoers as adulterers, homosexuals, and rebellious children. Strict Muslims sometimes still
seek to impose such rules of death. Judaeo-Christian ethics has
seldom understood these ancient civil statutes as abiding moral
rules. But the death penalty for murder is another matter.

After the great flood, when human history was given its
second beginning, the Lord God came to Noah to urge the renewal of the human race. In effect, he said, Life is good, so
multiply it on earth; and always respect it as the life of God's
own image. "Whoever sheds the blood of man, by man shall his

120 blood be shed" (Gen. 9:6). That is the mandate for capital punishment, it is argued. The reason for killing killers is the same as the reason for forbidding murder: the unique worth of human beings, "for God made man in his own image" (9:6). Capital punishment appears to be God's own idea.

If Genesis tells us that murderers should be killed, Paul tells us that it is government who should do the killing. The governor "does not bear the sword in vain; he is the servant of God to execute his wrath on the wrongdoer" (Rom. 13:4). There are established ways to do the grim job of sending criminals off; the Lord is on the side of order even in death. God did not provide government with a sword for bluffing, but for killing. Hence, only the government may—*and the government surely must*—execute those who spill the blood of God's image.

But a second look at these Bible passages will show how risky it is to pluck them from their setting for use as proofs that God directs all societies to kill killers of human beings. Genesis 9 is a profound religious statement about life's sacredness; but we confront some sticky problems once we turn it into a divine command for capital punishment.

There are other commands in this passage which almost no one considers valid for life today, for instance, the prohibition in verse 5 against eating meat with blood in it. From a deep sense that God's own life somehow penetrates our life's blood comes the word that even animal blood must be respected and not mixed with ours. Modern believers may or may not feel the same reverence for blood, but very few take it that the Lord has spoken forever against eating rare beef. Again, out of respect for life, the Lord God orders people to execute animals who have killed human beings (v. 4). Does this still bind us? (There is evidence that a pig was tried for murder in 1386, and a horse too. Both were executed after solemn due process. But to recall this medieval insanity only tells us how ludicrous it is to execute a sow for murder with malice aforethought.)[16]

In short, we can point to this ancient proverb—"by man shall his blood be shed"—as God's demand for capital punishment only if we inconsistently ask obedience to it while ignoring the rest of the context in which it is found. Besides, the ancient text sweeps with a much wider brush than most zealous advocates of killing killers would wish. It does not separate the cold-blooded killer from someone guilty only of negligent homicide or manslaughter. It also allows for executing children—a fact probably noted by British judges, who condemned children of nine and ten to die by hanging as late as 1833.[17] Most people today would at least narrow the hangman's loop so that it catches only adults and murderers in the first degree. But then, of course, they are no longer listening only to the text of the Bible.

If we are seeking an early expression of God's will on capital punishment, we should go back a few chapters in Genesis to the story of the very first murderer. Far from having a mind to kill all killers, the Lord went out of his way to protect Cain. He put a "mark" on him to ward off self-appointed executioners (Gen. 4:15). Cain was a cold-blooded murderer. He stewed in his jealousy, let hate percolate through his mind, and only then went for his brother's jugular. The Lord personally spared the original first-degree murderer. Would he then have ordered for all time the execution of anyone who kills, no matter how, in passion's fury or with cool calculation?

In short, Genesis 9:6 is too obscure, too broad, and too dubious to be a divinely issued mandate for all human societies to kill their killers. Perhaps it is a proverb like "Those who live by the sword die by the sword." If so, it is a shrewd observation of what usually happens to killers. But if we are claiming that the Lord of life demands the death penalty always and everywhere, we need more than a proverb to go on.

If Genesis does not require the death of killers, Paul's classic word on government falls far short of requiring every state to be an executioner. Paul affirms the authority of human government over its citizens, and he insists that Christians are duty-bound to respect that authority. To keep the unruly in check, government has authority to punish, and the "sword" is a symbol of that authority (Rom. 13:4). But authority to punish is not a mandate to kill. If Paul had a literal sword in mind, and the government's hold on the sword were a mandate to kill, capital punishment would be the primary punishment government had available. And if possession of the sword were authorization to use it for what a sword can be used for, the hideous practice of "drawing and quartering" criminals, cutting off their noses and genitalia, would be sanctified.[18] A sword, after all, is for cutting things off just as it is for thrusting people through. Literalism has its consequences.

Rational arguments for capital punishment often appeal to

122   a common sense of justice, a sense upheld by the Bible. Justice demands that criminals get the punishment they deserve—no more, surely, but no less either. Punishment ought to fit the crime, and the worst of all crimes should get the worst of all punishments. Since this worst crime is unique among crimes, its punishment should also be in a class by itself. Execution is the worst of punishments, in a class by itself, different from jail and fines. Therefore, it is argued, justice makes capital punishment mandatory.

Besides inflicting punishment on the criminal, retributive justice witnesses to society's own moral sense. Sentence the kidnapper of a child to three years in jail, and you advertise how much you value the life of a child. Sentence murderers to the same sort of punishment that you give a car thief, and you announce that you really put murder and theft in the same category. Thus, the argument runs, any society that wants to witness to its respect for life must punish murder by the unique and dreadful ritual of judicial death.

The plausible foundation of the argument from justice is the notion that only by taking a person's life can we match his crime. The eye is literally taken in exchange for the eye—no more, no less. The punishment is the *same* as the crime. But we are not and cannot be consistent with this trade-off. In the first place, "eye for eye" justice cannot work in a literal sense. A rape for a rape, or a theft for a theft, would be insane justice. Why, then, in the case of murder, must the punishment not only fit the crime, but be the same as the crime?

The argument that executions testify to the high value society puts on human life is less than convincing as a reason for killing killers as a regular policy. Why not be consistent then? We should reconsider the pedagogical value of public hangings, and televise executions during prime time. Were the Romans witnessing to their high esteem for life when they crucified criminals as a public spectacle? Is it not the other way around? Would we not testify to our own respect for life precisely by keeping the *worst* of murderers alive?

The thesis that revelation tells us that capital punishment is *required* falls short of being utterly convincing—which it must be. So horrible is it to kill a person that the justification for ever doing so must be uniquely compelling. By casting reasonable doubt on the assumption that the Bible makes capital punishment mandatory, we have destroyed the case.

Is capital punishment permitted by the Bible?

But if the Bible does not require us to take the life of those who kill, does it allow for that possibility by way of exception? May governments kill murderers?

What might make it morally right for governments to take human life? Most people believe that we may kill a person if killing him is the only way to defend our lives against him. One reason we justify killing in self-defense is that our intention is not to kill someone, but to prevent someone from killing us. Our purpose is to stay alive; killing is forced on us as the only means available. I assume, of course, when my life is attacked, that I have more right to live than my attacker does.

Capital punishment can be understood as a form of self-defense.[19] A government may have to defend itself and society from terrorists who threaten to destroy them. Or, we can think of government as an extension of ourselves, with the job of being our defender. Can we justify capital punishment on this ground?

Disaster can sometimes cripple a society and bring a society to the edge of chaos. Consider the months after a terrible war or a community which has just suffered a devastating earthquake. Picture the worst—free-wheeling terrorists bringing community life to a halt, wild gangs of killers shooting people at random. Does a besieged society not have the right to defend itself by killing terrorists? What Caiaphas said was true in its way: "it is expedient . . . that one man should die for the people, and that the whole nation should not perish" (John 11:50). We are talking, of course, about an extreme need, when capital punishment becomes a measure of last resort. But we have opened the wedge, and we admit that we cannot tell for sure exactly when the moment of last resort has come. All we can say is that a government has the right to defend itself if need be by executing killers.

The government may also be the defender of a private person and kill a killer for the sake of a person who would otherwise be a victim. If we use capital punishment in defense of potential victims, we kill people *in the chance* that they might kill others. We are not certain; we need to calculate the odds. Here, morality is uneasy. It listens cautiously to the conflicting predictions and

124 statistics of the sociologists and the divergent theories of the criminologists. If we are to overcome our moral presumption against capital punishment, we must be persuaded that the chances of its actually saving a victim's life are very favorable. And how can we know what the chances are?

Can we not use some common sense about what people are *likely* to do under certain circumstances? Take a homicidal person who is in prison for murdering three people. He is already under the maximum sentence by law. Will he not feel more free to assault a prison guard if he knows he will not get any punishment beyond what he has already received than if he knew for sure he would be executed? Or, imagine that a killer is set free after several years. Is it not reasonable to expect that he will feel more free to kill again if he knows that at worst he will go back to prison than if he knew he might be executed? Maybe the threat of death would not hold back the hands of every killer. But what if it restrained half or even a third of the potential killers, and what if each of those whom it held back would otherwise have killed three or four people? What we have are good odds that some executions would defend the lives of some potential victims.

The Sixth Commandment surely inclines us against capital punishment. The person who assaults human life is, for all his guilt, still human. But there is evidence that capital punishment might sometimes be society's only way to defend itself, or its people. So we have practical reasons to suppose that the cause of human life may be served if some murderers were killed. We conclude, then, that the commandment, filtered through the realities of life, allows for self-defense through capital punishment. But the commandment does not allow for it as a regular policy. The word from the Lord, especially when we read it through the lens of love, is "Do not kill any, not the weakest, nor the worst, of the human family, for everyone in it is the image of God."

C. ABORTION

If we accept the commandment in its austere simplicity as the word of the life-affirming God against the destruction of innocent human life, can we suppose that it might allow for killing an innocent fetus?[20] Can circumstances arise in which the Lord might approve of abortion? That question arises today in a society reeling over the issue of whether a woman's private right to control her childbearing counts as much as a fetus's primitive right to survive. We ask it in a world where some thirty-five million women arrange for killing the fetus within their wombs every year. We cannot turn away from the awesome magnitude of this fetal slaughter.[21] But the moral question is legitimately raised only if we are touched as deeply by the frightful anguish of many women who face the personal question of abortion in their own lives. Yet no matter how difficult the issue or how passionate our concern, we must ask the question: does the commandment of God against killing somehow allow for killing a fetus?

Abortion confronts us with two distinct moral questions. The first question is personal: is it right before God for me to kill this fetal being inside of me? This question requires a private answer from every woman who wants to terminate a pregnancy and every doctor who agrees to do it for her. But none of us escapes this question, for every morally serious woman or man needs to make a personal decision about abortion. None of us can avoid involvement in this life-wrenching issue. The second question is social: is it right for a government to prevent mothers from killing a fetus? This is the question that divides society today. The personal question asks whether abortion is a sin; the social question asks whether abortion should be a crime?

It is important to keep the personal and social issues apart. We must remember that abortion is not made right by making it legal. The law may or may not prevent a woman from getting an abortion; but it cannot tell her whether it is right for her to get it. Furthermore, abortion need not be a crime simply because it is a sin. What we need to show, if we believe abortion is a sin, is that it is one of the special kinds of sins that society cannot tolerate. If we believe that abortion is murder, we will also believe that it should be a crime. But our merely believing that abortion is murder is not enough; we also have to make a reasonable case for this claim among our doubting fellow citizens. For it is not clear to everyone that the law should prevent people from doing what their conscience allows them to do—even if some others believe it is murder. Thereby hangs one of the hardest moral questions of our time.

The personal question

The center of the storm lies at the point where two human interests intersect—those of the fetus and those of all the other persons involved in a woman's pregnancy. As we divide the ques-

126   tion into a consideration of those two spheres of interest, we must admit that we are giving priority to one over the other. First I will talk about the fetus, whether we can be sure it is or is not a person. Second, I will talk about other human concerns, to see if they may ever count for more than the continued life of the fetus. The ultimate moral question for any believing person will always be: given my special needs, may it be God's will that I act to kill my fetus?

Abortion is killing; this we know for sure. True, the doctor does not assault the fetus directly; he only evicts it from its hostess, the mother. The doctor's primary intent is to liberate the mother. But he also intends to doom the fetus as a living thing. We cannot disguise this by using medical jargon about "evacuating a uterus." Further, abortion is the killing of human life. A fetus is alive; if it were not, there would be no terrible problem about killing it. And the life it has is human kind; no fetus conceived of human mother and father was ever born a dolphin or a dog. If its life is not of human kind, what kind might it be?

But if abortion destroys life, does it destroy a *person*? Here the abortion issue becomes awesomely complex. We know the commandment forbids us to take the life of a human being. It throws a protective armor around all persons; especially the marginal members of the human family, the weak, the vulnerable, the unproductive, and the very inconvenient persons. We know that the fetus is weak and vulnerable, and we know that it contains the beginnings of the biological support system which sustains the eventual person. But the commandment does not tell us whether a fetus is a person.

The Christian belief in personal immortality does not let us identify persons with biological life. Though linked in mysterious symbiosis, body and soul are not one and the same. Therefore, the fact that a fetus has the biological life of human being does not of itself tell us that a fetus is a person. We know that on the other end of life's pilgrimage a human body can be alive, its lungs taking in oxygen, its heart pumping blood through the veins, though the person once supported by that body no longer lives on earth. Bible-believers often crusade against abortion on the assumption that a fetus is a person. But we must test that assumption.

When does a fetus become a person?

There are four ways to answer the question of when a person comes into existence. Finally we have to choose among them, difficult as it may be to do so on the basis of what we really know about this mysterious event. Our moral choice about abortion will depend in large measure on which of the four we accept.

1. *A fetus is a person at the moment of its conception.* The clearest position we can take is this: there is never a time when a fetus is not a person.[22] The instant a sperm fertilizes the ovum by joining its 23 chromosomes to the 23 offered by the egg, a new and unique person exists in our world. Here, at the very beginning, we have the complete chromosomic kit from which the very specific individual emerges who will live and die as God's very special image.

This view leads to the clearest decision about abortion. If we believe that the formless microscopic zygote is a person, we can brush aside as obfuscation all the complex moral distinctions that arise in discussions of abortion. We don't have to resort to talk about quickening, viability, or even implanting. Early or late in pregnancy, the decision is plain: we may not kill another human being. We may not kill it with a "morning after" pill. We may not kill it with an intra-uterine device. Whatever kills a fertilized egg is a murder weapon.

What the mother wants or how the conception happened cannot offset the awesome untouchability of the fetal person's life. If a choice had to be made between a mother's very life and that of the fetus we might listen to an argument that the mother's life comes first, but it would not necessarily convince us. Nor is it clear that a fetus conceived in rape has less right to life than a fetus conceived in love. Why should Person A be sacrificed because Person B raped his mother? The veto on abortion is final and uncompromising from the first moment if we know that a person comes into being when a sperm fertilizes an egg.[23]

But how can we know? There are two sets of data that persuade people that all fetal life is personal life. One set comes from the Bible, the other from genetics. In a few very personal passages of the Bible, we find someone looking backward to see God at the very beginning of his existence, creating him, knowing him, caring for him. The Psalmist, for one, rhapsodizes:

> For thou didst form my inward parts, thou didst knit me together in my mother's womb. . . . My frame was not hidden from thee

128   when I was being made in secret, intricately wrought in the depths
of the earth (Ps. 13:13, 15).

In the depths of a believing heart lies a consciousness of
divine care leading a person from a microscopic flake of organic
life into the full riches available to one who is created in the
divine image. Surely this is inspired poetry, religious confession
wrought in metaphor. But is the Psalmist also offering technical
information on which we may base a judgment against abortion?
Consider: if the words were meant as factual information, what
would we make of being "wrought" in the depths, not of the
uterus, but of the earth? But the Psalmist is not alone. Jeremiah,
doubting for the moment his calling from God, hears deep within
his consciousness a word from him who touched his life beforehand: "Before I formed you in the womb I knew you, and before
you were born, I consecrated you" (Jer. 1:5). *Before* the prophet's
body took on the form of a human being, before there was a
heart or heartbeat, a brain or brainwave, God knew Jeremiah
and consecrated him as a prophet. Is this divine sanction for
saying that a person is present the moment an ovum has 46
chromosomes, even before it clings to its uterine nest?
If you pin your hopes on one inspired confession, another
may come back to trouble you. Paul, for instance, knew for sure
that God chose us, and thus knew us, not when we were knit
together in a mother's womb, but before the earth itself began
(Eph. 1:4). The Lamb of God himself was slain before the world's
foundations were laid (Rev. 13:18). Is not this a testimony of
faith in the Lord who mysteriously knows people before they
exist, knows even Jesus the Lamb hanging on the wooden cross
before the seed of the tree was planted in the soil? God sets his
caring love on us unconditionally, sovereignly, independently.
One way to praise the God who cares for me from beforehand
is to say that he knew me before I was born, before I became
that zygote which one day would become me. When I meditate
on the Lord who tends my life, I look backward and see no
beginning; he was always there, and as long as he was there, so
was I, in his mind, in his love. In short, the confession is about
God, not about the precise status of fetal life.
The other line of reasoning, we said, comes from genetics.
At the outset, when 23 male and 23 female chromosomes unite,
we have the building blocks for an individual person. Made of

the mysterious DNA, these chromosomes provide the genes, more than two million of them, which determine the special human individual that each of us becomes. They contain the alphabet out of which our life stories will be written. For many people that settles the question of when a person begins. The person I am now, what I look and feel like, what I can do, was locked into that tiny bit of biological life called a zygote. Can we say, then, that all a person is going to be is compressed into what his genetic code has in store for him and a newly created fetus must therefore be reckoned a person with all rights pertaining thereto?[24]

But the genetic alphabet tucked into the DNA is not yet a short story. Building blocks are not a building; even if you have a pile of lumber, the tools of the builder's trade, and a carpenter standing by, you do not yet have a cottage.[25] What finally goes into the making of an individual person includes a lot more than his genetic building blocks. We become what we are as our bodies and our souls are touched by many fingers, including the finger of God. Bible believers who enlist genetics in support of their convictions against abortion may in the end lose more than they gain. They may pay the price of fatalism. If we admit that a fetus is an individual person because of its genetic bank account, we may also have to admit that we are what we are now, as whole persons, only because of what was stored to our future account in the chromosomal bank. So, to buy into the genetic "proof" may cost more than those who believe in personal freedom and dignity really want to pay.

The question of whether a fetus can be considered a person exposes a deep ontological ambiguity—the ambiguity of not being something yet and at the same time having the makings of what it will be. Every one of us, to some extent, lives with such ambiguity in his life. Early philosophers invented the word "potential" to express it. The Catholic anti-abortionist John Noonan takes hold of one side of the ambiguity when he says: "Once conceived, the being was recognized as man because he has man's potential. . . . If you are conceived by human parents, you are human."[26] But the fact is that the fetus is *only* potential and for that reason is not yet a person. An acorn is not an oak tree, even if it has sprouts; and no one in his right mind would equate crushing an acorn with cutting down an oak tree.

2. *The fetus becomes a person after it receives the one property*

130 *essential to personhood.* Many people believe that the fetus becomes a human being in one marvelous moment of transfor-
mation into the image of God. For many devout people, this
moment comes when God "inserts" a soul into the fetal body.
But even if there is such a moment, we need a physical signal
of it, for God and the soul are both invisible.

Some people hold that the sign that the fetus may be counted
is its implantation on the wall of its uterine guest-house. At that
moment, the fetus, which already has the genetic makings of
personhood, now has the environment it needs to grow into the
person it is meant to be.[27] For others, the marvelous moment
is that of "quickening"—when the fetus begins to stretch, shove,
wriggle, or kick within the womb. Quickening has been seen as
a signal that the soul has come, complaining of its confinement,
bringing human life to the body. We now know, however, that
quickening is what the mother feels, not what is really happening
to her fetus; in fact, the fetus is "quick" before the mother ever
notices.

For others the key moment is that of "viability," the moment
after which a fetus can survive outside the mother's womb. Viability once had a fairly stable meaning, but no longer. Even
apart from the prospect of test-tube babies surviving outside the
womb before they are ever planted within one, the moment of
viability is shifting downward. Until about 1970, a fetus had to
be a thousand grams in order to survive. By 1985, we are told,
neonatologists will push viability below the 500 gram mark.
Nathanson predicts that in the future fetuses of two ounces—
less than 60 grams—will be kept alive outside a mother's womb.
Viability seems to be obsolete as a fixed moment to mark the
arrival of personhood to a fetus.[28]

Another proposed signal of the soul's arrival is the presence
of an electrical impulse from the brain, which first happens near
the end of the third month. The reasoning here derives from the
ancient notion that a person is a thinking animal and from the
modern technique for testing whether a brain is able to think.
At the other end of the journey, we have allowed that when a
brain is irretrievably dead we can assume that a person has died,
though the heart may beat and the lungs take in air. So, at the
beginning, we may assume that before the brain is able to think
a fetus is not a person and after it thinks the fetus is a person.[29]

Do we now have a technical dividing line beyond which

abortion is clearly immoral, maybe even murder? Are brain waves registered on an electroencephalogram the same as thinking? Is an electrical impulse the same as a thought? Perhaps this is the best indicator of fetal personhood we have ever had, but is it enough?

Let us say that we could mark the marvelous moment— whichever moment we chose—that a fetus becomes a person. Would not that moment be the moral Rubicon for any decision about abortion? After the river has been crossed, whether three days or three months after conception, the fetus has a right to life that it did not have before. From that moment, we would have to respect its life almost absolutely. But what about the time leading up to the moment when the fetus became a person? In that "nonperson" period, the fetus' right to life would be weakened. If we spot a moment during its life in the womb when the fetus changes from nonperson to person, we also mark out a time period in which fetal life may take second place to the needs or desires of its mother.

3. *The fetus becomes a person when it is born*. The belief that a person emerges only when it is finally separated alive from the mother's body matches nicely the conviction that abortion is only a matter of a woman's private decision about her own body and her own procreative life. Dignified as a theory, this view holds that a person is essentially a social being. Unless a living being can interrelate with other people visibly, by sending and receiving various sorts of messages, it is not a person. A fetus, on this ground, is a subhuman guest which exists at the pleasure of its hostess. She may release the fetus from her body at any time with no more reluctance than she would feel if she removed a sick dog from a respirator. She may unplug the fetus if its existence happens to interfere with a trip to Europe she is planning this summer. Abortion on demand, at a whim, for convenience— it makes no difference. The only real immorality about abortion is the impertinence of busy bodies intruding into the private lives of pregnant women. The private right of a woman to control her body is the only moral criterion relevant to the abortion question.[30]

Any argument for abortion makes sense if you believe that fetal life is subpersonal until birth. It is not clear, however, whether people accept abortion on demand because they are sure a fetus is a nonperson or whether they believe that a fetus

132   is a nonperson because they want abortion to be right. But does this make sense? The only really new thing a baby does at birth is stretch its lungs and take in air on its own power. Breathing is probably closest to a biblical sign of life, for the breath of life is the very breath of God (Job 33:4). When he gives breath, we live (Gen. 2:7; Acts 17:25) and when he takes it away we are no more (Ps. 104:29). But a fetus already has the breath of life via the mother's oxygen supply.

The notion that a fetus does not become personal until birth gets a jolt every time a live baby is born during an abortion. A breathing infant, intended to be separated from its mother as a dead fetus, confronts an aborting physician with a grim paradox. At one moment he is using his skill to relieve a pregnant woman from an invisible life, and killing it in the process. At the next moment he is using his skill to save that same life. The purpose of the abortion was to end the fetal life. But the abortion by accident turned into a birth. The fetus was just as alive before the abortion as afterward; the only difference is that it is now visible. What must a doctor do? Should he finish the job he set out to do by wringing the baby's neck? Or should he let it die by abandoning it? (Dr. Kenneth Edelin, of Boston, was convicted of manslaughter for abandoning a post-abortion baby.) But if we agree that even post-abortion babies should all be kept alive, we make it a lot harder to believe that fetuses are persons only after they are born.

4. *The fetus develops into a person gradually, with no fixed turning point.* The key idea here is process. There is no marvelous moment; instead, the fetal life gradually develops from the fertilized egg toward personal life as the organism becomes more complex and enters ever more complex relationships with its environment.

There is, of course, an entity that is experiencing the process, becoming a person, but this entity is also a genuine being in its own right, not just a piece of its hostess' tissue. It is dependent on her, but it is distinct from her too, as Jonah was distinct from the whale or an astronaut is distinct from his space capsule.

To think of the fetus on its way toward becoming a person, in process, is to make the whole question harder. We cannot point to any moment in the process when we are sure that the fetus is *not* a person. Nor can we mark off a moment after which we know for sure that the fetus *is* a person, with the same right to life as a child dancing in the streets. How, then, are we to treat the fetus-on-its-way?

Must we think of what the fetus is becoming and treat it as if it already were what it is on the way to be? Philosopher Alan Donagan thinks so:

> If respect is owed to beings because they are in a certain stage, it is owed to whatever by its very nature develops into that state. To reject this principle would be arbitrary if indeed it would be intelligible.[31]

Bonhoeffer argued similarly from a theological point of view. We know God's intention: "The simple fact is that God certainly intended to create a human being and that [if aborted] this nascent human being has been defrauded of his life."[32] Most people would probably find a certain common sense to Donagan's logic and Bonhoeffer's faith. When the living entity you are tempted to kill is on its way toward being a person, you probably ought to treat it as if it were a person. If person-becoming is a process, the prejudice is always against abortion.

Yet we are bound to have reservations about the very early fetus. Most women do not feel that a fetus a few days old is a person. What does the most life-honoring woman do with the fetal tissue expelled from her body in a spontaneous abortion? She probably flushes it away with no sense of disrespect for the dead. No one holds a funeral service for a miscarried fetus, nor have we ever thought seriously of giving a zygote the legal status of a person. In the past we have not really believed that a fetus of early days is to be treated like a person.

Our attitudes match the unhuman form of the newly fertilized fleck. The process has hardly begun. The ovum has not made a nest in its uterine cavern. It may still, as millions of others do, slip off into miscarried oblivion, its existence hardly noticed. It has no form that even begins to resemble anything human; it performs no bodily functions to hint at what it may one day become.

We have said enough to cast doubts on an absolutist stance. The commandment is simple; life is complex. We do not mean to say that there is open season on a fetus for the first few days. But dare we condemn every abortion at this early stage as an act of murder? Do we not have sound reasons at this point for at least considering the matter from the mother's point of view—

and maybe that of others? Can we ignore the desperate claims of the people whose lives are sometimes awesomely burdened by the birth of a child—ignore them wholly on grounds that (apart from the very life of the mother) only the life of the fetus counts?

What counts besides the life of the fetus?

We are inclined to think of becoming a person as a process. But the hypothesis that the fetus gradually develops into the fulness of what a person is deprives us of clear-cut positions and certain absolutes. We eliminate the absolute anti-abortionism of people who believe a fetus is a person the instant an egg is fertilized. We eliminate the absolutism of pro-abortionists who believe that a fetus becomes a person only after it is born. The premise that fetal life is person-becoming life imposes on us the moral burden of protecting fetal life; we will be anti-abortion as a state of mind. But we admit that the early stage of life's development is so remotely connected with the later stages that we cannot simply identify the early fetus as a person. This concession does not mean that abortion for the first five weeks does not matter morally, but it does mean that the concerns of other people whose lives are deeply touched by the existence of a fetus will count for something in the moral deliberation. Let us consider the interests of three involved persons.

1. *The welfare of the mother.* "Abortion on demand" implies a woman's right to make any decision she wishes to make about her pregnancy. Our earlier insistence that the life of the fetus is the *prime* moral issue rules out that right. What we are talking about in this section, therefore, is not a blank check for women's rights, but the possibility that the pregnant woman's welfare might count for more than the early life of a fetus.

The mother's welfare is a wide net. It can hold everything from "being inconvenienced" to "psychotic depression." We need not draw up a list; it is enough to imagine a case situation in which we must at least balance out the conflicting needs of mother and fetus. Not every threat to a mother's welfare will count. It is not always the end of the world for an immature girl to have a baby. It is not always true that another child will send a harassed mother into a psychic tailspin. On the other hand, there may be times when giving birth is too much to ask.

Remember that we are comparing a mother's welfare to a fetal life of less than six weeks, plugged into the mother's life-support system before it possesses anything like human form. Now consider a woman who has been raped by a violent stranger, or maybe a young girl seduced by an incestuous father—extreme stories, I know, but they help us clarify the issue. Would we still put the rights of fetal life above the needs of a woman who would almost rather have died than conceive it? Someone will counter that the rape or the incestuous seduction was not the fetus's fault. Of course it was not; nor was it the fault of the mother. Consider a woman with severe bronchial asthma, who has four children, one of them mentally retarded, and a husband who is out of work most of the time because of his drinking problem. Will we insist that the sanctity of the early fetal life is so absolute that we cannot even bring the mother's needs into consideration?

Certainly we are on shaky ground when we open the door to a mother's needs. Who knows whether her desires might slip through under the guise of needs? We have to leave a good deal to personal discernment and individual responsibility—more, maybe, than the moral traffic will bear. But are we ready to rule out any and all abortion in the early stages on ground that people may get their wants mixed up with their needs?

2. *The welfare of third parties.* The further we move from the fetus and its mother, the harder it is to justify abortion. Yet, other people are involved when conception takes place, and their welfare can be deeply affected by the birth of a child. Most obvious, perhaps, is the woman's husband. Imagine that a woman gets pregnant in an act of adultery. Her husband forgives her infidelity, but he chokes at the thought of caring for a child fathered by the man who outraged his marriage. He demands that his wife get an abortion at once; if she does not, he cannot promise that we will have the love to bear with the child. Imagine two other children within this scene, and the effects of the father's anger on them. Set their complex needs, their unpredictable responses in a scale to be weighed against the life of a three-week-old fetus. Are we sure that sanctity of life forecloses on even a consideration of the husband's claims?

3. *The welfare of the future child.* No child, it has been said, should be forced to enter the world unwanted. Being unwanted is worse than not being at all, for to be unwanted is to be bru-

136   talized and dehumanized. Therefore, the death of a fetus, not
yet a person, is better than the life of an unwanted person.

We must weigh this future possibility against the life of great
value that hangs in the balance. The "wantedness factor" is very
slippery. Remember that "unwanted" is not really a description
of the child. The child is desirable even if the mother is unable
to desire it. We must not transfer a lack in the mother to the
fetus, as if the mother's failure to value it made the fetus less
valuable. Remember, too, that a fetus could grow into a person
who would rather be alive and unwanted than dead and forgotten; but of course we cannot consult a fetus on what it might
want were it to be allowed to become a person. Finally, remember that what a pregnant girl does not want during the first weeks
of pregnancy can become a child she passionately wants as a
mother who has given birth.

Nevertheless, children do suffer grievously from being unwanted. We may never underestimate the gruesome evil a parent inflicts on a child simply by turning his or her heart away.
Lives and minds are often stunted; and such children grow into
adults who cannot love, who in turn brutalize their children the
way they were brutalized.

And the fetus may be in for future tragedies more clear-cut
than the sadness of being unwanted. Here is a pregnant Jewish
woman whose fetus she knows—from amniocentesis—will be
a victim of Tay Sachs disease. Tay Sachs strikes Jewish children
of Eastern European background, kills them painfully after a
miserably brief life. This is her third pregnancy; the first two
times she miscarried. Now, three months after conception, she
decides to have this fetus disengaged from her body, as the
others had sprung loose on their own.

What shall we say by way of moral response? Was escape
from Tay Sachs worth losing fetal life for? Is it better not to exist
at all than to die at age two from a horrendous disease? Does
this case not suggest that there may be times when the welfare
of the child-to-be counts more than the life of the fetus-that-is?
May it be that in such time the commandment against killing
does not hold back the hand of the abortionist?

What can we say? It seems to me that no woman is morally
bound to condemn her child-to-be to die at two by Tay Sachs'
cruel hand when she has the power to release the fetus before

it becomes a dying child. A Tay Sachs child is a signal that the welfare of the child-to-be may sometimes count more than the life of the fetus-that-is. We weigh the certainty of a child's gruesome dying against the early fetus living, and we let the fetus die. Again, this is not to make a general rule that abortion is justified whenever a mother thinks the child-to-be will be better off.

We have, in conclusion, arrived at a not-quite absolute anti-abortion position. The commandment against killing human beings sends us into every tragic situation of unwanted pregnancy with a powerful bias against killing fetal life. But it was precisely in facing the key question of fetal life that we blinked when we considered the earliest period of a fetus's existence. The process of development not yet really begun leaves us with less than absolute certainty that we have a person as soon as we have conception. Growth into personhood is dynamic, gradual, complex; its beginning is obscure. Over against uncertainty about the fetus, we weigh the certainty of misery and pain for the living persons who would be driven to desperate disadvantage by the birth of the child. In the broken and disordered lives of human beings times and situations come when it would be morally irresponsible to refuse any consideration of their needs and their rights when confronting the question: may it ever be God's will that a mother abort a fetus? Once we admit the needs of people into our moral deliberations, along with the life of the fetus, we admit the possibility that we may justifiably choose abortion. In any case, we admit that we do better to suspend judgment sometimes than to condemn every abortion as murder and every abortionist as a murderer.

How can a woman, or a doctor, ever know for sure that in her case abortion is justified? I believe that no one can ever know for sure. The concerns for the welfare of the child-to-be, the needs of the mother, and/or the rights of any other people involved would need to be profoundly compelling, never trivial. The stage at which abortion is considered would need to be early, usually the first six weeks. Every person who, on balancing out the claims of the fetus and the needs of others, decides for abortion, will need to do it with fear and trembling before God and conscience, taking the risk that she may be doing some-

138 thing deeply wrong, and trusting a forgiving God to carry her through.

The social problem

The crisis abortion has created in contemporary society cannot be resolved unless one of the two principal adversaries has a radical conversion. The crisis centers on law, and whether women should be prevented by law from having abortions. Ought abortion to be made a crime? If you believe that a fetus is a person, consistency obligates you to answer this question affirmatively. If you believe that a fetus is only a growth on a woman's flesh, the effort to outlaw abortion will seem an insufferable invasion of a woman's private life. There is no evidence that believers on either side of this issue are changing their minds in massive numbers. How might we then cope with this crisis which we cannot resolve?

Not everyone, as we have seen, accepts either of the two choices held out by the radical antagonists. In our discussion of abortion as a moral question, we concluded that we cannot flatly declare that a fetus at the earliest stages is a person. So we cannot simply equate abortion and murder. On the other hand, we cannot concede that a fetus in any of the later stages is a nonperson. Therefore, we cannot dismiss abortion as a private matter between a woman and her obstetrician. Now we must explore the tough social question we face in this middle ground: is there a workable legal response to abortion that fits a mediating moral stance?

I will argue in what follows that using law to restrict but not absolutely prohibit abortion is the right response for our society to make. My argument on the social crisis will depend, of course, on the validity of what I have already said about the personal morality of abortion. As a background, I think we should consider, for a few paragraphs, the arguments of both of the extreme sides. If we tone down the volume of debate and try to listen, not to the slogans, but to the reasons behind them, we may help each other toward a responsible decision about this tragic dilemma.

Arguments for freedom of abortion

I will mention five arguments that have been advanced for keeping abortion private, out of the reach of law. Each argument follows from an important principle that most people accept about a free society. None of them is trivial; each takes a bead on a vital nerve of a free society. All are rooted in the assumption that a fetus is not certainly a full-fledged person with the same rights that any child riding a bicycle has. Without this assumption, all of the arguments wilt like a flower out of water. Aware of the assumption, then, let us look at the arguments.

1. *A mixed society ought not prevent people from doing things their own conscience approves of.* We live in a pluralist society; each of us makes a covenant with everyone else to tolerate the religions and the morals of people we disagree with. Freedom of religion includes freedom of abortion. How so? Some women believe it is right before their God to control their own pregnancy; in abortion they are practicing the tenets of their religious belief. In a mixed society, we may not prevent these women from living by the values implied in their faith.

The argument based on a religiously mixed society does not really work, however. The reason is that it is too loose, too sweeping. There are limits to everyone's religious freedom. Should we stand by to tolerate the suicidal madness of a religious leader like Jim Jones? Should we tolerate everything the Ku Klux Klan or the Nazis might do if they were free to practice all their beliefs? Is not religious freedom limited wherever its use by some threatens the rights and the freedom of others? The question is whether the fetal minority is fatally deprived of its rights when the aborting majority exercises its freedom of conscience.

2. *A free society ought not invade the privacy of a woman's decision about her own body.* A woman's pregnancy is her most private affair. What she decides to do with it is her secret, her problem, her decision and hers alone. Mary Mannes puts the case for a woman's privacy in compelling terms: "This is our citadel, our responsibility, our mental, emotional, and physical being." No law can be good that allows government to invade the holy of holies of a woman's life.

The principle is unassailable. But does it lead to the pro-abortion conclusion? Important as anyone's privacy is to a free society, it never surmounts the importance of someone's right to stay alive. And with this, the same fierce moral combat is joined again. Furthermore, we already draw many lines on privacy. A man who beats his wife or a parent who abuses his child cannot take sanctuary from interference in the privacy of his home. The privacy argument holds only to the extent that what a person does in privacy does not violate other persons. And this is precisely what is at stake in the abortion debate.

3. *A just society ought not pass laws that will inevitably be unfair.* Anti-abortion laws are always unfair to poor people, because the rich always manage to buy illegal abortions safely and cleanly. Poor people are doomed to put their lives in the hands of grubby butchers or they are forced to bear the children they desperately want not to have. Hence, abortion laws are bound to be unfair to the very people about whom God is most concerned.

The fairness argument troubles the conscience of every anti-abortionist who shares God's care for the poor and his hatred of systems that bring unfair advantage for the rich. And yet, concern for poor women runs directly up against our concern for the unborn. We must make an unhappy comparison: does injustice for poor women who want an abortion count for more than the existence of perhaps the three-quarters of a million fetal lives that might go on to live were abortion restricted by law? Until it is shown that the unfairness any abortion law will bring to poor people is worse than massive loss of fetal life, this argument will not be convincing even though it has great appeal.

4. *A compassionate society ought not pass laws that will force terrible handicaps on children.* A society ought to have compassion for its children. Blanket laws against abortion force existence on children whose handicaps of mind and body are all but insufferable. It is not justice but brutality that coerces women to have children who are unwanted or horribly handicapped or both.

No one can reject this argument as trivial or tendentious. Yet, empathy for handicapped children does not imply that someone has a right to decide for them whether they should exist on this earth or not. Being unwanted is not the same as being undesirable. And the struggles and disadvantages handicapped people face do not imply that any real, live handicapped person would choose not to exist. Tragedy lurks in the lives of children who are born of unwilling women, to be sure. But may we avoid the tragedy by giving healthy people the power to decide whether a future handicap disqualifies someone from having a share in this life?

5. *A wise society will not pass laws against behavior that does*

not injure society in any significant measure.[33] If a society is deeply divided about any exercise of personal freedom, the course of wisdom is to allow that exercise of freedom so long as no great harm will be done thereby. Some of us are deeply convinced that abortion is a sin. But, in the long run, societies that have permitted freedom of abortion have not been harmed by it. There is no reason to predict that ours will be much harmed either. Moreover, we do have reason to believe that forced birthing of unwanted children does bring much harm to society. Unwanted children are likely to grow up to repeat the cycle, bringing children into the world that they do not want, and adding more to society's burden of emotionally wrecked children.

The argument that a wise society does not outlaw things which do not injure it comes from a "live and let live" social morality. In many cases, indeed, people with strong moral convictions must respect other people's civil right to sin. We may feel that it is a sin to fornicate, but prudence tells us not to put fornicators in jail. But is abortion like fornication in this way, that it really does not hurt society much? Is any society unhurt if it offers no protection to its weak, defenseless, and marginal members? Is any society wise if it does not use its laws to protect innocent, helpless human beings? The wise society does indeed tolerate many morally debatable acts. But it does not follow that the wise society must tolerate also indiscriminate assault on fetal life.

Every argument for freedom of abortion appeals to a fundamental virtue of a democratic society, which it claims will be violated if we prevent women from choosing whether or not to abort a pregnancy. If society wants to be tolerant, free, just, compassionate, and wise, it must permit women to do what they wish when it comes to their own bodies. But none of these arguments works; nor do all of them added together.

The reason these arguments fail is that they depend on broad principles which seem to require us to permit just about anything at all. A tolerant society is not tolerant of everything. A free society does not permit everything. Nor does a just, compassionate, or wise society open the door for everyone to make any decision he wishes. In this case, it cannot be shown that a society with all these fine qualities *must* permit every women to kill a

142 fetus whenever she chooses. They all beg the question of whether fetal life deserves to be protected from other people's decisions to do what they want with it.[34]

The argument for absolute prohibition

People who think abortion should be outlawed need only one argument. For that matter, they need only to get the rest of us to agree to the fundamental premise that a fetus at any stage of development is a human being. Once you agree that a fetus is a person, you must concede that it has the same right to protection against assault that any visible person has. This argument is self-evident to anyone who agrees that all persons have an equal right to protection of the law against assault with intent to kill.

We are back again at the bottom line of the social side of abortion; can we live with a law that assumes every fetus to be a person from conception? Could we arrest and convict a woman because she aborted a fetus which was doomed to enter the world with Tay Sachs disease? Could we arrest an adolescent girl for aborting a month-old pregnancy that a rapist forced on her? What about a prison sentence for women who regularly use an intra-uterine device? If we pass laws on the premise that a fetus is a person from conception, will we be led to cruel and crazy positions that few responsible people would wish to defend? And would we make society more pro-life if we passed anti-abortion laws that we could not or would not enforce?

Flexible and temperate measures need to be found. Is there a way that will set us on the side of the fetus and against unrestricted freedom of abortion, and at the same time free us to deal honestly with the uncertainty most people have about the early fetus—let us say in the first six weeks? We must, it seems to me, in honest realism, prevent the anti-abortion crusade from carrying society to the cruel consequences of its own absolutism. On the other hand, we must, out of respect for life, prevent the pro-abortion crusade from carrying society to the cruel consequences of its own peculiar dogmatism.

The possibility of a temperate law against abortion

When the United States Supreme Court decided in 1973 to limit but not deny the right of every woman to have an abortion if she chooses, the court had two moral claims in mind: the claim of women to privacy and the claim of fetuses to life. It ruled that a woman's privacy was, for the most part, more important than a fetus's life. During the first six months of its existence, the fetus has no rights at all. During the last three months, the fetus has to compete for its very life with its mother's right to health. The result is that no state may prevent a woman from having an abortion at any time if she believes it is necessary for her health.

The present situation is morally intolerable. What is at stake is not primarily a question of good or bad argument; it is a fundamental choice of values. The court (under the thin veil of its incompetence to decide whether a fetus is a human being) decided that a woman's private decision to kill a fetus was her fundamental human right, a right more important than that of a fetus to continue its development toward birth as a baby. It seems clear to me that we, as a society, must reverse our values. We must once again—as a general rule—choose the life of the fetus over the privacy of a mother.

But we cannot, in all honesty, be absolutist. We ought not to legislate that every last fetus—regardless of its age—has unconditional priority over the needs of a mother. We ought not commit society to judge and sentence every woman who has an abortion as if she were a murderer. We must probe our way toward a law that will control and limit abortion drastically, while not prohibiting it absolutely. Let me propose some guidelines for abortion legislation that will protect the rights of the living fetus and be responsive to both the limits of our knowledge and the legitimate concerns of pregnant women.

1. *Abortion should be legally permitted during the first six weeks of pregnancy*. Many people believe that a woman is wrong to have an abortion at any time. They may do their utmost to persuade her not to do it; they may weep if she decides to go ahead. But if a woman does decide to have an abortion in the first six weeks of pregnancy, society must leave her alone, for she is doing what none of the rest of us can be sure is wrong. No one can reasonably be sure that the fetus is a person during the first six weeks. Indeed, the most reasonable view is that it is not a person. Whatever certainty people have is the certainty of their own intuitions or their own faith.

2. *Abortion should be severely restricted after the first six weeks and through the twelfth week*. Abortion should be permitted during the second six weeks of pregnancy only for the most weighty reasons affecting the mother or the fetus. The reason for the

twelfth-week cutoff point is that this allows ample time for amniocentesis and the discovery of serious—even monstrous—defects in the fetus. What sorts of reasons would legally justify abortion? If the pregnancy were a serious threat to the mother's physical health, the abortion might be permitted. If the mother conceived in the course of being raped, abortion might be permitted. If the fetus were infected with certain congenital diseases, abortion might be permitted. Lawmakers would be faced with hard questions of where to draw lines; boards of appeal would be hard pressed. But the alternative to working in the dusk is to work with no light at all. The alternative to difficult choices is to throw the door open all the way or to close it all the way.

3. *Abortion after the third month should be a crime.* By the end of the third month, a fetus has developed into a being so completely endowed with human qualities that we deny it legal rights as a person only by a violent exercise of our social will. At the close of the first trimester, the fetus has become a functioning human body. It weighs only about half an ounce, but the major organs are beginning to work. Besides, three months is time enough for a pregnant mother in dire distress to have weighed her own needs and the fetus's future over against her calling to respect the right a potential human being has to existence. To abort a fetus after this time is to commit a crime against society— a crime, however, for which extenuating circumstances might recommend suspension of judgment.

*   *   *

We began our discussion of the terrible and complex abortion question with a simple question: does the commandment of God against killing ever permit us to end the life of a human fetus? Our presumption was in favor of a simple answer: fetal life is human life and therefore killing it is morally intolerable. But we did not go very far before it became evident that we would never arrive at an absolutist answer from the facts. In looking at the route a fetus travels in its procession toward personal life, we had to admit that we could not affirm that a fetus in the early days is a full-fledged human person. So we had to admit that, during this early time, a mother's rights might be considered along with the rights of the fetus in any abortion decision. To say that a mother's concerns are a valid component in the decision is not to say that they should always prevail, or that any and

every abortion is right during the first months. It is only to say   145
that abortion is not *necessarily* wrong during that time. And since
we admitted a mother's interests into the discussion, we had to
agree that laws absolutely forbidding abortion were not good
laws. It is important to understand, however, that as we make
the concession we also insist that the laws of the land should,
for the most part, come down on the side of the right of the
fetus to live. Society should control abortion with the eye of a
moral hawk and the heart of a compassionate angel.

D. LETTING PEOPLE DIE

Anyone who has to decide whether to let a person die faces a
radical crisis. A *human* life is in the balance, after all, and we
who decide are *only* human. We cannot be absolutely sure of
what we are doing; we always make our decision on the basis of
a fallible diagnosis. We know we can make awesome mistakes in
this area with no chance of ever undoing them. A false judgment
could be paid for with a human life or with needlessly prolonged
suffering.

The real decisions are made in an endless network of complex human conditions. Any ethical discussion will only vaguely
reflect the astounding variety of real situations where people
decide whether other people shall live or die. But, while sensitive to life's ambiguity, we must think the matter through as
clearly as we can. Beginning with the assumption that we should
usually help people to live, we must go on to ask whether we
may nevertheless let some people die. Our discussion will center
on three questions: (1) *What* does it mean to let someone die?
(2) *How* can we know when to let someone die? (3) *Who* may
decide when it is right to let someone die?

What does it mean to let someone die?

Is letting someone die morally different from other ways of deciding that people should die? Almost everyone agrees that doctors should not kill patients or even help them commit suicide.
If there were no important moral difference between killing
someone and letting him die, the case would be closed: we
should not let people die. But doctors usually make a clean
distinction between causing death and allowing it, and most of
the rest of us agree that letting people die has a different moral
"feel" to it than does causing people to die.[35]

146   The two do have one thing in common: someone makes a decision and, as a result, someone else dies. A mere mortal takes on himself the responsibility for deciding that it is time for someone else to die. There is nowhere to run from the profound moral significance of this decision. We cannot avoid its implications by appealing to motives. The motives for letting someone die cannot automatically be assumed to be nobler than the motives for causing someone to die. We may imagine that most people who let others die always do so out of kindness. But it is not necessarily so. A person could let a rich uncle die instead of helping him, out of sheer greed for a slice of the old boy's fortune. And, on the other hand, people have sometimes killed purely for mercy's sake.

We can, however, identify some important differences between letting someone die and causing someone to die.

1. Letting someone die usually leaves everyone feeling better than causing someone to die does. The emotional scene is tidier. There are no ugly blotches of guilt left on the canvas. There are fewer chances of a litigious hangover for doctors. The family is not traumatized. It is risky to confuse aesthetics with morality; still, in crises, feelings are stronger than moral reasons.

2. Permission to let someone die involves fewer risks to life. The person whose life is at stake is usually already at the edge of the dark night. We are asking about the morality of letting someone die who is already dying or who has no meaningful personal life ahead of him or her. When we approve of letting a very sick person die, we are not really in danger of declaring open season on disagreeable neighbors or wealthy relatives.

3. If we do not let a person die, we may really be *forcing* him or her to live. We are talking about people who may want to die, or who in someone's judgment *would* desire to die if able to choose. We are talking about sticking the pads of our meddling modern machines on bodies to force them to stay warm, or forcing a child with Tay Sachs disease to live out a span of three painful years when we could let him die quickly of a kidney ailment. Put this way, the moral question is seen in a different light. The issue is between forcing someone to live and forcing someone to die, and we must ask whether we have a right to force *everyone* to live.

The difference between letting people die and causing them to die is not so great that we can leap to the thesis that letting people die is all right simply because it is different from causing people to die. But the difference is enough, I think, to reassure those who fear the domino theory—that if we say today it is all right to let someone die we are likely tomorrow to say it is also all right, in the same circumstances, to cause someone to die.

Is it ever right to let someone die?

We go into every medical situation with a presumption in favor of keeping a person entrusted to our care alive. If we act against this pro-life presumption, we must have convincing reasons. What sorts of reasons might they be?

One clear indicator that we are *not* in a situation in which we may let a person die is the will of a patient to live. Any sick person who has the personal power to desire life and to say so has a right to be helped by those whose calling it is to help him. A second indicator is potential for responsive personal life. Whenever a patient has a future as a person who relates to others, he or she has a right to healing help. For instance, a Down's Syndrome child has a personal future—even if it is a handicapped future—and therefore deserves whatever life-prolonging treatment he may need.

These two guidelines may sometimes work against each other. A doctor may think a patient has a personal future which makes healing obligatory, while the patient may be certain that the quality of whatever future he has is not good enough to make life worth living. When this happens, we face the crisis of whose decision is final.

Let us begin by dealing with a religious sense for life which may suggest that it is never time to forsake it.

We may call this the sense of *life as a gift*. The believer's sense that life is a gift of God may tell him that any human decision to let people die is an affront to life's Giver. Does God give someone this pearl of great price only to let a green-smocked medic decide to let it slip away? Must we not assume that the gift of life must always be worth keeping as long as God considers it worth giving?

Life is, of course, a gift of God. But this religious sense does not lead me to any clear conclusion. There are things about this mysterious gift of life that get between my gratitude for it and a conviction that we may never let people die.

For one thing some gifts are more important even than the gift of life, and we may do a good thing if we trade our gift of life for some more important things. One instance: "Greater love has no man than this, that he trade his (gift of) life for the life of a friend." Furthermore, the gift of life can turn very sour, so that by itself it does not compensate for the terrible price of prolonging it. The sheer fact that God gives life must be balanced by the fact that it may be good stewardship to turn the gift back, with respectful thanks, to the giver.

The second, and more important, reason that life's givenness does not clinch the matter is that life, awed as we are by its mystery, is not the most critical reality we deal with here. Believers are not worshipers of vitality; we are respecters of persons. Life is a necessary condition for a person; but a person transcends the life that supports him. The question of letting someone die always centers on a specific person, not life in general.

If we keep our focus on the specific person rather than the general value of life, we are better able to take account of special circumstances. We will not value life the less, but our sense of its value will—in any particular instance—be qualified by the question of whether life is in each case supporting a human person in a genuinely personal existence. Human life is subordinate to personal ends. Therefore, we should go beyond the single issue of the gift of life itself and face the question of whether the life we have in our hands is, in fact, a personal life or whether it has a future as a genuinely personal life.

Are there also some clear signals that tell us it is time to let someone die, to turn life-support mechanisms off and leave the person alone? Can we describe typical situations in which it is always right to decide not to do what is needed for life? It is likely that such situations are not enough alike to allow for generalizations. I shall suggest some *sorts* of situations in which we may be permitted to let someone die, in which, perhaps, we even ought to let him die.

1. *Bodies without persons.* We can contrive to keep bodies alive after the persons they once supported are missing. A warm body may be no more than a breathing corpse. But can we ever be sure? When we stand beside a very specific living body, can we be sure the person has taken flight? We have no clear, normative definition of personhood that we can use to test every body for the presence of a person in it. But we can use reasonable standards. For instance, the definition of the death of per-

sonhood as the permanent absence of any function in the cerebral cortex seems like a reasonable criterion. If we know that a patient's brain will not function again, we have no reason for sustaining his or her life. A living corpse is not a living person.

May we decide only on absolutes? That is, must we always have a continuously flat electro-encephalogram? Must the brain's function be at absolute zero? I think not. But such relativities only push us to make more distinctions.

2. *Dying people.* There seems to be no good reason to prolong anyone's dying. But when does dying begin? What is the difference between a person who is going to die soon and a person who is actually dying? Surely the difference is relative. Yet it seems very real. Do we not often have a rough sense that a person has entered the process of his dying? Are there not indicators, clear enough for physicians to recognize, that further ministrations are pointless and that therefore to keep the patient breathing is only to stretch out his dying? And if these indications are present, is the doctor not relieved of obligation to prolong the dying process?

3. *People without a personal future.* Now and then, children are born into our world with no apparent possibility of living a personal life. I do not mean a child whose personal life will be handicapped or a child who lacks the qualities parents desire for their children. I mean a child who will, as far as we can tell, never respond to another person, never convey a message, never receive a message, never enter into a conscious relationship. Perhaps a virtually anencephalic child would be the clearest example. A Down's Syndrome child would surely *not* be. But what about others who will exist in a grey zone? The distinctions between a life with no personal future at all and a life with a terribly diminished personal future are sometimes fine. We need to face these with fear and trembling. What we need to decide ahead of time is whether the lack of a genuinely personal future may indicate that we may withhold life-supporting measures. Thereafter, we would need to define "personal future" more clearly than we can now.

4. *People with horrible burdens.* There may be persons—whose life will be undeniably personal—for whom the burdens of life are so horrendous that they might responsibly desire to die. Their desire to die may be a warrant for doctors not to persuade them to accept life-saving help. May there also be children for

whom the future is so horribly burdensome that responsible people may act as if they knew that these children themselves would prefer to die?

Caution flags wave at every corner of this question. One caution is this: No person has an undeniable right to live without burdens, even horribly heavy burdens. The lives of handicapped saints remind us that a person handicapped in one part of life may develop another part far beyond the rest of us, and shine as a bright star in the human galaxy. Her handicap may be a special reason for keeping her alive; to let her die may rob the human family of a saint or star.

Nevertheless, we must be skeptical of the heroism of the healthy. I am leery of healthy, wealthy, and wise doctors who announce too glibly that other people's grotesque burdens are mere ladders to the stars. I fear comfortable Christian doctors who tell patients that their pains may be turned into praise, and then force them to live to make the doctor's pious dream come true. Handicapped people with terrible burdens may seize their own possibilities; our question is whether others should thrust them on them.

We cannot leave the question of when we may let someone die without considering the distinction between ordinary and extraordinary means.[36] We may agree that normally we should always use ordinary means to keep persons alive; we should feed them (intravenously, if need be), keep them warm, provide medicines regularly available, and do routine surgery for them. And we may agree that sometimes extraordinary means need not be used. But "extraordinary" is a quality that shrinks and stretches with each situation. What must be said is that a given means is not extraordinary *simply* because it is scarce or expensive or risky. Means become extraordinary when the life prolonged by them ought not be prolonged. Ordinary surgery to remove a stomach blockage in a normal child may become an extraordinary means in the life of a child with Tay Sachs disease or some devastating defects in the central nervous system. "The means is extraordinary because the infant's condition is extraordinary."[37]

We must be clear, before going on, about some things that we have *not* said. We have not said that the future productivity of a patient is a relevant criterion for determining whether we may let him die. We have said nothing about relieving the burdens a person may impose on other people if kept alive. That is, we have not hinted that a person's usefulness to others or his burdensomeness to others is a test of whether he should be allowed to die. The tests all apply only to the patient himself.

Who may decide?

The moral question of letting a human being die centers on doctors because they have the vocation and the art and the tools for keeping people alive. But other people are involved, too: the patient, the patient's family, the nurses who care for the patient hourly, and pastors, who represent the care of God for the whole person. Doctors may be the ones who pull the plugs or remove the respirators, and face the question as a vocational crisis; but it is often an equally terrible risk for many who are close to the patient.

Who is permitted to decide—who has the burden of deciding—whether a person's future is so bleak that it may be better if others do not use their skills to keep him alive? Several people, each playing a distinct role in the patient's life, may have a voice. None of them, probably, has the sole right to decide. But some voices may need to be heard ahead of others.

1. *May God alone decide?* Believers with a strong sense of divine sovereignty may claim that God alone has the *authority* to determine life's end for his children. Only the Creator of life has the *right* to decide when a person should die. For mere human beings to assume the role of determiners of death is to play God.

Religious modesty does not strike me as a reason to avoid decisions to withhold life-prolonging treatment. "Playing God" is what rational human beings are meant to do as God's stewards on earth. Of course that is dangerous: we must make sure we are playing the right God and that we are playing him faithfully. But we cannot run away from the responsibility to act as God's agents.

Modesty before God's authority is, in fact, double-edged. A good deal depends on how we construe what we are doing with our machines. When we give life, we believe that we are cooperating with God, because God supports personal life. But suppose that our machines are forcing someone to live whom God wants to die, and who would die if we left him alone. Would that not be just as arrogant? A mere human medical technologist says to a patient, in effect: "You will die when *I* get ready to let you die." Isn't this also to make believe we are God?

2. *The person whose life it is*. Should not the person involved have the right to decide? To borrow the title of a recent film: "Whose life is it, anyway?" The answer is that the patient probably does have a right, but not an absolute right, to decide about his own life.

Take John Gather, for instance. John is a victim of the "elephant man" syndrome. He has, against enormous odds, managed heroically to live a "meaningful life." Now, at 42, he has a tumor at the bottom of his brain which will kill him within months if it is not removed. The neurosurgeon has told John that if he has surgery chances are about 80% that he will be both deaf and blind. When John heard the prognosis, he was traumatized and unable to reason. Later, he decided not to have the tumor removed by surgery. I do not know whether John made the right decision. I believe the neurosurgeon was right when he did not try to persuade John to change his mind.

Must we always honor the patient's desire without arguments? I think not. A depressed person can be terribly wrong in seeing no future, no purpose, no joy in life for himself. John Gather may have been enabled to live as a blessing to his neighbors because of his terrible afflictions. Who can be absolutely sure? Yet there may be times when one's life, after healing, may be so terror-ridden, so burdensome, that others should step aside and let the patient's own will be done.[38]

Here, our respect for persons should lead us to respect their own evaluation of their own tragedy. Even if we believe that, with God's help, they may live to be a blessing to others, and even a joy to themselves, we must stop short of coercing or manipulating them into living by our hopes for them. Respect for persons ordinarily means that we help them if they need our help; here, respect for persons may mean that we stand back and let them reject our help.

3. *The medical team*. Every physician, by community consent, is entrusted with our lives. In simpler days, we assumed that he would do everything he possibly could to keep us alive. Now medical lone rangers are out of date, at least when it comes to deciding not to try to keep us alive. Now we want a team. Sometimes a patient is denied the benefit of a team of medical people. A single doctor may arbitrarily act on his or her own. But who can be objective about an operation that will net him a five-

thousand-dollar surgeon's fee? Or the team may be too restricted; for instance, doctors may exclude nurses from the field
of decision-making, even though nurses live and work more
closely than doctors do with the patient after a decision is made
to let him die.

Medical decisions are made most responsibly with counsel.
Many hospitals organize crisis committees to give advice to physicians in ambiguous situations; they invite professional ethicists,
pastors, social workers, and psychologists, as well as medical
colleagues, to discuss difficult cases and offer their judgment.

What ought a medical team to do in the case of infants whose
parents are not able to make a decision of their own? Take little
Helen Fallow, for example. She was born prematurely with in-
adequate lung power. She was set on a respirator at full capacity;
without the respirator, she would be dead in minutes. But sooner
or later the respirator itself would fatally damage the child's
heart. Her mother could not make a decision. She was all alone;
her husband could not even muster the courage to come and see
his child. She had no parents near enough to help her. So Mrs.
Fallow lived by blind faith in the doctor's power to "do something." She was not even able to hear the doctor when he told
her that her baby was probably going to die.

The doctor has two responsibilities to Mrs. Fallow, it seems
to me. First, he should be tough-minded enough to compel her
to hear; putting gentle manners aside, he must do what she needs
done to help her understand her child's real condition. Second,
he must summon whatever resources the hospital has—the chap-
lain, social workers, anyone—to help the mother assume some
of the responsibility for dealing with her tragedy. If she is a
member of a church, he should ask her pastor or priest to translate the situation for her. In any case, it is the medic's task to
use whatever team he can get to enable parents to make the
decision that is uniquely theirs.

Sometimes the doctor has the task of freeing patients from
their families. Where children are deciding whether an aged parent should be treated, the doctor may be the only person who
can provide space for the elderly parent to freely decide for
himself or herself. Some of the children may exert subtle pressure on the parent to forgo surgery—maybe for the parent's
sake, maybe for the family's sake. Other children may press for

154   surgery—maybe for the parent's sake, maybe only to avoid the risk of a bad conscience. Either way, they may pressure the parent to decide on grounds of what the children want and not what he or she wants. Thus, it may be a doctor's task to provide information and encourage a patient to use it to determine his own future. The doctor, then, acts as a guardian of the patient to see that he is free to take responsibility for his own life.

*   *   *

I will now try to sum up what I have said about letting people die. First, letting people die becomes a moral question when everything we see tells us that dying might be better for a patient than living. Second, letting people die is a moral option only when the alternative is forcing them to live. Third, in most cases we cannot determine beforehand that we would do well to permit patients to die; the best we can do is indicate the sorts of situations in which it may be appropriate to make such a decision. Finally, while no one has exclusive or absolute authority to make the decision, the patient or his family have special authority to decide with respect to their own lives and the lives of those in their care; the others, including the doctors, ought to help the family to decide responsibly. Where neither the patient nor the family is able to decide, the doctors on the case, as the fiduciaries of the patient's life, must decide.

It is medical success, not failure to respect life, that has forced us to cope with the problem of letting people die. Technology makes it possible to keep people living "beyond their time." And we have no precise rules to cover all situations. We have a sweeping law of love that tells us to let people live. What we need besides love is the gift of discernment, awareness of how delicate are the fibers that hold us together in a community of respect for one another's right to live. What we need is spiritual wisdom, purity of soul, and clarity of vision to know the right thing and the courage to do it. We need a community of prayer to help us, and a readiness to hear special signals from God that it may be time to let "the dust return to the earth as it was; and the spirit shall return unto God who gave it" (Eccl. 12:7).[39]

CONCLUSION

We have been considering God's command that we must always

respect the life of human beings. Most of us sense deeply the sacredness of our fellows. We fear that where that sense is not shared widely, the human community is at the edge of disaster. For this reason we had to consider carefully and fairly the possibility that we are sometimes permitted to kill people or to let them die when we are in fact able to keep them alive.

We have spent some time on four such possibilities—that it may be right to take our own lives, to kill killers, to destroy fetal life, and to let some people die. Each possibility has its own claims which we have tried to hear out. But we could not emerge from our discussion with any unqualified permission. We could not say, "Yes, it is permissible as a general rule to commit suicide, to execute killers, to have abortions, or to let people die." Nor could we say, "No, it is never, under any conditions, permissible to cause or permit death in these sorts of cases." What we had to say was that causing or permitting people to die must *always* be a tragic situation in which not doing so would bring intolerable suffering to someone.

The assumption must be that, living together as children of God in human community, we ought to keep killing hands off our neighbors and ourselves. We ought to do all we can to help, to lend them a hand when they need it, to support them in their struggles, to persuade them to undo the injustice that might inflame oppressed people to kill them, to heal them when they are sick, and to feed them when they lack food—in short, to help them live and not to die. Any decision to treat a neighbor in ways that diminish his or her life is a wrong decision unless there is an inescapably clear and utterly urgent reason that compels us to act against a particular human life for the sake of other human lives. Whenever a life is taken or permitted to die, it must only be with fear and trembling, with hope for grace, and with clear understanding that we are acting, not in arrogant disregard for life but in the only way possible, given this ironic and tragic situation.[40]

QUESTIONS FOR DISCUSSION

1. Do you believe that only human life is protected by the Sixth Commandment? Or do you think that animals have some right to life as well as persons?

2. Do you think it makes any difference, practically, whether we stress the sacredness of persons instead of the value of life?

3. Do you agree that the mental attitude of the person doing it makes a difference as to the rightness or wrongness of committing suicide? Why? Give an example.

4. Do you think that people who are against capital punishment necessarily have more respect for the life of persons than those who are for capital punishment?

5. The starting points for our argument often are crucial. How would you state the difference between the starting point taken by Karl Barth and that taken by Gordon Clark (or John Murray) in the discussion of capital punishment?

6. Do you think we should separate our personal views about the morality of abortion from our political views as to its legality? Why?

7. Do you think we can know "for sure" when a fetus is a human being? Do you think we need to know "for sure" before we can make a decision about the right and wrong of abortion?

8. Do you think there are other matters to think about in abortion than the welfare of the mother and the life of the fetus? Can you give an example?

9. Do you think people who have abortions, other than to save a mother's life, should be arrested for murder? For something less than murder? Why not?

10. Do you think we should consider the possibility of a miracle of healing before we ever let someone die? Why not?

11. If capital punishment were slightly helpful, sometimes, in deterring crime, would you be persuaded that it should be used? If you knew capital punishment did not deter crime, might you still think it should be used? Why?

12. Do you think we can responsibly treat a patient as a person "with no future"? Do you think we can responsibly think of a breathing being as a "former person"? Explain.

13. Do you think we should pass laws to clarify the times when it is permissible to let people die?

14. Do we have a right to live in relationship to God? Or is life only a gift with respect to our Creator? What difference does it make when we consider letting people die?

15. Do you think the Bible alone tells you what to do in cases of abortion, capital punishment, and "letting people die"? How might the Bible help you know what to do?

RESPECT FOR COVENANT: ⑥

"Thou Shalt Not Commit Adultery"

Adultery slashes the fabric of that fundamental but delicate human alliance called a marriage. Marriage is what the commandment is about; adultery is what it forbids.

Most people agree with the sense of the commandment. Not many husbands encourage their wives to escape the tedium of marital routine in the arms of a stranger. Most wives still feel jealous if they suspect, and damaged if they discover, that their husbands are making love to another woman. Over cocktails newly liberated suburbanites may hail the advantages of open marriage, but alone with their spouses few hail open adultery. More than half of the married men and more than a third of the married women in American society commit adultery at some time, but most of them still keep their affairs hidden even from their closest friends. In sum, the commandment still speaks to the conscience, even if it does not shape the desires and actions of most people.

The concern of the Seventh Commandment is not merely with sex; its real business is with marriage and its wholeness. The commandment is about sex only insofar as sleeping with someone other than one's marriage partner is the most blatant and exciting way to commit adultery. But there are other ways to violate the commandment. Adultery, defined Christianly, is anything that violates a marriage—including divorce. Since most people, however, mean by adultery illicit sexual intercourse, I shall use the word this way too. But I will try to keep the bigger issue of marriage and total fidelity close by, so that we do not forget that human respect for the covenant of marriage is what is at stake.

Now we can go on to ask the three questions we have been posing to all the commandments. *What* does the Seventh Commandment require of us? *Why* does the commandment require it; is there some innate tendency in human life to which sexual

158   fidelity is tuned? And, finally, *how* can we best manage to honor it within the pressures, needs, seductions, and ambiguities of our lives?

I. WHAT DOES THE SEVENTH COMMANDMENT TELL US TO DO?

The people who heard this commandment intoned at Israel's annual festivals understood it, in its narrowest sense, as a warning to Israel's males to keep away from their neighbor's wives. A concern of this commandment, just as with all the others, is our neighbor's rights—in this case a husband's right to the integrity of his marriage and certitude about his descendants. A man, married or not, committed adultery against a woman's husband when he slept with her. But a married man did not commit adultery against his own wife by having intercourse with another woman. A male broke the covenant of another man; he did not break his own covenant with his own wife.

A husband could sleep with a prostitute, and nobody much cared. No judge's finger was pointed at Samson for his sallies into the boudoirs of liberated Philistines (Judg. 16); nobody observed that Judah was a married man when he slept with his daughter-in-law Tamar under the impression that she was a prostitute (Gen. 38:12ff.). When Nathan condemned David for his disastrous affair with Bathsheba, the prophet did not say a word on behalf of David's own wives (2 Sam. 11, 12). In short, adultery was almost always an injustice only to the cuckolded husband, whose human right to descendants unquestionably his own was being abridged by his wife's dalliance with a stranger.[1]

Adultery was not a private peccadillo, therefore, but a social crime that called for retribution. In early Hebrew society those who lost their heads to sexual passion and committed adultery could also literally lose their heads to the executioner (Deut. 22:22; Lev. 20:10). The straying wife was especially vulnerable; at first she was to be stoned, but later, following the Talmud, she was to be divorced without the privilege of marrying her lover. The innocent wife of a straying husband might also suffer, if Job is to be taken literally. Boasting of his own sexual innocence, he hints how he would allow vengeance against his own wife if he had violated another man's:

If my heart has been enticed to a woman,
and I have lain in wait at my neighbor's door;
then let my wife grind for another
and let others bow down upon her.
For that would be a heinous crime. . . ,
an iniquity to be punished by the judges (Job 31:9-12).

It was only fair, as David learned, that if you slept with your neighbor's wife, he or somebody else would sleep with yours—an eye for an eye, a wife for a wife (2 Sam. 11, 12).[2]

Adultery takes on a radically new look in the New Testament. The wife comes into her own as a full partner in the covenant; it is she who is sinned against when her husband violates his commitment to her. Jesus, for example, speaks of divorce as adultery, as a breakage of the covenant. But, he says, when a man or a woman divorces a spouse (and remarries), he violates his own wife or she her own husband. For Jesus, two whole and equal persons made a marriage; those two are the primary persons hurt in a violation of the marriage partnership. Paul supported the New Testament's "equal rights amendment" to the Old Testament regulations when he insisted that a man owed sexual allegiance to his wife as much as his wife owed it to him (1 Cor. 7:4).

Violation of marriage is basically what the Seventh Commandment forbids. Adultery, as illicit sex, is prohibited as a most likely and most threatening assault on the partnership. But is this commandment also perhaps a kind of catch-all putdown of pleasure?

The Reformed tradition has tended to spread the net of this commandment over nearly every improper sexual impulse—against "any filthy or lustful intemperance of the flesh."[3] To the question, "Does God in this commandment forbid nothing more than adultery and such like gross sins?", the Heidelberg Catechism replies: "He forbids all unchaste actions, gestures, words, thoughts, desires, and whatever may entice one thereto" (Lord's Day 41). Old-time Reformed sermons on the commandment zeroed in on "whatever may entice": short skirts, bobbed hair, the cinema, ballroom dancing, and lipstick—all came in for attack. A husband might have "lustful intemperance" if he wanted intercourse more often than his wife did. Sexual fantasies were

160 as serious as adultery itself. No one escaped the finger of the Seventh Commandment, for everyone had reason to cringe at some "lustful intemperance" in his own life.

It is a mistake, I think, to use the Seventh Commandment as a club against sexual passions. What happens when we do is that eros seems totally defiled and passion an ugly product of sin. The real issue is obscured. We do the commandment more justice if we focus its clear light on one's duty to his or her marriage.

A. COVENANT-KEEPING[4]

The question of adultery is a question of what sort of people we want to be. Not that only bad people commit adultery, but our attitude toward adultery as a way of life depends much on the kind of person we are. In this arena, there are two kinds of characters—and both of them live within each of us. The two characters are covenant-keepers and self-maximizers. Culture tells us to be self-maximizers; the commandment tells us to be covenant-keepers.

A covenant-keeper is loyal, trustworthy, committed, dependable, even heroic—qualities that hardly throb with sexuality. The covenant-keeper in us is not what excites people with our erotic energy. But he is a person who keeps faith with people who trust him, a person who holds relationships together and in the process keeps life humane and decent.

A self-maximizer is open, self-asserting, expanding, and erotic. A self-maximizer evaluates relationships with others in terms of how they contribute to his own growth. He thinks of marriage romantically—a deep personal relationship with rich potential for mutual fulfilment. He marries in order to enrich his life, and in analyzing his marriage, he is likely to ask: is my marriage giving me all I need to stimulate my growth? Probably the time will come in a self-maximizer's marriage when a sexual affair promises more than he is getting in the marriage—and he may grab the promise.

The self-maximizer turns life into an exciting quest for maximal happiness. Extra-marital affairs can offer a lot to anyone who earnestly joins the hunt. They offer new love to a person whose spouse has forgotten how to love, intense passion to a person whose marriage has gone flat, beauty to people whose marriage has turned plain or ugly, new growth to a person stifled by a spouse. Few experiences seem more justifiable than a love affair to a person who feels robbed of all the glittering promises of a romantic marriage. This is why we said that the issue is basically one of what sort of person we want to be. We need a profound reason to justify staying home nights when home is next to hell. Why stick with what you are stuck with when the bright, beautiful people of our Camelot culture are living endorsements of the prevailing hunch that self-maximizing is a lot more fun than covenant-keeping?

Yet, the commandment asks us to become covenant-keepers, people who subordinate the right to maximize their potential for sexual happiness to their responsibility for a covenanted partnership with another human being. In short, the natural, human erotic urge to stretch ourselves and reach for the maximum experience must take second place to our commitment to care for the partnership which, as it were, we are stuck with. The commandment calls us to make a deep decision, not simply about sex, but about the meaning and purpose of human life.

B. VOW-KEEPING

Covenant-making is a uniquely human way to begin an alliance. Perhaps the greatest mystery of our humanness is the power to make and keep a vow. For in a vow you freely give yourself over to a permanent identity in the face of an unpredictable future. You will change, the person to whom you make the vow will change, your circumstances will change. Moreover, the person you vow to live with is in some ways the wrong person for you—no one ever marries the right person. But, if you are a vow-keeper, you are likely to do in the changing future what you promised in the unchangeable past. No other creature manages this. A dog can be born and become attached to a human master; only a human being can promise to create a permanent identity for himself or herself as a partner to another person.

The commandment calls us to be vow-keepers in defiance of our culture. Our culture urges us not to define our life in terms of past commitments but in terms of present needs and future possibilities. The command calls us to subordinate our

162   needs and accommodate our possibilities to the special history
we began when we vowed to be a partner in marriage.

C. KEEPING EACH OTHER
Within the unique relationship of marriage two people care for
each other's total welfare. Each, in a total sense, becomes the
spouse's keeper. Each is dedicated to the growth, healing, pleasure, and freedom of the other.

There is a reserve clause in person-keeping that prevents it
from suffocating the other person in our care. A person-keeper
cares for the freedom of the other person. A husband seeks his
wife's freedom to be what she is capable of being, and she nurtures his freedom in turn. Care for one another's growth brings
a risk into person-keeping, for the person we care for may, in
growing into a fuller person, grow away from us. And growing
away within a marriage increases the chances of growing toward
someone outside the marriage. But the commandment asks us
to take that risk.

"Freedom in Christ" is the biblical model of freedom in marriage. The Lord is married to the church; it is "subject" to him
(Eph. 5:23) and he is bent on its freedom (Gal. 5:1). We are not
truly experiencing subjection to Christ unless we are being set
free by it. Christ's goal is always the freedom of the church. In
the same way, each partner in a marriage is faithful when working
at the other's happiness, healing, wholeness, and freedom. Paul
was probably asking married people to be "person-keepers" when
he told them to be "in subjection" to one another (Eph. 5:21).

D. KEEPING OUR RELATIONSHIPS
The inner essence of a marriage is a human relationship, rooted
in sexual difference and human oneness. It is the one relationship
that joins two people on every human level: emotion, intellect,
spirit, and body. So, too, this relationship can break down at any
of its levels, not just through sexual unfaithfulness. Fidelity to
a marriage is therefore a steady *commitment* to the fragile network
of communication between two partners. The vow is the moral
foundation; the relationship is the personal essence. And fidelity
is the mortar that holds the relationship together on the grounds
of the vow. Hence, fidelity is an all-embracing moral call to
devote our energies to the growth, enrichment, and repair of

the tender relationship of two people within the personal union of marriage.

The commandment forbidding adultery, then, comes within a compelling call to fidelity. Fidelity is a dynamic, positive posture that needs renewing and recreating constantly. It is not achieved simply by staying out of other people's beds. The question is whether it can be achieved in spite of a little "playing around." Can a husband or wife be truly faithful, in his or her way, even though making room in married life for extra-marital sex? The question may seem flippant, but we cannot answer it without facing up to the further question of why human beings, alone among sexual creatures, are morally bound to confine sexual intercourse to a marriage covenant.

II. WHY IS ADULTERY FORBIDDEN?

The Bible does not explain the reason for the Seventh Commandment in so many words. Some people may believe that adultery is wrong just because God forbids it. Others might propose that this commandment is just an ancient male trick to keep women in tow and bloodlines pure, so that it has no more validity for a modern marriage than the Hebrew legislation forbidding intercourse with a menstruating woman (Lev. 20:18). A third option is to say that, if a reasonable God forbids married people to have sexual intercourse outside their partnership, there must be a good and a profound reason for it, which we will find if our minds are clear and our hearts pure. This third option encourages us to go ahead and look for reasons even if they are not explicit in the text.

Why, in the light of the commandment, is adultery to be considered a human failure, not just an infraction of a rigorous religious rule intended mainly to keep eros in check? We are not inquiring whether a single foray into illicit love is a *particularly* bad wrong as wrongs go—though it probably goes deeper than forgetting an anniversary. What we want is a signal of how fidelity is woven, like an invisible fiber, into the design for humane living.

A. BORDERLINE REASONS
People have believed adultery to be wrong for reasons that touch only the borderline of marriage and sex. Immanuel Kant, for

164   example, thought that adultery reduced a man to his animal nature. A married man carrying on an affair of passion was losing his head.[5] Kant was wrong; hot passion is as human as cold intellect. Besides, people commit adultery for many reasons other than lust. Sometimes extra-marital sex is an adventure of true personal devotion outside a marriage torn by hostility. Kant saw all evil as a fall from rationality; we who see it as a fall from love must take our cue elsewhere.

Thomas Aquinas believed adultery was wrong because when people have sex outside of marriage they wish not to conceive a child.[6] A natural sex act lets the procreative process have its own way. But adulterers always interrupt it if they can. If they do gamble with nature, they are doing wrong for another reason: they would force a child born of their illicit union to come into life at a disadvantage. The main thing wrong with adultery, however, is that it blocks nature by interfering with its urge to procreate through sex. Most of us today probably resist this strict and limited view of the purpose of sex. We want sex to be the source and symbol of personal union, the expression of fulfilled love. So "blockage of nature" is too impersonal a reason to convince us that adultery is a serious moral lapse.

A more personal approach to adultery holds that it is wrong because it hurts people.[7] It hurts adulterers, especially if they care for each other; the deeper their secret, fragmented, and finally aborted love, the worse their pain. The spouse who finds out is hurt by a sense of being unlovely, unwanted, and unrespected. And adultery may hurt many others besides—the friends who know and care, and the community whose frame is shaken a little by every stricken marriage.

If adultery hurts people needlessly, it is no doubt a bad thing. But suppose everyone's feelings were to change, so that we all accepted a measure of "healthy extra-marital sex." And suppose, then, accepted extra-marital sex brought only a pain that was quite tolerable compared to its pleasures and its opportunities for self-maximizing. If pain is the reason adultery is forbidden, we may be able to render the commandment obsolete by making adultery painless as we make it popular.

B. ADULTERY IS WRONG BECAUSE SEXUAL INTERCOURSE FITS WITH MARRIAGE

The reason sex outside of marriage is wrong, in the biblical way of looking at it, lies in a notion of what a marriage is. But what does sex have to do with marriage? Why is sex so tied into marriage that the Lord God should command the human race not to enjoy sexual embrace outside of marriage? To answer this, we must ask what a marriage is for and how sex fits into the purpose of the partnership. We want a biblically informed view of the connection; but to make good sense, a biblical view will have to be consistent with our own experiences and supported by what we experience and see around us.

Marriage as a sexual covenant

A marriage is a covenanted partnership between two people who give themselves to one another in committed love. We call it a covenant for two reasons. First, it is created by the free wills of the people who make it and lasts as long as those wills determine. In this sense, a covenant is different from an "estate of matrimony," indestructibly set within reality by sacramental power. Second, marriage is meant to be a personal life-sharing union; what marks it is the unreserved sharing of two human lives. The life-sharing of a covenant makes it different from a contract; a contract calls for an exchange of goods and services, and can be cancelled as soon as the arrangement is completed. The essence of covenant is different; it is a wholeness of life-sharing, not merely an exchange of goods and services to meet the needs and desires of the partners.

Sexual activity, with all its joy and sorrow and tedium, fits within the wholeness of the covenanted partnership. This is the meaning of the biblical metaphor of "one flesh."[8] I am not saying that voluptuous or joyful sex is the secret to a good marriage; but sexual intercourse *as such* is close to the core of any marriage. Happy sex does not necessarily make a happy marriage. Two people, with healthy erotic drives and a little artistry, may create sexual symphonies in the bedroom yet make life miserable with the discord of their quarrels in every other room of the house. All that I am saying here is that without any sex at all you have no marriage at all.

The intimate bond between sex and marriage is ultimately a statement of faith, for which we need some support besides our own hunch. Paul's tough words to those Corinthian Christians who apparently sought their Saturday nights' recreation at a local brothel gives us a signal. He did not say it was degrading to buy sex, nor that it was wrong to have sex with prostitutes because they are not nice people. What he did say was that in having sex you become "one flesh" with the person you are having sex with (1 Cor. 6:6). Sexual intercourse—whether with a prostitute or the man next door—somehow bonds two people in a deep personal union. Coitus is a unitive act, not because it is fun, but because its intimacy has a meaning that only someone cued into the Creator's design can fully appreciate. Sexual intercourse has a mystique beyond what can be registered on electrodes. Its mystique is that it signifies and somehow seals a personal life covenant. This is why it is of the essence of marriage. A life-unitive act fits into a life-uniting covenant.

We cannot prove that sex and marriage belong together: the intimate bond is something to be believed. But I think it gets support, not only from Paul's teachings but also from our own experience. There may be hints in our own feelings that Paul was right, hints that what most of us (believers or not) feel with regard to marriage and sex fits with Christian belief about it.

1. *A hint from the experience of sex*. Not every experience of sex reveals its deeper meaning. Sex can be flippant or frustrating or fragmented, so that some people's experience of it tells them it has no meaning at all beyond pleasure and pain. Even at its joyful best, sexual intimacy has enough variation to keep it from being stereotyped. Still, we can capture a few signals that flow from experience. The physical intimacy—two uncovered bodies entangled in closeness, one entering the very body of the other—hints that sex belongs only where the two *persons* are very close and committed. The orgasm—two people out of their senses in ecstatic abandon—hints for most people at the need for trust, for confidence that such self-giving ought to be matched by a self-giving of the persons. And the memory—two people who have slept with each other never again see each other through the same eyes—hints that nothing which happens between two people can compare in depth with sexual intercourse.[9]

2. *A hint from the experience of adultery*. Consider the *jealousy* a man feels when he even suspects that his wife is sexually involved with someone else. He feels as if something of his own self is being ripped off, as if he is being crowded out of his own place. It is the feelings of pain at losing a person who gave herself to him. Consider the *secrecy* of adultery. Most people still keep their affairs hidden from their own friends, and very few tell

their spouses, except in sorrow or revenge. Then there is the *pain*—for everyone affected, most of the time. We have already mentioned this; here we ask only why it should hurt so much— unless it is because sexual intercourse for married people just does not fit well outside their own covenanted relationship. Again, these are only hints; every reader must sense for himself or herself whether the experience of adultery signals something deeper about sex than what meets the eye.

Marriage as a link to the kingdom of God
We need a large vision of what marriage is for as well as a notion of what sex is for. Only a fool would claim to know *all* that marriage is for. But perhaps our culture has made fools of us all by getting us to believe that marriage is only for making people happy and that successful sex is its dream come true. I suggest that we need a sense that marriage is not for making people happy, but for giving people a future; a sense that sex is God's gift for making a good future possible; and a sense that even a barely tolerable marriage can achieve its purpose.

The ancient Hebrews at least recognized one element of reality when they identified adultery as a threat to their future in the ongoing community. They recognized sex as a force for the future of God's family and their place in it. To play around with sex was to play games with the future of God's people. The kernel of truth in the Hebrew notion is that in the birth of a child God is signaling his ongoing commitment to the future of his family and kingdom. Our culture would ignore this kernel of truth, which we need—for it points to the one large vision that makes it reasonable to subordinate our needs for maximizing our sex lives to the heroic demands of fidelity in a marriage.

The line of reasoning goes this way: Families are for the kingdom of God. Marriage is for families. And therefore, since sex is for marriage, sex is for the kingdom of God. Maybe only a logic like this can counterbalance the seductive "nowness" of our romantic culture. This view of fidelity manages, I believe, to set sexual fidelity in a picture larger than the profile of your own and my own marriage covenant. It sees sex and adultery within the setting of the history of one's own future family and of God's future family. The questions it poses to an ordinary married person are these: Are you willing to be the sort of person who lives with an eye on the kingdom of God? Are you

168   willing to be the sort of person who subordinates your understandable erotic needs to what you see ahead in God's future?

To say this is obviously to link sex closely with conception.[10]
But I do not mean that sex is only for having children or that
adultery is wrong because people who commit it try to avoid
conception. It is not always wrong to have sex without wanting
a baby—or for that matter to have a baby without sex. I am saying
that sex and conception are the means God normally uses to
continue his family through history until the kingdom comes on
earth in the form of a new society where justice dwells. And for
this great cause, fidelity to a marriage is reasonable. Fidelity is
a way of opting for the ongoing pilgrimage of a people toward
the renewed family of man, a way of enduring the pain and
boredom of a sexually unsatisfactory marriage for the sake of a
great purpose that transcends even our rightful longing for sexual
fulfilment.[11] In the big picture, sexual escapades are a blur on
the scene and a distortion of the view that fidelity is meant to
keep clear.

If we believe the evidence from the Bible and if we share
the signals hinted at by experience, we are likely to see the *why*
of the commandment against adultery. The reason is the singular
appropriateness of sexual intercourse to the sort of thing marriage is. We move, as it were, from this sense that sexual intercourse is very appropriate to marriage to the conviction that it
is inappropriate outside of marriage. A crucifix has such intense
symbolic meaning within the Christian church that it would be
inappropriate hanging in a mosque. The hammer and sickle would
be inappropriate in the offices of the Chamber of Commerce.
And sexual intercourse is inappropriate outside the covenant of
marriage because sex fits in a sexual covenant and nowhere else.
And this explains why there is a primal duty to honor marriage
by avoiding adultery.[12]

III. FIDELITY IN THE CONFLICTS OF LIFE

The Seventh Commandment commits us to fidelity to our sexual
covenants. But fidelity is an ideal so full and flexible that we
take it as a goal we need to keep reaching for. Adultery, by
contrast (at least in its specific sense of illicit sex), is so specific
you can take pictures of it and record the hour it happened.
Between adultery avoided and fidelity never achieved, lies a

spectrum of fascinating relationships between men and women
that raise a host of delicate questions of moral propriety. Besides,
while adultery is presumably a failure in fidelity, we must face
the question of whether unusual circumstances can ever make
extra-marital sex consistent with fidelity to the marriage itself.
We must also ask whether every case of adultery is as wrong as
every other case, or whether some adultery might at least be
excused, even if not completely justified. So we are back to the
job of drawing some lines. There is a variety of sex outside of
marriage. How does each variety match up against the command
to respect our covenants?

A. SEXUAL FRIENDSHIPS: THE FRINGES OF FIDELITY

Does the law of fidelity leave us free to experience some of the
joys of personal intimacy outside the "estate of matrimony?" I
raise the question in this legalistic jargon in order to pinpoint
the issue where moral people feel it. Are married people morally
safe as long as they stay out of a third person's bed? Or are all
close friendships a subtle failure in fidelity?

We will have to depend here on discernment rather than
rules. We must trust our sense of propriety and keep it in tune
with our beliefs about sex and marriage. If a married woman
becomes a close friend of a man other than her spouse, she
needs to be mentally tough with herself. What do I want from
this person? What does he want from me? What am I asking
from him, what do I need from him, what can I expect him to
give me? What is he asking from me, what does he need and
what can I give him? How much of myself am I prepared to
share with him? How much of him can I share with my husband?
What is really going on between us?

Every person in this situation has to ask questions like this—
only he or she can answer them. But there are, I think, five
things that need to be said about friendships and fidelity.

1. *Sexually tinted friendships are almost inevitable.* Married
men have always made friends with women who excited them
sexually, and today's married women are more free than ever to
make friends with other men. All of us get around more than
people used to. But it is not as if extra-marital friendships are
merely inevitable; we need them—at least most of us feel that
we do and we are willing to concede that our spouses have the
same needs. A commonplace in marriage psychology has it that

170   none of us is able to meet all our partner's needs for interpersonal relationships. Any husband who thinks he can satisfy all his wife's needs is kidding himself. And fewer people tolerate a double standard anymore—women friends for husbands mean male friends for wives. Friendships outside of marriage are likely, if not inevitable, and are more to be commended than suspected.

2. *Sexual friendships are not necessarily innocent.* It would be morally shallow to sanctify a sexual friendship simply because the friends stay out of bed together. It seems silly to suppose that lovers can frolic freely and passionately in guiltless fidelity just so long as there is no sexual intercourse between them. Technical fidelity, which reserves adulterous guilt only for penetration while it winks at all the other sexual games our fantasies can inspire, is complacency bought too cheaply. More important still, a friendship free and clear of sexual touch could in fact be an emotional seduction away from one's commitment to the love of a dull spouse.

3. *Sexual friendships are risky.* A great risk comes along with the fascination we feel when we share the mystery of our personhood with a new person. When a man and a woman enter each other's lives, their separate mysteries almost immediately begin to unfold to each other. And as they begin to unveil their mysteries, they are taken into an emotional flow that will carry them to places neither has been before. The woman has hidden reservoirs of feeling and need she has not yet explored. The man has emotional resources he has never come to feel. Unsuspected yearnings, unexplored needs, and untapped feelings begin to unfold. Each has a mystery moving within waiting to be evoked, and once evoked, it opens the door to still more untapped personal mysteries. At this moment, two people are on the verge of losing full control of their futures precisely because neither knows what mysteries the other will reveal and, for that matter, both are unsure of what mysteries of their own they will expose. They cannot know for sure how their lives will be changed, or how deep will be the bond their shared mysteries creates. But the promise of further revelations and the need for further sharing can be so intense and seductive that the emotional promise overcomes prudence. The adventure has begun.

When this happens, it is time for the married person to test the flow of the game. Is it time to fold the cards and walk away? The stakes, if he continues, may be bigger than he knows. But

every morally responsible person will weigh all odds and take
the risk only if he can be sure his spouse will not be the loser
either way.

4. *Sexual friendships are tested by what they do to our covenant*.
How can we know whether our friendships have become illicit
relationships except by testing them with the law of fidelity? The
issue is this: How does an extra-marital friendship affect the
primary covenant we have with our spouse? This is a rough test,
easily misused. No one can provide a map of body zones that
are untouchable or a list of emotions that are unsharable. We
must ask at every stage: Is the next step into a deeper relationship *appropriate* for me? Can it fit into my covenant commitment
and take its honest place within my primary loyalty?

When a married woman devotes so much time and energy
to an outside relationship that she robs her husband of prime
time and high level energy, her friendship has probably compromised her covenant. When a man's friendship with another
woman becomes so complex that he needs to contrive it through
secret negotiations, he may be creating an illicit alliance. When
friends meet only in secluded places, their friendship has probably slipped into borderline infidelity. If a woman's husband gets
wind of her friendship and her only assurance to him is: "Bill
and I have never slept together," she is probably evading the
real issue.

5. *Sexual friendships can be consistent with fidelity*. We have
no precise rules because circumstances and persons intertwine
to make each friendship unique. A kiss may be appropriate in
one case; a look into each other's eyes may have the engrossing
vibration of psychic adultery. Only a legalist would claim that
intense forms of intimacy are innocent merely because there is
no genital contact. Only a legalist would brand all deep friendships as morally tainted. What we need in this expanded arena
is moral responsibility, and a good sense for "whatever is honorable, whatever is just, whatever is gracious" (Phil. 4:8) in our
relationships outside of our marriages.

Freedom for friendships outside of marriage is a gift that
comes with fidelity. A covenant-keeper does not have to worry
much or moralize a great deal about the proprieties of relationships outside of marriage. Within commitment there is room for
surprises, risks, and adventures. Loyalty is limiting but not con-
stricting. Bonhoeffer put it remarkably well: "If I love my wife,

172   if I accept marriage as an institution of God, then there comes
an inner freedom and certainty of life and action in marriage; I
no longer watch with suspicion every step that I take; I no longer
call into question every deed that I perform."[13] Fidelity is freedom from legalistic fears because it keeps one's focus on the
essence of covenant keeping.

B. IS ALL ADULTERY ALIKE?

Only in a technical sense is all adultery the same. In terms of
persons and their circumstances, adultery comes in more varieties than anyone could guess. Most people know whether they
have committed it—no matter whether their memories bring
them joy or shame. The commandment simply speaks to adultery as a class; it creates the same moral bias against ecstatic
adultery as against banal adultery. Yet, in its personal dimension,
adultery comes in many shapes and many moods. If all adultery
is wrong, it is not all wrong in the same way.

There is such a thing, Paul reminds us, as being "overtaken
in a fault" (Gal. 6:1). Most people know what the apostle means;
in the heat of passion we have all done things we would never
do under reason's cool control. A person who falls into a loving
sexual relationship, foolish but unplanned, is a very different sort
of adulterer from one who orchestrates weekends around extra-
marital conquests. It is one thing to fall in love; it is another to
select an adulterous life-style. The difference is not between
innocence and guilt, but between degrees of responsibility.

People move into adultery with differing sets of needs, as
they do with differing degrees of intention. Some people need
assurance: a man whose wife treats him with contempt needs a
loving affair with a woman who assures him that he is worth
loving. Some people need hope: a woman fears that age is cutting
down her power to attract the attention of her husband and
needs someone to reassure her that she still can be attractive.
Some people need affection: a man married to a woman who
fears intimacy needs someone to embrace him in warm and
tender love. Some people need to express anger: a woman who
has suppressed her rage against her husband's brutality for fifteen
years needs to get even with him by having an affair with someone else. A few people simply need the experience of sexual
embrace: a man whose wife became paralyzed two years after
their marriage feels the need occasionally for a passionate meet-

ing with a sexually active woman. The needs that drive people to adultery are subtle, complicated, and individual. Some of them are neurotic, others are healthy in themselves. None may be enough to justify adultery; some may be enough to excuse it.

Self-deception lurks at every corner here. There is probably no self-deceiver like an adulterer. A person may be persuaded that she was an innocent victim of her innate gift of passion, seduced by a charm beyond any mortal's power to resist, that she was a helpless child, gasping for pure love as an asthmatic gasps for oxygen, and therewith wholly forgivable and quite excusable. But she may also be guilty of fooling herself. She may have chosen to be vulnerable and then used her vulnerability as her excuse.

Nearly everyone assumes that he plunged into adultery to satisfy an unbearable need. Other people may have "cheap affairs"; he has a "need-filling relationship." Being the sinners we are, we like to relabel the fiery desire we take into our hearts as a human right. A responsible person will begin his thinking about adultery with the conviction that, though some adultery may be excusable, the odds are against it in his case.

C. IS ADULTERY EVER THE RIGHT THING TO DO?

May a married person ever sleep with someone outside his or her marriage with a good conscience, with a sense that God himself approves? We are not now asking whether adultery may on occasion be excusable—which only means that we temper our judgment of it because we understand the extenuating circumstances. The question is whether some extra-marital sex deserves no negative judgment at all, no need to be forgiven or excused. How can we go about testing adultery for moral permissibility? At the risk of over-simplification, let me suggest three ways to test the possibility of legitimate adultery.

1. *The test of the beautiful story.* No one has come up with a better "good adultery" tale than Joseph Fletcher's story of Mrs. Bergmaier, a German lady captured by the Russians at the end of the war and imprisoned at a camp in the Ukraine. Her husband had been sent to Wales as a prisoner of the Allies. When he was freed, he returned to Hamburg, where he rounded up his children and tried to grub out an existence for them all. But the children needed a mother. Through the underground Mrs. Bergmaier had gotten word that her husband and children were

174   safe but needed her desperately. The only way to get out of the
camp would be to get pregnant, in which case the Russians would
probably release her. So she asked a camp guard to sleep with
her. He did, and made her pregnant. She was dismissed from
the camp, returned to Hamburg, and joined her family. Eventually she gave birth to the child who, by the miracle of conception, resurrected her for her family, and "they loved him more
than all the rest."[14]

Mrs. Bergmaier's story reminds us that cruel circumstances
compel some people to do things they would not justify in kinder
times. But Fletcher does not tell Mrs. Bergmaier's story to persuade us only that she did a right thing—as an exception to the
rule—when she slept with the guard. The point Fletcher wants
to make is that a love like Mrs. Bergmaier's, certainly love for
one's children, *generally* justifies extra-marital sex, just as it justifies most things. That is, he means his story to illustrate *a
general principle* that love can justify almost everything.

It seems to me that the most we can draw from Mrs. Bergmaier's agapic adultery is that justified adultery is not unthinkable. To say for sure whether or not her adultery was justifiable
we would need to know more. For instance, what if she might
have gotten out of jail two months later—without getting pregnant? Even if Mrs. Bergmaier was right to seduce the guard, her
story would only illustrate that the Seventh Commandment, like
the others, might allow for an exception in extreme situations.
But we already admit that. What we need, besides a story, are
some general criteria by which true life stories can be tested.

2. *The test of benefits gained.* Is adultery right if it has good
results? Put this way, the test is terribly vague. For *whom* might
the results be good? Take a man who gets the affection and love
he needs from a woman other than his wife; he is served. But
what of his wife? What of the other woman once he leaves her—
as almost always happens? What of his children and his friends?
The good results of adultery are unfairly divided. So we must
decide on *who* should benefit before we apply the test of good
results.

What is at stake in adultery is not only the happiness or pain
of individual people, but the marriage itself. So the test of benefits gained must first require that the results of adultery be good
for the marriage. May we argue that adultery is permissible if it
can revive a dying marriage or even improve a sickly one?

Perhaps there are two kinds of extra-marital sex from a moral point of view: marriage-building and marriage-destroying. Perhaps the word "adultery" should be confined to negative, marriage-destroying affairs. Psychologist Carl Rogers says that in his therapy he has often seen people use sexual experiences outside of their marriage as part of their struggle to recreate their marriages; it is "frankly ridiculous," he says, to label marriage-healing extra-marital sex "adultery."[15] The O'Neils, in their best-selling *Open Marriage*, were even more positive: "Sexual fidelity is the false god of closed marriage, a god to whom partners submit . . . at the cost of the very relationships which that god is supposed to protect."[16] If an extra-marital sexual affair can nurture your marriage, then it is not a sin at all, but a duty; having sex with outsiders can be fidelity's best friend.

How might extra-marital sex improve a marriage and thereby be justified as a boost to fidelity? The O'Neils talk about the "magic" of love: the more love you give, the more you will have to give; the more people you give it to, the more you will have for your spouse. It is ironic, I suppose, that license for adultery should grow out of such a "Christian" sounding notion of love. But the O'Neils confuse their loves. Agapic love, the love of God shed abroad in us, does grow as it is shared. But erotic love, the love that drives us to seek another to enrich our life, does not grow as it is scattered. The wider I spread my eros, the less I can love anyone in particular. This is why the eros of married love needs the boundaries of covenant fidelity. We have limited erotic energies and great erotic needs; if we scatter our energies, someone gets shorted—and in adultery the person who deserves more and gets less is usually the spouse left alone while the other "seeks his own" with another person.

But if adultery does not increase love, maybe it can be justified on the narrower grounds of improving our sexual performance. Gay Talese suggests that married people learn how to be better partners at Sandstone, the California mecca of sexual license. Couples reaching for new adventure beyond the boredom of their own bedrooms become re-eroticized by contact with expert lovers at Sandstone. Later they channel that charged-up sexual energy back into their own marriages. A man who noticed that other men were aroused by his wife became newly aroused by her and strove to repossess her; women, particularly those who had been monogamous in long-term marriages, could re-

176 experience their glorious feelings of being sexually desired, and thus recapture "the elan of youthful courtship."[17] Sexual clods become virtuosos by making love with artists; adultery is marriage therapy.

Some people may even claim that there can be spiritual fringe benefits from adultery. A woman falls in love with a man who brings her fantasies to life. Then she falls into guilt and confesses everything to her husband. At first crushed by the revelation, he is given grace to forgive and takes her back. She gains from the experience of repentance; he grows through the exercise of magnanimity. Both benefit, and their marriage abounds in saving grace.

How should we evaluate the proposition that adultery can be justified, as a rule, if it benefits one's marriage?

The "good results" test for adultery has at least three flaws. First, it is too broad and unqualified to be trusted. What sorts of "good results" count? How enduring should the benefits be? Must both partners agree that the advantages outweigh the disadvantages and the pain? Can only certain sorts of people, with long experience in sexual liberty, reap such benefits? And how do we compare the benefits with the pain that follows? Too many questions are left dangling and unanswered and too much is granted to the adulterer's own rationalizing talent for us to trust the test of good results.

Second, even if this were an exact test, it could only be used after the fact. Beforehand a prospective adulterer can only gamble on the results. How could a married woman know that her marriage will abound in charity if she has an affair and confesses it afterward; how can she be sure that grace will abound if she sins boldly?

Third, even if adultery has some good results, does a wrong thing become good just because benefits follow it? Take this horrible example: two parents are brought closer together in love after their ten-year-old son is run down in the street by a drunken driver. In their grief over the lost child they find each other at new depths of love. Would it not be outrageous for someone to justify the drunken driver on the ground that by killing a child, he actually saved a marriage? I am not comparing adultery with negligent homicide, of course. I use the illustration only to dramatize a simple point: moral evils cannot be justified by beneficial results.

Grant that by grace some extra-marital affairs do end up happily, with both partners in loving embrace. What would happen to marriages generally if adultery were endorsed as a method of marriage therapy because it might improve some marriages? Do we not invite marital chaos? There is plenty of evidence that for every marriage helped by adultery, five are seriously hurt.[18] Marriages do well to survive adultery; only a rare marriage is improved by it.

3. *The test of evil avoided.* One test of whether it is right to violate a moral law is this: if you obey this particular moral law, will you break a more important one? For instance, it is not too hard to imagine situations that might, as Bonhoeffer put it, call for us to tell a "robust lie" to save a life. Can we imagine situations that call for "robust adultery?" We are not talking now of someone sneaking off to a motel room to make secret love with a neighbor's wife. We are talking about a person boldly and honestly (and maybe lovingly) seizing sex as a justified way to save a person from serious harm.

Here our problem is not so much with the logic of the test as with the limits of our imagination. I am sure that a married woman could conceivably avert a great evil by sleeping with someone other than her husband. Imagine a man mad with violence who threatened to kill a woman's child unless she yielded to his sexual aggression. Imagine, for that matter, a married woman yielding to rape in self-defense. Most people would grant, I suppose, as a universal rule: It is right for a married person to have sex with a stranger whenever it is the only way to save a human life, including one's own. So certain are we that self-defensive sex is right that it would seem offensive to speak of it as adultery.

Once we get beyond life-saving, however, adultery to avert evil opens up an endless catalog of sexual remedies for anything that ails us. Adultery could cure the bad self-image of a man married to a woman who is reluctant to go to bed with him. Adultery heals the pain of living with an impotent male. And consider the suffering of a single woman, crippled and inordinately plain, moving into middle age with no hope of every being loved physically; would not somebody's husband be an agent of healing if he proved to her that she could be loved?

Arguments to justify adultery as a way of averting evils tend to prove too much. They seize on extreme cases and argue from

178   them that adultery is good if it soothes any sorrow or salves any sore. As if by magic, almost any affair becomes an adventure of redemptive love. No one has ever, I suspect, launched a sexual excursion outside of marriage without the confidence that he or she was thereby healing somebody's wound. Thus every adulterer is sanctified by his or her good intentions.

It is one thing to concede that, *in extremis*, a person may be justified by the intention to save someone from harm. But such situations are unique in their irrationality. A person being raped does not choose to have sex; she does not want to have it at all, but submits to violent and irrational coercion. Such moments lie outside the arena where we make ordinary free decisions. We cannot use them as the starting-point for a line of reasoning that could finally justify adultery as a way of coping with the everyday burdens of living.

D. DIVORCE AND REMARRIAGE

Far from relaxing the Seventh Commandment in the softening agent of grace, Jesus stretched its demands almost beyond human limits. One of the hardest applications of the commandment he ever seemed to make was to divorced people who wanted to get married again. The words, as Mark gives them, went this way: "Whoever divorces his wife and marries another commits adultery against her; and if she divorces her husband and marries another, she commits adultery" (Mark 10:11, 12). Jesus seems to be saying that while a married person committed adultery by having sex with a single person, a single person—if divorced—could commit adultery by getting married. People who remarry after a divorce violate the Seventh Commandment. Does Jesus really label every twice-married person an adulterer and obligate every divorced person to be a celibate for the rest of his or her life?

Our task here is only to understand how to obey the law of respect for marriage covenants. We cannot interpret all the ins and outs of Jesus' hard words about divorce and remarriage. Whether or not Jesus on another occasion made an exception to this rule for people whose spouses committed adultery, leaving the "innocent party" to remarry if he wished, is not important for us here.[19] We want to know whether any divorced person who gets married again commits adultery by doing so.

If Jesus condemns every remarriage, he certainly leaves us bewildered as to why. Why should a compassionate Lord judge every loving couple as adulterers when they get married, just because one of them has been married and divorced before? The answer that convinced Christians for a long time was that marriage is indestructible except by death (or maybe by adultery). So, even if a person got a legal divorce, he was still morally married. Marriage is wed*lock*, a holy estate, and no one breaks out of it by a legal decree. Thus, when a divorced man sleeps with his new bride he commits adultery; he is still married to his first wife.

The myth of the indestructible marriage was created out of a metaphysical notion that few of us even understand today. What we can understand, and what is true to reality, is that a marriage is a covenant between two people, a covenant created by their wills and therefore breakable by their wills. Human will is the invisible fiber that holds a marriage together. When will fails, the marriage dies. It ought not to have died; but it did die.[20] If a marriage is left behind to die after a divorce, it makes nonsense of the notion that a divorced person is still morally married—and nonsense of the notion that remarriage is a kind of adultery for this reason.

People can be drawn into bizarre and even cruel dilemmas by the myth of the indestructible marriage. Consider the "guilt" of a young woman who marries a young man at 18, and lives with him for one terrifying year during which he brutalizes her in jealous, frustrated rage. She divorces him, mainly to stay alive. Suppose she later marries a decent man and loves him faithfully. Is she guilty of adultery on the ground that she is stuck forever to her first brutish partner?

Or consider the strange innocence of a man who divorces his wife and marries another woman. After a few years, he visits his former wife who herself had remarried. He sleeps with her one night, but of course he is not committing adultery with her because he is still morally married to her. He is committing adultery, rather, when he sleeps with his own wife.

Roman Catholic morality at least allows for the merciful escape route of annulment. To most Protestants this often seems like a charade, but it is a humane way to avoid the consequences

180   of the "indestructible marriage." Without the option of annulment, Protestants who believe the myth of an indestructible
marriage are stuck with the painfully unreasonable conclusion
that divorced people may not remarry—unless perhaps they are
lucky enough to have had a partner who committed adultery
during the earlier marriage.

Does Jesus really tell us that a person commits adultery if
he or she marries again after his earlier marriage ended in a
divorce? I do not think so. I believe Jesus was not here speaking
of adultery as illicit sex; sleeping with one's second spouse is not
the sin he has in mind. He is using the word adultery in the
deeper sense of breaking the covenant of marriage. The adultery
is the divorce, not the remarriage. Jesus says that a person commits adultery (breaks a covenant) when he or she divorces a
spouse.

Divorce is an assault against life's most complete covenant,
a partnership that calls for a sharing of everything one is and has
in life. Sexual intercourse outside marriage is one form of adultery. Divorce is another. So Jesus is simply using the word
"adultery" as the equivalent of covenant-breaking. Other passages in the Bible also speak of adultery in this way. People who
do not keep faith with their Christian commitment are, in James'
words, adulterers (James 4:4). Israel was an adulterer because it
repeatedly broke covenant with its Lord (Ezek. 16). And now,
Jesus tells us, people who break covenant with each other by
means of divorce are doing something called adultery.

Why, then, does Jesus mention remarriage? The answer is
that he lumps divorce and remarriage in one package; he simply
assumes that a divorced person will get married again, maybe
even that he divorces *in order* to marry again. So he simply says:
"Anyone who divorces his wife [and, naturally, remarries] commits adultery." The indictment is against divorce. Remarriage
was thrown in, not because it involved sex with the second partner, but as the almost inevitable appendage to the divorce. It is
the divorce that breaks covenant and thus violates the basic intent of the Seventh Commandment.[21]

If we see that Jesus is indicting divorce and is not sin-
gling out remarriage, we are free to deal with the past in a realistic manner, and to hold out hope for a new beginning. The
important issue is whether after a divorce a previous marriage
is really over, assuming both ex-partners will it to be. We would

then have a scenario that—in its endless variations—reads like this. A vow was once made and then broken. No divorced people can make believe that the failure did not occur and act as if the past never existed. Over any remarriage lingers a moral and psychological shadow from the past. But it is only a shadow; and shadows can be lived with or dispelled by the light of forgiveness and renewal. The human reality in history is that covenants made and dissolved are dead; maybe they *ought* not to have been dissolved, and often not made, but once made and dissolved they are past and done with.[22]

Paul's vision of future possibilities is relevant to remarriage: "forgetting those things that are behind," he wrote, "we press on toward the high calling in Christ" (Phil. 3:13). The past does not wholly bind us. We need not be shackled to our past mistakes any more than we can rest on our past successes. The possibilities opened by grace do not veto Jesus' words. We cannot forget the past in a psychological sense: a failure of covenant-keeping is a deeply regrettable chapter in our history. People who remarry ought never make light of the moral seriousness of their divorce. But the past can be forgotten in the sense that it no longer determines our future. When a marriage fails, really fails, and reconciliation is impossible, the marriage is dead, and has no claim on us. The gospel of grace then opens up new possibilities for a new vow, a new commitment of two selves in the face of an uncertain future, and a new entree to a life of covenant-keeping.

*   *   *

Marriage is one of God's ways of ordering human life and even redeeming it. Sexual intercourse is essentially bound up with the nature and purpose of marriage. It is therefore appropriate only within marriage. The important concern throughout this chapter has been marriage and our moral duty to honor its integrity. Sex outside of marriage becomes a serious moral issue only because marriage is of enormous importance to the human family and the future God has for his people. Adultery is called into question, not because sex is suspect, but because marriage is so important to life.

In discussing adultery, I have tried to keep a steady focus on the main issue, respect for our covenants. I have not sought to peg the act of adultery somewhere on a scale of human failures;

182   I am not at all sure that sexual adultery is the worst way to fail in fidelity. Moreover, I think that fidelity can digest an act of adultery. One whose husband or wife commits adultery should put fidelity to the marriage above revenge against the offender. Fidelity is the main thing. Keeping away from sexual affairs outside of marriage is one way of keeping the decks clear so that we can work at fidelity without a lot of moral clutter. But what it finally comes down to is this simple order: marriage is for families (though not *only* for families) and, for this reason, sex is for marriage. The order is built in, part of the human design. It is the better part of moral responsibility to keep the order.

QUESTIONS FOR DISCUSSION

1. Do you think that adultery takes on a radical new look in the New Testament?

2. Do you agree that without sex we have no marriage?

3. Do you agree that the sexual act is somehow life-uniting?

4. Do you think that adultery necessarily produces feelings of *jealousy* and inflicts *pain* on all involved?

5. Do you think that some sexual friendship outside of marriage can be all right? Or do you think this is usually harmful?

6. Do you think that God could ever approve of a married person having sexual intercourse with someone not his/her spouse? Do you think he would excuse some adultery even if he could not approve of it?

7. Do you think that honesty and care between married people outweighs the technical sin of adultery?

8. Do you agree that it is unrealistic to suppose that adultery could break a marriage at a single blow?

9. Do you agree that when a marriage fails, really fails, and reconciliation is impossible, that the marriage is dead and has no further claim on us?

RESPECT FOR PROPERTY: 7

"Thou Shalt Not Steal"

In the Eighth Commandment, the Lord God invades the mysterious world of our personal relationship to things. Between persons and things is a bond we call ownership, and God tells all people to respect that bond. Behind "Thou shalt not steal" must lie a permission to keep things. Respect for persons, the common thread we see running through all the commandments, here requires a particular attention to persons in their relationship to things which are truly their own and therefore bound up with their very selves. There is a wrong of taking because there is a right of keeping. Wrong taking and right keeping constitute the dialectic of the command against stealing, and we shall be asking questions about both.

The commandment confronts a modern culture which accepts greed as a style of self-affirmation and whose systems of exchanging property are so complex that recognizing the difference between stealing and dealing is a lost art. We still know that when a thug snatches a woman's purse, he is stealing; we are not sure whether or not a creative ad writer who woos money from people by seductive lies is stealing. We know an embezzler is stealing from a bank when he falsifies computer data; we are not sure whether or not a corporation that bribes its customer is stealing. We know that a burglar who takes a poor family's television set is stealing; we are not always sure whether a company is stealing when it exploits a poor nation's resources. One yearns for the day when a thief was a mere rogue, not an executive in a three-piece suit.

Some thieves are violent thugs who break the law; others are more refined and may steal by taking advantage of the law. A thief may mask himself as a philanthropist. Most thieves only rob from the poor and we despise them; some thieves rob much from the rich, and we create legends to glorify their exploits.

In all its varieties, there is more to stealing than meets the eye. It somehow violates a fundamental sector of human life and sets order and justice of human community on its head. But stealing is as complex as life. We must look at all the angles to see if we can understand *what* God asks of us when he says

184   "Thou shalt not steal," *why* he asks it, and *how* we can obey this command in the complex and crazy way in which things are distributed among the people of our world.

I. WHAT DOES THE EIGHTH COMMANDMENT TELL US TO DO?

The Eighth Commandment is a moral broadside against taking things that belong to someone else. It assumes that things sometimes do belong to some person or some institution who wants to keep them. Not all taking is stealing. If I take something that belongs to no one, I am not stealing. Since the beginning of time, a person who comes on land that no one has conquered or claimed stakes a claim and calls it his. If I take what my neighbor invites me to take, I am not stealing; if he tells me that I may collect the fruit that falls off his trees, I am not stealing when I harvest his fallen oranges. So the commandment seems only to forbid taking something that another person or group truly owns and intends to keep.

The commandment forbids taking people as well as things, a fact that complicates the sin of stealing. Some scholars believe that the Eighth Commandment aims specifically at stealing people.[1] Kidnapping is a sin against what is stolen more than against who is stolen from. You reduce a person to a brute thing; you shrink him to something you can steal like a machine and sell for profit. No wonder that the Old Testament treated kidnapping as a capital offense: "Whoever steals a man, whether he sells him or is found in possession of him, shall be put to death" (Exod. 21:6; Deut. 24:7). A kidnapper was stoned to death, not out of respect for an owner who was robbed, but out of respect for the person stolen, who was stripped of the divine image.

If the Eighth Commandment was a rule against kidnapping, the Tenth Commandment, "Thou shalt not covet," may be our general rule against stealing. To covet something is to put your finger on the trigger of your will, to crouch like an animal poised to pounce. In the words of one translator, when you covet a thing you are already putting "your hooks out" for it.[2] The Tenth Commandment might read: "Keep your heart and your hands off your neighbor's property." It registers against the whole process, from intent to act.[3]

Our concern here is not with the technical question of whether it is the Eighth or the Tenth Commandment which forbids stealing things. We want to understand what the commandment tells us, not which commandment does the telling. So let us be content to acknowledge the textual problem, appropriate some lessons from it, but then go on to speak of the Eighth Commandment as a rule against stealing.[4]

The commandment, as it stands, gives us a "live and let live" morality of property. Illuminated by the law of love, however, it leads beyond minimal morality. As we noted earlier, if taking is wrong, having must be right. But if having things is right for those who do indeed own them, it must be wrong for others to own nothing. Property is not something that is merely around us for us to hold or sell like shares in a company we care nothing about. Genuine property is proper to us, close to what we are. It follows, then, that a person without property is bereft of something very important. Let the light of love's law be shed on this closeness between property and person, and the negative rule becomes an affirmative law.

The positive law could be put this way: Always do what you can to help people get property they have a right to have. Help others get what is coming to them. There is a limit, of course. The commandment does not urge us to help an oil baron add to his holdings. It compels us to help those who have nothing to get something, for no person can flourish as the image of God without something to call, to shape, and to make his own. The Eighth Commandment requires those who are strong to help those who are weak to get what they need in order to be and to grow as persons. The Old Testament prophets saw the duty of God's people this way. Isaiah, for instance, accused the powerful of grotesque larceny against the weak: "You are the ones who . . . conceal what you have stolen from the poor. By what right do you crush my people and grind the faces of the poor?" (Isa. 3:14f.). But he wants the powerful to do more than "live and let live." He wants them to turn themselves around and go into action for justice.

> Search for justice,
> Help the oppressed,
> Be just to the orphan,
> Plead for the widow (Isa. 1:17).

186 Behind the negative rule lies a positive law that requires active pursuit of property for the dispossessed. "Do not take another's property" is the rule of "live and let live." "Seek property for those who have none" is the law of love.

II. WHY IS STEALING WRONG?

The Eighth Commandment matches the Creator's design for persons and their lasting affair with things. It matches the nature of human community, too, because brute things are woven into the fabric of human relationships. How we exchange things with each other may tell us more about how we are getting along as persons than how we exchange ideas. So, the command that forbids stealing emerges from the way we are meant to relate to each other.

What insights into *ourselves* can we use to help us see that it is reasonable to respect property? How does the rule fit nature?

A. OUR RELATION TO THINGS

Our identity with things

If you respect a person, you must respect his property, for if you take what is truly his you take something proper to his self. A thing truly becomes my own when I stamp an image of myself on it, set it in new relationships, reshape it, put it to my special use. Brute and inanimate by itself, it can nevertheless take on a bit of my mind and spirit, and thus become uniquely mine. When I have truly made a thing my own, I can demand a respect for it as a respect owed to myself.

The relationship works both ways. A person can get his or her identity from things. What we own can put its stamp on us. The things we surround ourselves with reveal the sort of people we are. Tell me what you claim as your very own, and I will know something—though not everything—about you.

Of course, some things bear our image more than others do. It all depends on what we have done with them. My son reshaped an ordinary Volkswagen into a unique automobile. It bears his image, while my showroom model Rabbit bears none of mine. But my house bears my image more than my friend's condominium (which he paid a professional to decorate, and in which he does little more than sleep) bears his. On the other hand, you can learn much more about me from looking over my books than you can by looking at my house. My books are my own, my property; my house is less my own; but my car is only my possession, and not really my own property.

The fact that persons can make things their own and, in turn, get their identities (in part) from them, suggests that ownership matches a facet of our human beingness. It also hints that stealing things which other people own violates more than civil rule; it violates persons. There is something right about persons owning things and something very wrong about ripping them off.

A lot of the things we possess may be alien to us: we never really come to own them. A woman possesses stock in a corporation she has never seen or cares to see; yet she owns it in an impersonal way. A man possesses an apartment building that he uses as a tax write-off; it is not really his own, yet it is his alien property.

Stealing things a person really makes his own has a special perversity about it, to be sure. Thus if you steal my son's rebuilt VW Beetle, you do something which is on the face of it worse than stealing my VW Rabbit. But of course people often badly need things they merely possess. If I need that car which I "merely possess" in order to make a living as a salesman, and you steal it, you take away my power to support my family. In that sense my Rabbit does give me identity and power. It is a thing that helps make me what I am, and you reduce me by stealing it.

In any case, we can see a deep reason in the command against stealing, a reason located in the heart of God's creation of human souls that naturally and caringly makes brute things their very own.

Our calling to be caretakers

Human beings seem created to take care of something. Caretaking is of the human essence. The prime showcase of human caretaking is the natural relation of parents to their children. But we are placed here to take care of the things of earth as well. From this fundamental fact of humanness the right to own things arises. Add to human caretaking the fact that things need taking care of, and a prime reason for ownership becomes evident.

188   When the Lord God created a being who transcended brute creation and set him in control (Gen. 1:26), the primary purpose was to provide a caretaker; we were given dominion *over* things *in order to* take care of them. Man and woman were set within a finite garden and made tenders of it for God and for his future caretakers.

Because the human population would grow while the garden remained constant, careful nurture was necessary for the earth to remain a fitting habitation to the third and fourth generations. As Genesis 3 tells us, in a great moral disturbance, known as the Fall, humanity took one of its most calamitous turns. Cavalierly, we cast off our calling to be caretakers. We have consumed the precious wealth of the earth as if it were an infinite resource. We have corrupted the air and water as if no one would ever need to breathe or drink after us. We have buried our chemical and nuclear poisons in its bowels as if it had an infinite digestive tract. We have subdued the earth, as God said, but we have done it without care. And careless subjugation is inhuman exploitation. Therefore, we have undermined the foundation of our property rights at the core, for we were made to own only so that we could take better care.

Adam Smith was obviously mistaken to suppose that private property is an intrinsic good, that humans left alone will be guided by an invisible hand always to use private property for the common good. In fact, ownership has often been a moral evil because we have often chosen not to use it in order to care for what we owned with regard for its own value and its own laws. Karl Marx was equally wrong to suppose that private ownership is intrinsically evil. My ownership is an evil only if I exploit what I own rather than care for it, or care for it only with an eye to my private pleasure in it and not with an eye for other people's needs. Owning things is good only if our owning keeps faith with our calling to take care of the earth and of our brothers and sisters who inhabit it.

Our need of things
Persons need things because we are dependent creatures as truly as we are transcendent spirits. We are body-persons, not souls who drive bodies about for a brief earthly journey and easily discard them as a man trades in an old car. So we depend on

things—food to fuel our bodies, shelter to protect us from winds and rain, clothing to cover us and make us pleasant to look at, medicine to cure our bodily ills. We need such things to survive as spiritual bodies, and it is our need that justifies our owning them.

I cannot say how much of these things I need. But I have a sense that my need makes it necessary for me to own at least some things. If I always ate other people's food, if I always slept in other people's shelter, and if I always wore other people's clothing, I suspect I would be diminished in spirit. The transcendent spirit housed in my dependent body needs to make some things its own.[5]

I need things, too, because I am a creative spirit, superior to things. I depend on things which I can recreate. I need things because I am a member of the human family that was, in its primeval goodness, told "to have dominion . . . over all the earth" (Gen. 1:26). To exercise my dominion requires tools. It also requires a place—a home, a shop, some land. I need objects of art and books so that I can participate in the recreative works of other people's hands and minds. My very transcendence over things puts me in need of them.

Transcendence and dependence are set in a delicate dialectic which is broken by the foul sumptuousness of "conspicuous consumers." It can be difficult to maintain a decent balance between legitimately enjoying things and debauching ourselves. Some things—roses, sunsets, and high art—are on earth for no reason that we can sense except to bring us pleasure. Hence, we must not moralize ourselves into joyless austerity. But excesses can make a travesty of the created symbiosis between persons and things and at the same time divide the human community. When people strain to find gifts for "the man who has everything" and end up buying him a gold golf club, when parents celebrate a daughter's wedding with a $10,000 reception, when women keep scores of dresses in their closets, some worth as much as a thousand dollars—and when these massive indulgences are flaunted in full view of poor people—God's intention for a humane relationship with material things is turned into a debauchery that alienates human beings from one another. Let no one suppose that the design for life which makes it right to own things ever justifies grabbing everything we can.

B. OUR RELATION TO OTHER PERSONS

God's commandments are all rooted in the respect for each other without which human community cannot exist. The Eighth Commandment calls for a respect that lets people freely do the job of caring for the things they own. Respect compels us to keep our distance, to allow a person to be what he is with his property. The rule against stealing, therefore, at least lets people alone, and so allows for the possibility—though of course it cannot create the reality—of a human community.

Stealing violates human community because it destroys trust. Only where most of our relationships are built on trust can we live together as persons. Trust breaks down with fear. When people sense that their private places are vulnerable, they fear every stranger in their midst. And so they shut strangers out. They build walls, bolt doors, and install electronic vigilantes. They call the police if a stranger lingers too long in their neighborhoods. Thus, community shrinks to confined quarters where only proven friends are allowed. The open spirit of hospitality shrivels to an intimate dinner party for close friends. Stealing closes us in on ourselves and paralyzes us; love is frozen when people live in fear of thieves.[6]

But community is also broken when persons are systematically deprived of things they need to live humanely. Bereft of justice, they will eventually be possessed by rage and hate against those who deprive them. It matters little whether they are deprived because persons steal from them or because the system ignores them. Further, community is broken when one class of people enjoys and displays much more property than they need. Conspicuous consumption alienates those who have much from those who have very little.

To protect their own feelings, the well-to-do make believe that the poor do not exist. Driving in their air-conditioned cars from downtown Los Angeles to the outlying valley, they shut their minds to the ghetto sprawling beside the freeway just as they shut out the hot smog from their automobiles. They ride the train from Westchester to Manhattan and deliberately ignore the squalor around them as their train clanks through Harlem. The poor meanwhile turn into themselves, digging themselves deeper into the culture of poverty. Thieves among them steal from their poorer neighbors. And so the human community becomes an inhuman jungle.[7]

In summary, God's command not to steal fits the primal design of the human community because persons need things to own and persons have a right to own things they need. The command mirrors the nature of humans as persons who need to care for things, and in the need of any community for a fair distribution of things among its members. These are insights that come from a biblical view of things. They provide faith's own reasons for what most reasonable people affirm as a moral duty.

III. RESPECT FOR PROPERTY AT THE BORDERLINES OF LIFE

The Eighth Commandment tells us that it is right for us to own things and wrong to steal things. Is it *always* right to own and is it *always* wrong to steal? How do you know whether you have a moral right to your property? When is it right to steal? Are we not ready to excuse a person who steals a loaf of bread for a hungry child? But then how do we know when we can steal with God's approval? Can we find a guideline for justified stealing? Or do we improvise, play the moral tune by ear, and take our chances? Let us reason first about the matter of the moral right to own and then about the moral right to steal.

To have a moral right to property means to be justified in claiming it as one's own—justified before God, justified before conscience, and justified before the judgment of human reason. I can appropriately thank God for all the goods to which I have a moral right. I may enjoy them, give them to my children, sell them for a profit, or distribute them all to the poor. No matter how I dispose of them, no one—neither God nor man—can fairly blame me.

Moral right to property is more important than legal right, though it is far more difficult to assess. Legal rights are settled by experts in points of civil law. And so thieves may well succeed in getting the legal right to their loot. Tyrants legally siphon personal fortunes out of the people's store; robber barons become society's models of industry and ownership. But no court is competent to decide whether you have moral title to your wealth. To settle the question of moral rights to property, we need to turn the floodlights of revelation and reason on the ambiguities by which society deals with its commonwealth.

192   A. CONDITIONS THAT MAKE FOR A MORAL RIGHT
TO OWN SOMETHING

How we obtained it

How does a piece of God's creation get locked into a specific
person's dominion? The trail from God's creation to one person's possession is difficult to trace. Christian believers may be
inclined, like Calvin, to explain it theologically: our right to own
a thing, he said, was given by "distribution of the Supreme Lord
of all." We own it because God gave it to us. Robber barons
with a touch of Calvinism in their blood may be comforted by a
cheap assurance that what they grabbed was really bestowed by
God's sovereign hand. But Calvin was no fatalistic fool: he did
not mean to justify a person's property on grounds that God
gave it to him. Calvin's purpose was pastoral: he wanted the rich
to be thankful and thus generous, and he wanted the poor to
hold back their souls from complaint and their hands from theft.[8]

Thomas Aquinas, with his sharp eye for realities, recognized
that our right to own things is arranged through human institutions.[9] He was right, obviously. And it may also be true that
God gives things *through* the strategies of society. But we shall
have to focus on the human strategies.

The many ways by which a person can come to own things
may, I think, be categorized under three headings: conquest,
contract, and creation. In briefly discussing these we should recall that we cannot claim moral right to anything simply on
grounds of how we came by it.

1. *Conquest*. No means by which people come to take possession of things has less moral support than conquest. Conquest is
a nationalist euphemism for grand theft. What people take by force,
they usually take away from someone who already owned it.

Yet, for a long time western Christendom blessed a feudal
system based on conquest. You owned land in those days if your
fathers had taken it from someone else and held it by force. The
church itself was given a good share of valuable land as a reward
for blessing the conquerors. The passing of time dulls the moral
edge, but it is nevertheless true that the lands we call ours probably began their trek to modern ownership as "stolen goods."

We cannot decide the moral question, however, by how the
property was obtained in the old days. Too much time separates

us from the original conquerors and those from whom they stole the land. My people may have driven native Americans off land which their people had possessed for time unrecorded. But my people since then have cared for the land and made it yield an abundance of tall corn and bulging steers. The descendants of those native Americans who were ravaged by my ancestors may now lay claim to my land. I will argue that my parents' and grandparents' care for the land over a century and more gives me and my children rights to it. But that claim of care must be balanced against their claim of blood ties with ancestors who got it straight from the hand of God. The moral claims are strong on both sides; neither side has an absolute case. In the ambiguity of life, right is often gained only by compromise.

2. *Contract*. Most people who own things today have either bought them, inherited them, or earned them as pay. Society arranges to validate that ownership by pieces of paper verifying that the property has legally passed from one owner to another. The legal right thus given usually coincides with a moral right. But not always.

When I meet the terms of my contract with you, I have a right to what you transfer to me. But some contracts are immoral. A contract is immoral if the parties did not agree to it as free and responsible persons. A contract between a slave-owner and a slave, or between a clever crook and a mentally retarded person, is immoral because one party was not responsible. These are clear-cut cases. Between these obviously immoral contracts are innumerable ambiguous cases. The point is that my getting something according to contract does not mean that I have it morally.[10]

Some societies arrange for the ownership of almost everything to be arranged by contracts which individuals make with one another. Other societies allow major properties to be owned only by the corporate group. Even the most individualistic society allows for public ownership of most highways and airports, and even the most socialistic of societies allows a woman to buy her own pots and a man to buy his own bicycle. For example, American society sets aside a little land and some enterprises for public ownership, and then limits what I can own privately by means of antitrust laws and inheritance taxes.

194

Hence, my right to contract for ownership of something is limited by the strategies my society uses to keep some things in public domain and to keep private ownership from being intolerably unfair. I cannot claim moral right to something just because I am able to make a contract to buy it or because my father has contracted by way of a will to give it to me. My moral rights to own are conditioned by the society I happen to live in. Within that limit, any contract made with a free and responsible person ordinarily gives me a right to own. But even then it does not give it unconditionally.

3. *Creation*. The strongest moral claim that I can make on my property is that I have created it. When I make something, I have given a thing my image, as God gave me his. It is my own as nothing can be that I buy or conquer. Ownership comes to its own in creation. As the universe he made is truly God's, so the things I make are truly mine.[11] If I paint a portrait, it is mine as it can never be another's. If I write a book, it is mine as it can never be a reader's. If I build a house, it is mine as it can never be the property of a speculator.

Not even creation, however, gives me unconditional right to own what I have made. If I paint a woman's portrait on commission, the portrait is rightfully hers. If a book I write is published, it belongs to the publisher and, one may hope, eventually to a reader, and I must pay for a copy of "my" book at the bookstore. If I build a house on consignment, I will need an invitation to enter it once it is given over to the owner.

Remember that we never create anything out of nothing. Whatever I have made is also a gift to me. I have many partners in the slightest creative act. Someone had to teach me how to make it. I needed others before me to bequeath a genetic legacy which then became my gift. I needed material and tools that others produced for me. And I needed the Creator Spirit who alone finally makes creators of his creatures. The thing I make, before it is begun, is a gift to me. This puts a moral limit to my claims on what I make. I do not own anything as if I were God; I am always a co-creator.

In sum, none of the ordinary ways of getting legal title to property gives us unconditional moral right to own something. Every way of gaining legal title to something must meet certain conditions if it is to give moral right as well. If I conquered it,

I must prove that no one owned it before I took it. If I contracted for it, I must demonstrate that the contract was fairly and freely made. If I created it, I have to show that I did not contract to make it for someone else.

The sort of property it is

There are as many kinds of property as there are kinds of things in the world. But if we look at them from different points of view, we can cluster property within a few broad categories. Each category brings out certain crucial aspects of the property. For instance, we can distinguish *real* property (things you cannot easily move, like land and buildings) from *personal* property (things you can easily move around, like jewelry and cars). Or, looked at from another angle, there is *non-renewable* property (land, minerals, fuels beneath the land) and *renewable* property (apples, TV sets, and airplanes). A third way of distinguishing one kind of property from another is property for *production* (like factories, railroads, and farms) and property for *consumption* (like all the things we use and enjoy, what we eat, live in, and wear).

We will consider here only two kinds of property—land and factories—and ask what goes into the making of a moral right to own each of them.

1. *Land*. The land and the resources beneath it are limited; only so much land is available to any society. The trend is always in the direction of fewer people owning ever more land. Anticipating this tendency, the Old Testament provided for semi-centennial land reforms. Every fiftieth year, called the Year of Jubilee, the land had to be returned to its original family owners.

> And you shall hallow the fiftieth year, and proclaim liberty throughout the land for all its inhabitants; it shall be a jubilee for you, when each of you shall return for his property and each of you shall return to his family (Lev. 25:10).

Behind this regulation lay the conviction that land ownership was conditioned by the need of farming families to have a place to keep the family together. The concern of the law was for family life as much as for property. It aimed to protect the larger community; for the fellowship of the whole human family breaks down when the land on which it lives is owned by a few,

196   while the people who work the soil can never actually make it
their own. Human community was what the Lord of the law
meant to rescue with the Year of Jubilee; this is why the year of
land reform became the augur of the kingdom of God (Luke
4:13). Whether the jubilee land reform was regularly or seldom
or for that matter never put into effect does not alter the vision
behind the law: survival of the family within a caring community
limits our moral right to possess land.

Of course, owning and working the land in our time is not
the same experience as it was in Bible times. Then a person
belonged to the land; it was the land that told him who he was
and where he stood. Working the land, he was personally, indeed
spiritually, one with it. His place on earth was, in a way, his
perpetual womb. To own land was to embrace the land as
proper to one's own self. To question the right of ownership
would have been to question the right to one's own life.

Unlike the sweating figure bent over a hand-forged plow,
chopping a furrow into topsoil before the sun has warmed earth's
crust, today's farmer is often an absentee agro-businessman, a
capitalist who has never made the land his own by putting himself into it, turning the soil, planting the seed, or harvesting a
crop. Once, the farmer personally belonged to the farm; today
the farm often belongs legally to a non-farmer.

Who produces the harvest in our time? A vast network of
hands help bring forth every bushel of grain: the people on
assembly lines building combines, the biochemists and geneti-
cists at the university, the oil riggers in Saudi Arabia who provide
fertilizer, the airplane pilots who spray insecticide on the crops.
And this short list mentions only a few platoons from the army
of people who help produce crops from the land today.

This radical change in how people actually relate to the land
they possess is bound to touch on their moral right to own it.
The moral right of an absentee landlord obviously no longer
emerges from his symbiotic oneness with the land. Nor can it
come from the sheer fact that he has bought and paid for it. It
must now come from the effects that his kind of ownership has
on other people and on the land itself.

An absentee landlord must answer questions such as these:
How does my ownership affect the quality of food that people
eat for nourishment and delight? How does my ownership of
the land help starving people far away get enough to eat for their

children? How does my ownership help those who till the soil and pick its fruit to get a fair return for their sweat? How, in short, does my kind of caring for land touch on the lives of people who need the fruits of the land in order to live?

More, how does my use of pesticides affect the balance of animal life around my land? How does my management of crops affect the future fertility of the soil? The moral right to a specific piece of land comes down finally to one issue: how do we fulfil our destiny as caretakers—of people and goods—through our ownership of the land?

2. *The factory*. Its Latin derivation tells us that a manufacturer was once a person who made things with his own hands. The place where he made them was, naturally, a factory. He used his skills and tools to make things other people needed or wanted enough to pay him for them. He took care of his factory because it was all his; the skills, the tools, and the products were all his own. He was a true owner.

The economist Adam Smith believed that an invisible hand guided such factories into blessing for their owners and their society.[12] No one would take care of a factory like the person who owned it, and therefore private ownership of production was part of eternal wisdom. What Smith did not foresee was that success would fundamentally change the privately owned factory. Good caretaking turned factories into corporations; and corporations required a new kind of ownership, absentee owners, who gave neither skill nor sweat to the factory, but trusted everything to a corps of managers.

The moral factor in ownership of production has thus been turned on its head. Owners are usually not caretakers; all they have to attest to their ownership is a certificate tucked away in a safety deposit box. If owners are to regain their moral right to own factories they must again become caretakers of their property. The moral issue is not whether a factory is socialized or whether it is owned by a mass of individuals. The moral question is whether owners of factories can be brought back into the task of caretaking.

One way to turn owners back into caretakers is to turn workers into owners. If workers are owners, they are also co-responsible for the factory, and thus are directly pushed into the question of whether they will be caretakers or only profit-takers. If workers not only owned shares, but were represented on the board of directors, they would bring ownership and caretaking into a working relationship. All that would be lacking, then, would be to turn the stockholders into responsible partners, converting them from mere investors looking for a return into owners accepting a share of responsibility for the factory.[13]

Caretaking ownership involves more than the ownership of the means of production. It must include the vision of the factory as a small community, a human fellowship of work. In this vision, men and women give their sweat and skill, imagination and capital, to a corporate enterprise in which everyone has a chance to exercise his or her gifts as a person created for community in work. Paul's vision of the church as a body that models a redeemed humanity must emerge in the factory as well as in the family:

> The body does not consist of one member, but of many. . . . God arranged the organs in the body . . . giving the greater honor to the inferior part . . . that the members may have the same care for one another (1 Cor. 11:14-25).

Somehow caretaking in a corporation must attend to the human side of the productive community, the side that encourages the members to see themselves as people cared for by others. No owner, in this vision, may ever think of labor as a commodity to be bought and sold. Nor may working people be robots pushed around by efficiency experts. The company must show signs of a fellowship in which everyone, from custodian to president, is a valuable human being contributing his or her gifts to the community of production.[14]

The owner must also be caretaker for the community within whose boundaries and by whose leave the corporation is able to produce things for people to consume and use. Every owner suffers jitters at this point: the competitors for his supportive care are legion, and every call for care seems to divert him from his own business. Consider a few of the items on the agenda that clamor for care from the owners of any corporation:

—Work for handicapped people

—Advancement for women equal to that of men

—Equal opportunities for members of all races and ethnic groups

—Support for the cultural life of the community

—Care for the environment, even to the extent of radical changes in product design and waste disposal.

Owners are not gods, and they cannot care for everything. But they are inescapably caretakers. Their moral right to own a factory is valid only if they intend and try to be. They may need to pray each night for vision. They need badgering and criticism from outside, for like all people they suffer the myopia of self-interest. But if morality touches the heart of things, they will be focusing on what matters most to them as human beings when they ask themselves again: by what moral right do I own this factory or this share in this corporation?

Some may argue that any talk of a moral right to own a factory has become an anachronism. Perhaps the corporation in a technological society is a monster beyond all moral restraint and moral ownership is an idyll. It may be that a valid claim to moral ownership can be made only by new visions and methods. At any rate, if we talk at all of our moral right to own a factory, we must be caretaking owners.

We have looked at only two kinds of property, land and factories. We might have discussed the ownership of technology or "intellectual property." But we have seen enough, I believe, to establish that the right to own things is not absolute, but relative, and that it depends largely on our dedication to the care of what we own, a care that reaches out to the larger community of people whose lives are touched for good or evil by the things we claim as ours.

How much there is to go around

My moral right to a slice of bread depends on how large the loaf is and how many people need to share it. The ratio of bread to bread-eaters helps settle my moral claim to the piece I have. I cannot expect God to approve of my slice if it is so large that I keep others from getting what they need. I have surely lost any moral place to stand if the size of my portion keeps some people from getting any at all. Thus, everything depends on how much is left after I get mine. It is not simply a matter of whether I have more or less than others; a billionaire in a society of millionaires can sleep with good conscience. A person who eats a large meal in a community of starving people needs to worry.

In today's global village, everyone's right to a large part of the world's wealth is under a cloud. Americans cannot be morally secure when they enjoy a huge slice of the world's wealth while two-thirds of the people on earth are destitute. We must think about the moral right to own things in a world of hungry people in terms of how our ownership decreases or increases the share others can own.

Traditionally, the "commonwealth" is thought of in political terms. When one makes a claim on his share in the commonwealth, it is assumed that it is his share of his nation's wealth which is in view. A poor Frenchman does not claim a share in the riches of California, nor can a starving Ugandan claim a fair share in South African wealth. If a nation's loaf is very small, everyone in that nation has a moral right only to a small piece, and everyone may be treated fairly even if his or her share is a starvation diet. Thus, on the nationalist view of property rights, if I starve I cannot complain of unfairness as long as my countrymen are starving with me, even if people across the border are living in splendid plenty.

Is it not clear that, Christianly, we must stretch justice beyond traditionally nationalistic terms? Political boundaries are accidents of history: even if God liberally "determined the boundaries of the nations' habitation" (Acts 17:26), the human community is more basic than any political community. Therefore, in a time when most of the world's limited wealth is consumed by a few nations, we need to globalize our sense of justice. When two-thirds of the world's people are hungry, they are not getting their *just* share of the world's food. And when they plead for a share, they are not asking for charity but claiming justice.

Is there a moral reason why people who by divine providence live in Iowa should have exclusive claim to the richness of that black earth just because they happen to live on top of it? Is there a moral reason why people who were set on Saudi Arabia's sand should claim to own all the oil beneath it, just because they happen to live above it? The tradition of distributive justice which answers Yes to these questions is morally insane in the global village. Who dares to say that starving children in Uganda are getting a "fair share" just because most children in Uganda get little? Do my children have a moral right to stuff themselves with junk food just because American wealth can create a huge pile of junk food to distribute? If my share of the world's goods helps bring a stranger to poverty and his children to starvation, I cannot claim before the God who made the earth for the whole human family that I own my goods with good conscience.

The upshot is that no one in the human community has an

indisputable right to what he calls his property. God makes it right for members of the human species to make things their own. But every individual has to justify his or her ownership of things before the bar of moral reason and the God of moral law, because he owns everything in trust as a member of the human community. True, in relationship to the Lord God we own nothing at all; we are only caretakers. But we do own things with respect to our fellows, and in view of this we need to justify our ownership.

Beyond our basic right to things we need to survive, our right to ownership is highly relative. We cannot take it for granted that what we have may never be taken from us. We cannot assume that our owning is blessed by God. Much depends on the answers to three questions: Is it fair? Do we take care? Do we share? If we obtained it unfairly, if we do not care for it responsibly, and if we refuse to share it with others, we are morally dispossessed, regardless of bills of sale and deeds of trust. And we are in as much moral danger for keeping as a thief is for taking.

How we care for it

Any person's moral right to a thing depends, in some part, on whether he takes care of it. We are born to be caretakers of God's things on earth; our right to own is rooted in our calling to care. So our moral claim to God's blessing on our ownership needs to be supported by evidence that we have used our ownership to take good care of what we own. A man who wants the moral right to own a forest must show, at the very least, that he is replacing the living trees he saws down for lumber. A woman who makes claims to moral ownership of an apartment building forfeits her right if she allows the building to slip into a decayed ruin unfit for human habitation. The owner of animals cannot claim moral right to them if he mistreats them.

We are dealing here with simple morality in a complex network of property laws. But the moral equation *is* simple: if we are given the right to own things in order to take care of them, our right is reduced to the extent that we are careless.

Yet, even though I take superb care of my own property, my right to it is called into question if I harm other people and their property by the way I tend my own. I may take excellent care of my shop, yet pollute my community's rivers with its garbage.

202 I may take fine care of my bank by ruthlessly foreclosing on poor people's homes. If I care for my things at cost to people, my moral right to own is not supported by my carefulness. Our moral right to property is not absolute even when we take tender care of our own; we are moral owners only within a community.

B. WHEN IS IT RIGHT TO STEAL?

Judy lives on welfare in the Watts section of Los Angeles with her two sons, Michael and Tiger. Every month, after she pays her bills, she is about $25 short. There is always a lag between the time her money runs out and the food stamps come in. If the food stamps are late, she and the boys go hungry. They were a week late this time. She grew faint and vomited from hunger.

Michael lay on the bed next to her: "Mama, what are we going to eat?"

"Suck your thumb and take a drink of water," Judy answered.

Michael sneaked into a neighbor's house, raided the kitchen, and came back with bacon and eggs.

"Son," Judy said, "it's wrong to steal this stuff."

"Hell," Michael replied, "we got nothing to eat."[15]

Are we not willing to excuse Michael's raid? Some of us will turn our moral fury on a system that creates such misery, and say that no matter how wrong it was for Michael to steal, his sin was trivial compared to the social obscenity that made it necessary. We are inclined to take extenuating circumstances into consideration. Most readers of Jesus' parable would have excused poor Lazarus had he stolen a few husks from Dives' barn; after all, it was the rich man's brutal tightness that made it necessary for Lazarus to steal some food. When stealing is a necessary evil, it is easily excused.

The tougher ethical question is whether we can *justify* Michael's stealing. If Michael's theft is justified, he may—with God's own endorsement—say to his mother, "No, Mother, it is *right* to steal this stuff." What would it take to convince us that in this instance Michael owes nobody an apology and needs no one's forgiveness, because stealing was the right thing for him to do— as it would be for anyone else in the same circumstances?

We can grant at the outset that some wrong thefts are worse than others. Most of us will agree that some thefts may be justified, right, even good. What we want to know is *how we can tell* when they are justified. We must look for some sort of standard for justified thievery. Is there a test that will work?

Stealing from owners who have no right to what they own

As we observed earlier, some people have no moral right to own things that they legally possess. General Rodriguez, a Latin American dictator, has deposited public funds into his Swiss bank account, building a personal fortune as a hedge against the day when his regime is overthrown and he goes into exile. With faked drafts, however, a few of the dictator's countrymen manage to siphon money from his account. Herman Menton, a venal Dutch art collector, has bought several paintings dirt cheap from a former Nazi who stole them from Eastern museums. A young artist, in love with the paintings, burglarizes the art shop and steals two of the precious works. John D. Rockefeller, Sr., it is said, ruined a small oil refiner by the name of George Rice through unfair competition; someone then stole five hundred barrels of oil from the refinery that Rockefeller had taken over. And what of Robin Hood who stole only from the greedy rich? Can we justify such stealing on grounds that those stolen from had no right to what was stolen from them?

I do not think we can, for two reasons. The first is that the character of a victim does not give other people grounds to abuse him. We cannot claim a right to hurt people on grounds of their morals. It is just as wrong to rape a prostitute as to rape a prude. It is wrong to murder a murderer just as it is wrong to murder a minister. For the same reason, it is wrong to steal from someone whose right to his goods you happen to question. If we may steal from anyone who does not deserve to have what we steal, we open the door to violence against anyone whose character is not up to our standard.

The second reason is that we are not all competent judges of other people's moral right to keep what they own. If everyone were free to judge other people's right to keep their possessions, we would all be hostages to self-righteous cutthroats who rob as a crusade against the unworthy. To declare open season on the goods of "bad guys" is to invite a reign of self-righteous terror.

Stealing when "no harm is done"

Petty thefts from giant owners often seem justifiable on grounds that the victim will never feel the loss. Will General Motors

204   suffer if a worker on the assembly line pockets a drill bit from the tool crib? Will a supermarket chain be hurt because a poor lady sneaks a steak through the checkout stand? Will a company notice the difference when a salesman pads his expense account to cover a night at the theater? Can the government really mind when a congressman uses franking privileges for personal mail? It is wrong, for all to see, when a rich thief steals a widow's mite. But can a poor typist really do wrong if she takes home a few office supplies from Ford Motor Company?

"They will never miss it" lets such persons sleep well. But we are not interested in the self-solace of petty thieves. We are interested in moral warrant for theft in general.

What would life be like if *everyone* were free to steal whenever he was sure he would not hurt his victim? I cannot justify my own action if I am unwilling to justify everyone who does the same thing under very similar circumstances. But precisely when I make such an allowance, the premise of not hurting the victim becomes doubtful. For if everyone were morally permitted to steal, the victims *would* be hurt. Employee pilfering and customer shoplifting are already the final cost that sends some firms into bankruptcy. In short, the more people who adopt this argument, the more likely its premise will be invalid. If everyone follows it, there will be no "harmless" stealing.

It is not only those whose goods are stolen who are hurt by theft. Most firms anticipate such losses and compensate for them by charging more for their products. So it is the poor who get hurt most by "harmless theft." But the whole community is hurt. Trust is destroyed; people treat each other as potential crooks. Managers employ spies to snoop on the workers. Customers at a clothing store submit to the indignity of a television camera in the changing rooms. Executives must make long reports to bureaucrats whose job is to police corporate morals. And thus civility in a trusting society gives place to surveillance of one another in a distrusting society. And we all pay for being watched by strangers.

Stealing to meet a human need
Human needs come in all kinds. There are trivial needs and urgent ones. People need things because of their own failure and they need things through no fault of their own. A justification for stealing, if it is to be adequate, must cover all kinds.

An unemployed father is arrested the day before Christmas for stealing children's clothing which a department store had discarded into its trash bin. A vice president hooked on gambling and hounded for bad debts is arrested for embezzling $20,000 from his bank. Both men needed something more than its owner did. But the situations are different enough to give each theft its own moral hue. We justify the poor father; we may understand the embezzler, but we do not justify him.

If we were to make a moral calculation of stealing based on needs, only a divine catalog would help us. A drug addict needs some heroin more than a pharmacy does. A young man six months behind on his car payments needs cash more than his employer does. In his own eyes, every thief needs the thing he steals more than its owner needed it. Yet there are real and important differences. The need to feed a drug habit counts less than the need to feed a hungry child. The need to pay gambling debts does not count as much as the need to pay medical bills. What we do not have is a universal standard for testing when my need for something justifies stealing from you to satisfy it. Lacking a standard of comparison, we are left with the conclusion that "need" is not a workable rule of thumb for righteous stealing. We may be able to recognize the Jean Valjeans of the world when we see them; we cannot define them in advance.

Stealing to avert a greater evil

We can easily imagine situations in which stealing might avert a serious evil. A penniless man believes his wife will die without medicine, so he breaks into a pharmacy to steal it. A company will suffer if a competitor breaks through with a new product; so it steals the competitors' secrets to protect its workers' jobs. Daniel Ellsberg was sure that the President had deceived the nation about the war in Vietnam; he stole the Pentagon Papers to prevent such a tragic deception from happening again. A relief agency wants to distribute food to starving Cambodians, but vast piles of food tied up by political bungling lie rotting at the docks; its agents steal the food from the government warehouses in order to prevent hundreds of children from starving. What these situations have in common is that a person breaks the rule against stealing in the belief that not to steal would cause more harm than stealing.

This test stands apart from the others in a few important

206 ways. First, it is an exceptional test. We are not called on every day to avoid evil by stealing. Second, people who respond to crises by stealing are not likely to become habitual thieves; the Daniel Ellsbergs of the world are not likely to get in the habit of larceny. Third, these thefts are usually less selfish than the others; people who steal to avert great evil are not usually trying to line their pockets. So the risks may be affordable.

Even here, however, we need to hedge our bets. What we want to know is not merely whether stealing can ever be justified, but whether there is a general guideline by which everyone can tell *when* stealing is justified. Does this test provide it?

To use this test to justify stealing, we must make two comparisons. The first is between the actual evils we choose between: the evil done by stealing and the evil averted by stealing. Second, we must compare risks: the *certainty* of the evil done by stealing and the *possibility* of averting evil. So we must compare *certain* smaller evils (stealing) with *possible* greater evil (averted by stealing). And this makes the comparison very hard, especially if you or the people you love are the ones who are spared the evil.

Sometimes it is easy. Letting a person die seems worse than stealing a thing. Here the evils are so uneven that we can probably concede a good deal on the question of how sure we are of saving a life. We may even be willing to give odds: if we have a 50-50 chance of saving a human life by stealing, we are justified in doing so. The greater the stakes, the greater risks we can take.

To concede this point is probably not to make human society vulnerable to a plague of larceny. But have we, by doing so, lost control of the situation? What about relieving any human suffering through stealing? The Robin Hoods of the world cry out for moral support.

The test of human suffering is, obviously, too flexible to be of much help. What sort of suffering, and how much of it, can counterbalance the evil of stealing? A population's pangs of undernourishment is an enormous evil—and most of us would not flinch at stealing if necessary to relieve it. But even here, the scale has not flopped totally to one side. Would any relief agency want the relief programs of the world to be reduced to steal as steal can? Would it not be a horrendous evil if relief of human misery had to be done through plundering and pilfering. Thus, even a concession to the relief agency seeking to feed undernourished Cambodians through a single spectacular theft needs watching.

The Eighth Commandment supports a morality of trust without which human life gradually slides into barbarity. The stakes are high, especially when we confront an erosion of common respect for property which may cause the cliff of civility to slide into a sea of distrust and deceit. For this reason, any justification for stealing must be weighty and clear if it is to overrule the moral commandment. We need not blind ourselves to moments when deepest need compels people to take something that belongs to someone else. What we have to see is that these are exceptions which underscore the rule, not weaken it.

Almost every common test for justifying stealing is unworkable as a general rule. Just one—life versus theft—sounds like a workable test, but we had to add some qualifiers to that one too. The conclusion is that we must go through life with a firm bias against stealing, a bias furnished by the divine commandment and supported by reason. It is a strong bias, rooted in the very design for humane existence. It should not be watered down easily; the results may be more than we bargained for.

C. THE MORAL IMPERATIVE OF SHARING

The law of respect for property gives no peace to those who have property as long as there are poor people who have none. We have seen that our need for certain minimal property belongs to our being human. This means that to be wholly without property in this world is to lack something we need to be body-persons in community. Therefore, the presence of poverty-stricken people is intolerable within the law of respect for property.

We have seen that none of us who has property has absolute moral property rights. We have property so that we can be caretakers of God's earth and God's people. This law gives a more particular content to the fundamental principle of love. Love requires us—and enables us—to move out toward our neighbors in ways that bring them at least what they have coming to them by virtue of their presence among us as human beings. The Eighth Commandment prevents us from spiritualizing the law of love; it forces us to embody love in action which puts material things in the hands and around the bodies of poor people.

We can know the right means to help the poor get the property they have coming to them only by considering the available options. Within limits, we can say that the right way is simply the most effective way. But those limits are very important. It may be effective to lop off rich people's heads. A revolutionary regime may share property among all the poor people by means of unlimited violence against the propertied rich; the means is suspect because such violence in the long run may cause a greater evil than poverty. A dole method of giving property to the poor at the cost of their own human dignity is suspect because the loss of dignity may be worse than poverty.

But the trade-offs are seldom simple. We need wisdom and intelligence to choose means that are both effective in the short run and respectful of humanity in the long run. But the commandment hovers over all our reasoning as the law of life, and it confronts all people with God's design for a human community where every person has a right to have and to get what he needs to live a human life as an image of God.

QUESTIONS FOR DISCUSSION

1. Do you believe that the commandment against stealing requires us to do what we can to help people get the property they have a right to have?

2. Do you agree that man's identity with things, his calling to care for this world and his need of things in order to live, gives him a moral right to own things as his/her private possession?

3. Do you agree that stealing is wrong because it tends to destroy community? Or is it wrong simply because an owner loses something that belongs to him?

4. Do you agree that the lands we call ours probably began their trek to modern ownership as "stolen goods"?

5. Do you agree that my moral rights to own and do what I please with property are rightly limited by the society I happen to live in?

6. Do you agree that private ownership of things is neither intrinsically necessary nor intrinsically bad?

7. Do you believe that the conspicuous consumption of the very rich is a violation of morality—or do you think we have a right to eat or wear or live in anything we can afford? Why?

8. Do you believe that if there is not enough land, food, and things available to be shared among all people, we lose our moral right to keep or consume what others need to survive?

9. Do you believe that since no one has an absolute right to own any particular thing, governments have a right to take from the very rich and redistribute it to the poor?

10. Do you agree that it is morally wrong to steal something even the owner does not need?

11. Do you agree that it is morally right to steal things to save human life? Heal sick people? Feed hungry people?

RESPECT FOR TRUTHFULNESS ⑧

"Thou Shalt Not Bear False Witness"

In this commandment, the Lord God bans lying—a poisoner of human communication, a destroyer of trust, and a dehumanizer of our neighbors. Lying breaks the tissue of faith that holds every human community together. Lies diminish everyone we deceive because by lying we treat persons as if they had no right to share in the mutual trust without which we cannot be human together. In marriage and commerce, in politics and law, everywhere people must trust each other, lying casts doubt on the survival of humane and civilized relationships. When we haggle over the sale of a used car, tell a dying child his real condition, whisper promises into a lover's ear, or negotiate an arms treaty, we are bound by the primal duty of truthfulness.

Still, the Ninth Commandment sounds like an alien echo rumbling from another world into an age in which deceit is almost a life-style. In our society the plain truth often puts one at a distinct disadvantage. The "credibility gap" that once alienated the public from people in high places now seems to separate us from one another in all walks of life. Americans lie on their income tax return to the tune of millions of dollars a year. Doctors fake reports in order to profit from Medicare patients. Prize athletes at great universities are kept eligible for competition through bogus credits and forged transcripts of academic records. Children soon acquire the cynical assumption that lying is the normal tack for TV advertisers. In the words of a *Time* magazine essay, ours is "a huckstering, show-bizzy world, jangling with hype, hullabaloo, and hooey, bull, baloney, and bamboozlement." After a while, people tend to expect not to hear the truth anymore; in 1976, a national poll showed that 69 percent of Americans believed that the country's leaders had, over the last decade, consistently lied to the people.[1]

Into this context comes the word from the Lord: "Don't lie." For most of us truthfulness comes very hard. Pascal observed that no one should expect to meet more than three or four honest people in a lifetime. Honesty is an almost superhuman

212   task, more like the promised end of life's moral purging than an
easy moral accomplishment.

The human heart, the Bible pessimistically asserts, has been
"deceitful above all things" (Jer. 17:9) since Satan, the father of
lies, deceived the world with his blandishments (Rev. 12:9). But
it is hard to be honest, not simply because we have cheating
hearts, but also because our individualistic society offers so many
incentives to lying.[2] And there is another factor: there are so
many good reasons to lie, compelling and loving reasons, that
we are seduced into lying, not for ours so much as for our neighbor's sake.

In examining the meaning of the Ninth Commandment for
life in our times, then, we must be keenly sensitive to the tough
time truthfulness has with us. Rather than parade pious slogans
about the evil of lying, we shall probe the profound reasons why
God commands truthfulness and the plausible reasons we often
give for lying. First we shall ask *what* the commandment tells us
we ought to do and not to do. Then we will try to see *why* the
commandment lays truthfulness on the human race as a moral
duty. What makes it a reasonable law of life? For the rest, we
will take a hard look at many sorts of lies we tell and the sorts
of justifications we give for them.

I. WHAT DOES THE NINTH COMMANDMENT REQUIRE?

A. THE COMMANDMENT TELLS US NOT TO LIE

The ancient Israelite heard the Ninth Commandment as a rule
against lying in court, or, as it was called, the Gate.[3] A false legal
suit here could deprive a person of his goods, his land, his reputation, even his life. An accused person could not hire a shrewd
defense attorney to cross-examine false witnesses and perhaps
trick the truth out of them. He had to plead his own case and,
while he may not have had a fool for a lawyer, he did have to
rely on the judge's knack for sizing up character. Everything
could hang in the balance while the prince or the judge drew on
his own personal ability to recognize an honest person when he
saw one. In the last citadel which ancient society offered for the
weak to seek protection against the strong, the simple from the
crafty, the poor from the rich, the one thing needful was a willingness to tell the truth. No wonder, then, that the Gate is

singled out for cleansing from deceit and calumny: "Speak ye every man the truth to his neighbor, execute the judgment of truth and peace in your gates . . ." (Zech. 8:16, 17).

The command against false witness is a specific example of God's total hatred of deception. In the courtroom the wrong of lying is transparent: it can ruin a brother. But the Bible's horror at deceit extends to all human communication. All lies, in the biblical view, are the vomit of the Devil; he spews deceit over the cosmos (John 8:44). Falsehood is the demonic obscenity of the age of darkness (Eph. 4:22-25; Col. 3:9, 10). The redeemed community, therefore, manifests itself first of all as a community of sincerity and truth: "Therefore, putting away falsehood, let everyone speak the truth with his neighbor, for we are members one of another" (Eph. 4:25). It should come as no surprise, then, that it was lying which first spoiled the life of the blossoming Christian community, nor that it should have been answered by a bolt of sudden death. Ananias and Sapphira's lie to the Holy Spirit was an intolerable offense, for the lie broke the bond of unity in the new creation (Acts 5:1-11). And so, we may conclude that the commandment, while directed specifically to the witness in the stand, points its compelling mandate to all who speak the human language.

Deceiving our neighbors

I lie whenever I intend to deceive my neighbor. Deception is the heart of all lies. There are two currents flowing in every lie: one between my mind and my message and one between my message and my neighbor. I lie when I purposely corrupt the current between my message and my neighbor. "Message" includes all the ways we express ourselves—gestures, symbols, facial movements, and silences. All are "words" that carry thoughts to the haven of a neighbor's mind. The key to lying is an intention to deceive a neighbor with our "words."

Of course, a person may not be lying when his words are untrue. He may be mistaken or deceived or merely ignorant. Nor is a person necessarily lying when a listener is misled. The fault may be with a listener who wants to misconstrue or is not able to understand what is said. We can also lie when our words are true to fact. Penny Baxter shows how. He wanted—in *The Yearling*—to get rid of a worthless bear dog he had. So he set out to trade the dog to Lenn Forrester. In that country, a man

214   was expected to brag about his hunting dog, stringing out his hunting prowess on a line of lies. The more you bragged, the more everybody knew you were lying. Penny brought his dog to Lenn's place and said: "He ain't wuth a good twist o' t'bacey. . . . Sorriest bear dog I ever . . . followered."

Lenn perked up: "I never heered a man run down his own dog that-a-way." Next day, Lenn carried a fine shotgun over to Penny Baxter's house. "Don't argue with me. When I want a dog, I want a dog. Take the gun for him or by God, I'll come and steal him." So the trade was made. Penny got rid of his dog and made a good deal. But his conscience began to flutter.

His son reassured him: "You told the truth, Pa."

"Yes," said Penny, "my words was straight, but my intention was as crooked as the Ocklawaha River."

We can err without lying, and we can lie without erring. The crux is in the intent. Words we aim at a neighbor's mind with a deceiving intent are lying words. Deliberate masking of the mind—this is the lie that is prohibited by the commandment.

Deceiving ourselves

If we ought not deceive others, it seems reasonable that we ought not deceive ourselves either. Again, I am not talking about being misinformed. All of us sometimes turn truth away because we do not understand it or we are not persuaded of it. Who blames the people before Galileo for not believing that the earth traveled around the sun? A ten-year-old boy is not morally wrong to believe that romantic love is absurd.

Self-deception is a fine art. It is a balancing trick in which we hover between knowing and refusing to know. In one corner of our mind we know that something is true; in another we deny it. Or one moment we know something and the next we deny to ourselves what we just knew. We see it for just an instant, long enough to feel its threat, and we close it off. We "know," but we refuse to know.

I am talking about what we see today, not about suppressing into our subconscious a terrible experience from early days. A wife sees clear evidence that her husband is carrying on with another woman. He often comes home late with feeble excuses; there are strange motel charges on his credit card and mysterious phone calls. But she knows that "Fred is faithful." When the truth cannot be covered any more, she says: "What a fool I was.

I should have known." But she did know; she just told herself a lie. A smart doctor sees all the symptoms of his own alcoholism. He knows. But he persuades himself that it cannot be so. The pain is too great to bear.

Religion is fertile ground for self-deception. Believers, for instance, are tempted to deceive themselves about the reality of evil. Tragic horrors in life challenge our faith in a good and powerful God. The horror itself demands to be known as evil, and it is, for a moment. Then fear crowds out the thought that evil can really exist where a good and powerful God is in charge of one's life. We "know" that it is evil; but we refuse to know it. So we call it a "blessing in disguise"—an "apparent evil" that one day will be seen as a God-given reason for greater heights of praise. Thus, we deceive ourselves when we refuse to look evil in the face and call it real, horrible, and against the will of God.

If believers are tempted to deceive themselves about evil, unbelievers are equally tempted to deceive themselves about God. In Paul's eyes, unbelief is at its core an exercise in self-deception. God is so close to every person that denying him is like denying the sun at high noon. He scratches at every person's soul. He displays himself unmistakably in creation (Rom. 1:20). He is there, in full view; there is no escaping him. But many sinful humans refuse to "see" him even though they cannot help seeing him; they know and they refuse to know. At some moment that slips by them unfelt, they choose not to know what they cannot help knowing. "So they are without excuse; for although they knew God they did not honor him as God" (Rom. 1:20-21). Unbelief is not merely a point of view, nor mere ignorance, but self-deception, a refusal to face up to the truth that lies plain before the heart.

B. THE COMMANDMENT TELLS US TO BE TRUTHFUL

Speaking the truth

A commandment that forbids me to lie compels me to be truthful. It obligates me to be faithful to what I think, what I believe, what I feel—and so to be faithful to the person with whom I am communicating. I may not always be in control of the truth about things, but I am always obligated to give my neighbor an authentic impression of what is on my mind. Mind and message

216 must be one so that through the message my neighbor knows my mind. Truthfulness, like lying, is not a matter of accuracy but of intention.

The commandment tells us to speak truthfully whenever it is appropriate for us to speak at all. Respect for truthfulness does not compel us to reveal our minds to everyone or on every occasion. The Ninth Commandment assumes, no doubt, a situation that calls on us to speak. It does not ask us to tell the people at the next table in a restaurant that their manners are repulsive. It does not obligate a nurse to contradict a physician at a sick person's bedside. Nor does it require me to divulge all of my feelings to a stranger on the bus. We are called to speak the truth in any situation in which we have a responsibility to communicate at all.

Further, the command requires only a revelation that is pertinent to the situation. A politician ought to speak the truth about public matters as he sees them; he does not need to tell us how he feels about his wife. A doctor ought to tell me the truth, as he understands it, about my health; he does not need to tell me his views on universal health insurance. A minister ought to preach the truth, as he sees it, about the gospel; he does not need to tell the congregation what he feels about the choir director. The commandment does not call us to be garrulous blabbermouths. Truthfulness is demanded from us about the things that we ought to speak about at all.

The commandment sends us into all human relationships with a bias toward truthfulness. If the tender lies that keep communications smooth are morally right, they must be justified against the sweeping commandment that requires truthfulness in an unqualified way. Liars always have the burden of proof.

An avalanche of qualifications falls over the commandment at the start. Surely, we wonder, the moral law does not rule out a good joke, the high art of fantasy, or the low art of the tall tale. Does it rule out the acting profession?[4] What about bargaining at a bazaar, where the rules of the game call for suspension of truthfulness? Could poker survive if candor were an absolute moral law? Must every wife tell a boring husband that he is a clod? Ought a parishioner, on leaving the Sunday service, tell the pastor his sermon was a tedious blend of trivia and platitude? I note these qualifications only to remind the reader that we do not expect each other to live by an absolute code of truthfulness.

Being the truth

Truthfulness is a straight line between what we say and what we *are* as much as between what we say and what we *think*. It touches our being as it touches our thinking. We all draw profiles of ourselves with the messages we send to others—no matter whether the media be words or actions. The moral question is whether we intend the profile to look like what we really are.

Truthfulness about what we are may be even more important than truthfulness about what we think. Being a hypocrite seems worse to most people than merely being a liar. Phoniness, pretense, dissimulation—these are awesome accusations against any human life. Jesus scourged the shams of his day: "You are like whitewashed tombs, outwardly appearing beautiful, but full of dead men's bones and all unclean within. So you also appear outwardly righteous to man, but within you are full of hypocrisy and iniquity" (Matt. 23:27, 28). Being "full of iniquity" may be the common lot of sinners; but acting out a charade of virtue makes iniquity doubly nauseous. Satan's pernicious influence is at its most dangerous when he parades as an angel of light. And when those who do not really share the faith disguise themselves as Christian apostles, they have Satan as their model. They are "false apostles, deceitful workmen" and their "end will correspond to their deeds" (2 Cor. 11:13-15). Pretending to be something you are not is the epitome of untruthfulness.

Pretending is making believe we are what we do not intend to be. We must not confuse our intentions with our feelings, however. I may intend to be hopeful, positive, and helpful, but at any moment I may feel like a hopeless, negative, person and want to help no one but myself. What I must be true to is my intention, not my feeling. So I am not hypocritical when I act hopeful and helpful even though I do not feel that way. I am hypocritical only when I deceive people into thinking I am what I do not intend to be.

Being true to what we intend to be does not require us to reveal all that we are in the corridors of our hearts. Just as we are not obligated to tell everything, we are not required to act out everything. In forbidding deception the commandment does not demand full exposure. To decide in the name of truthfulness that our inner hate might just as well be actual murder, that our inner lust might just as well be actual rape, or for that matter that we need to rip people into shreds with words just to be honest with our feelings would be mad, not authentic. The place to purge ourselves of meanness is not at the coffee table, but the altar. The one person who can digest all that we are is not our curious neighbor but our gracious Creator.

Truthfulness of being is an ideal we struggle toward. It is hard for us to be whole—inside and out—because we are complicated and confused within. We do not express our real selves because we do not know who our selves are. In a sense we are all like the demon-possessed man whom Jesus healed. When Jesus asked him to identify himself, he said: "My name is Legion, for we are many" (Mark 5:9). Dmitri Karamazov, feeling like a man torn apart, said: "Man is too complicated, I'd have made him simpler." How fatuous was Polonius' admonition to Laertes: "To thine own self be true...!" What Hamlet cried for was someone to tell him who his own self was. We are all only on the way toward our real selves. On the way, as the hymnwriter put it, we are assailed by "many a conflict, many a doubt."

We are also hypocrites for reasons less innocent than our complexity. We are fakes for profit. We make believe because we are afraid of being disliked for what we really are. We are phonies because we hate the reality of what we are. My point, however, is that even with the best intention truthfulness is hard to come by for mixed-up human beings.

Seeking the truth

The positive law that lies beneath the specific commandment thrusts us into active defense of truthfulness for the sake of our neighbor. As a concrete form of justice, read in the light of love, the Ninth Commandment compels us to "defend and promote the honor and reputation of my neighbor" (Heidelberg Catechism, Lord's Day 43). It obligates us to come to the defense of people whose lives are hurt by gossip, innuendo, and rumor. When we hear a story that demeans or maligns another person, we need to expose it. When we are privy to slander, we must refute it. When our friends pass along half truths that distort the image of another person, we must supply the other half if we can. We must, in short, expend ourselves to protect people from untruth about themselves. This is the work of love; for love not only "rejoices in the truth" for one's own self, but protects the truth for others.

Listening for the truth

The final moment in our clumsy try for truthfulness comes when our message finds its way into a listener's mind. But what he hears is not what comes from our mouths. Before he hears, he filters the message through an internal grid created by his own past impressions and current feelings. In the closet of his own subconscious, ghosts long hidden interfere with our message before it gets to his mind. By the time he hears our message, its shape has been slightly changed. What he hears is never exactly what we say. Thus our truthfulness can become his falsehood.

And so we must listen to how our neighbor responds to what we say. If we do not listen we cannot know what he has heard, and if we do not know what he has heard we really do not know whether we have been effectively truthful. We cannot speak and run if we want to be truthful.

Listening is a patient and delicate art. It is not as if we can listen only once and be done with it. A dialogue is necessary, in which we listen many times over, because after our neighbor responds to what we have said, we filter that response through our own interior grid. A counterpoint to Paul's "love rejoices in the truth," is this: "love listens long."

II. WHY MUST WE BE TRUTHFUL?

Truthfulness is neither neat embroidery on the fabric of life nor a disagreeable chore laid on us by an unsympathetic deity. The law of truthfulness emerges from our character as rational creatures who are fully what we are only in communication with each other. When we infuse our communication with lies, we are not only using a devious tactic for getting along; we are denying who and what we are as the images of him who "cannot lie" (Titus 1:2).

In this section I shall try to illumine that special quality of our lives which makes lying wrong and truthfulness a primal obligation. Two possibilities are open to us. One concentrates on the speaker's words. On this view our words must correspond with our thoughts because only then is the rational nature of speech respected. Another way of putting this first option is "truthfulness for the sake of truthfulness." The other possibility concentrates on the relationship between the speaker and the neighbor: our words must correspond with our thoughts in order to keep a right relationship between persons. In other words, "truthfulness for the sake of the neighbor." Much depends on which of these explanations we favor.

A. TRUTHFULNESS FOR THE SAKE OF TRUTHFULNESS

Can truthfulness—or for that matter a lie—be achieved by a person alone on a desert island? Those who define the essence of truthfulness as a correspondence between what we think and what we say would answer this question affirmatively.

Correspondence and contradiction, the core concepts in this view of truth and lying, are notions crucial to sheer rationality. Behind them is the portrait of the truth-telling God, whose revelation always corresponds with his mind, whose words always match his thoughts. His is truthfulness itself; he cannot lie (Titus 1:2; Heb. 6:18). His word is truth, not only because it speaks accurately of all things, but because it faithfully reflects his *thinking* about things.

The more we fix on truthfulness for its own sake, the more absolutist we are likely to be about truth-telling. A lie, said Kant, "violates the source of law"—the source being rationality—and it is this fact about lying which makes truthfulness "an unconditional duty which holds in all circumstances."[5] In all circumstances? Yes, as the famous Kantian example went, even if a lie might save your friend from an assassin. The fault of lying comes with how things hang together logically; the world of rational consistency falls apart at our feet if we allow for any lies at all— and the death of consistency is worse than the death of a friend.

It isn't easy to be an absolutist about lying in the face of the pressures of real life. Most of the great theological teachers who were inclined to be absolutists conceded that some lies were at least much more wrong than other lies. If you lied about God, in Augustine's view, you were the worst sort of liar, far worse, for example, than if you lied to save another person's soul.[6] St. Thomas, too, divided lies according to one's reasons for lying, and agreed that we can excuse a useful lie,[7] maybe even a lie told for the fun of it. But neither Augustine nor Aquinas would concede that a good intention could turn a lie into a good act. John Calvin seems to agree; the Reformer could not quite accept Rahab's lie even "though it was done for a good purpose." Anybody who thinks that even her noble lie could get God's approval, said Calvin, has not reckoned with the fact that *any* lie, even when it helps people, is "contrary to the nature of God."[8]

Every absolutist struggles with the conflicts between the demands of love and the rigors of truthfulness in real life. Some absolutists take a way out called "mental reservation." It is possible, sometimes, to defend even the biblical heroes against the charge of lying by showing they were actually telling the truth as *they* saw it. John Murray, as absolutistic as Christians tend to be, defended Elisha's lie (2 Kings 6) by claiming that he was only practicing the martial art of mental reservation. A band of Syrian soldiers came to the city of Dothan to capture Elisha. But the Lord smote them with blindness just as they arrived at the gates. Elisha, in on the Lord's strategy, went out to meet them. The soldiers asked him for help in finding Elisha. Oh, said the honest prophet, "this is not the way, and this is not the city; follow me, and I will bring you to the man whom you seek." So Elisha brought the trusting soldiers to an Israelite camp, where they were of course captured.

An unskilled interpreter of this account might say, "Elisha lied to the soldiers in self-defense. Why not?" But Murray argues that Elisha did not lie. He merely took the truth on a detour. He was, after all, standing just outside the city gates. Thus he was being literally accurate when, pointing to the ground they were standing on, he said: "This is not the city you seek." Moreover, he kept his promise; he brought them to the man they sought—after he had brought them to their enemy. Elisha told the truth, even though only he knew the truth he told. So, says Murray, Elisha's words were "strangely and wonderfully true." Using mental reservation to defend Elisha will sound like flimflammery to some readers; for Murray, it is a serious defense of the absolutist view of truthfulness.[9]

One gets the sense that a mental reservation is a dodge from truthfulness. That you deceive someone for a good cause poses no moral problem. For the absolutist it does not matter that your intent is as crooked as the Ocklawaha River if your words are consistent with whatever you have in your private thoughts.

222 B. TRUTHFULNESS FOR THE SAKE
OF THE NEIGHBOR

The primary reason for truthfulness, in my opinion, is in
the point of view of truthfulness for the sake of the neighbor,
in the relationship between the speaker and the listener. We
should not think of truthfulness as consistency between our mind
and our message so much as honesty between us and our neighbor. Lying is less a discrepancy between our thoughts and our
words than it is a deception of our neighbor. Of course, consistency is important, for without it we would not have honesty,
but the moral weight falls on the effects our inconsistency has
on people who expect honesty from us and do not get it.

Three things may be said in favor of a view of truthfulness
that sets the neighbor above consistency as the reason behind
the command to tell the truth. First, God's truthfulness is primarily trustworthiness, according to the Bible. Second, life in
human community depends on the ability of people to trust each
other. Third, personal freedom depends on trust.

1. *Truthfulness, for God, is equivalent to trustworthiness.* "Let
your Yea be Yea and your Nay, Nay"—or, in other words, say
what you really mean, and no more (James 5:12). The model of
such speech is God himself (2 Cor. 1:20), of whom one thing is
true above all else: he can be depended on to mean what he
says. This side of truthfulness evokes words like loyalty, commitment, faithfulness, and promise-keeping. When I speak truthfully in this sense I not only say what I think today, but I will
stake my own life on it for tomorrow. Therefore my listener can
trust that his expectations will come true.

In a heated passage in which Paul is debating God's character
with his Jewish opponents, he makes it clear that the core of
God's truthfulness is his promise-keeping. Israel did not keep
its promises, but God kept his. What, then, if "some were unfaithful? Does their unfaithfulness nullify the faithfulness of
God?" Paul thunders his answer: "By no means!" Then he suddenly changes his language. "Faithfulness" is changed to "true"
and "faithlessness" becomes "false." "Let God be true though
every man be false" (Rom. 3:3, 4). For Paul, truthfulness and
faithfulness were one and the same. Thus, the divine model
signals a basic concern in truth-telling. It is not sheer consistency
between word and thought, but faithfulness and the trust that
people can put in it.[10]

2. *Community cannot survive without trust.* The character of human community is a root reason God commands us to be truthful. Speaking of the church, which is meant to be the model of community life, Paul makes it quite clear: "Therefore, putting away falsehood, let everyone speak the truth with his neighbor, for we are members one of another" (Eph. 4:25). The reason for truthfulness lies in our relationship with one another. Our neighbor deserves the truth from us as a fellow-member of our community.

Imagine a society in which no one trusted another to keep a promise, in which every leader was expected to lie as a matter of course, in which every teacher was suspected as an academic cheat and every preacher a moral fraud, in which contracts were expected to be honored only when they paid well and a friend's word was no better than a cigarette advertisement. No person in such a society could ever confide in a friend or seek help from a counselor. No partner could ever bank on the loyalty of another. No one could make decisions in assurance of having the facts in hand. No one could be certain of his neighbor's next move. Life would be brutalized. Without trust, we change from a community to a pack, from a society to a gang.

3. *The neighbor needs to trust in order to be free.* My neighbor loses his freedom if he cannot trust me. To be free in making decisions, we need to trust that we are deciding between real options. But if I lie to my neighbor, I take reality away from him. I force him to decide on the basis of falsehood, of unreality. If I tell a person who wants to buy my car that it is in spendid mechanical shape, although I am selling it in fact because it needs an expensive valve job, I rob him of freedom to decide on the basis of reality. If you pretend that you are pleased with your daughter's report card when in fact you are furious because she has not been studying and her grades show it, you rob her of the freedom to respond to your anger and force her to respond to a charade instead. Thus, lying demeans our neighbors. We treat them as non-persons, whose freedom is of no consequence.

This is why my neighbor has a right to trust me to be truthful; he cannot be free without that trust.[11]

Now we must face this question: if we are truthful for the sake of others, may we lie for their sake too?

"What harm would it do," asked Luther, "if a man told a good strong lie for the sake of the good and for the Christian

224   Church? . . . a useful lie, a helpful lie. Such lies would not be against God; he would accept them."[12] A helpful lie? A useful lie? Luther brings a new dimension into our thinking. The commandment forbids lies *against* people, lies that hurt people. But what of lies that help people—"at the gate" or anywhere else?

Have we made truthfulness optional, to be used when it helps and ignored when a lie will do better? Have we, at this point, accepted the utilitarian point of view that "when deception is designed to benefit the person deceived, common sense seems to concede that it may sometimes be right?"[13] Bonhoeffer tells the story of a brutal teacher who, in front of the class, asked a young boy: "Is it true that your father still comes home drunk every night?" Suppose that the boy had neither wit nor courage to tell the teacher that it was none of his business. Suppose that, as a loving son and frightened pupil, he said: "No sir, it is not true."[14] We would all be quick to excuse the boy. But do we have grounds for believing it was right for him—and for everyone in his situation—to lie?

III. HOW TO BE TRUTHFUL
IN THE CONFLICTS OF LIFE

While the commandment is rooted in the thesis that human community dies without truthfulness and that lying hurts people, life gives seductive hints that individuals are sometimes better off with a little bit of lying. Can we respect truthfulness and also concede that now and then it is right and good to tell a lie? And if we grant the possibility of justified lying, can we find guidelines to help us recognize a good lie when we hear it? My plan in this section is to examine a few of the more commonly used justifications for lying, to see if they really do tell us when a lie is a good thing to tell.

We want to be clear about what we are looking for. We are, in the first place, looking for good lies, lies which we can thank God we have the wisdom to tell. We are not talking now about *excusable* lies; nearly everyone is willing to temper judgment on lies told under pressing circumstances and with loving reasons. Nor are we referring to *forgivable* lies; almost any lie is forgivable, I suppose, depending on the grace of the forgiver. What we are looking for is a species of lie that we can call a "just lie"—

the kind you need never ask to be excused or forgiven for telling.

In the second place, we are looking for a workable test to identify just lies, a test that will help reasonable people know ahead of time whether the lie they consider telling will be a good lie or not. We are not merely seeking examples of some lies that feel good for us, but a reliable criterion for separating justified lies—the kind we are permitted to tell—from bad lies—the kind we ought not tell. From the standpoint of the Ninth Commandment, our prejudice is against any lie. The burden of proof is always on the liar.

Let us begin by identifying four categories of lies of which we tend to think rather well, which we commonly tell, and which are generally tolerated by others. One test of a justified lie, then, may be whether it fits any of these categories.

A. THE "HARMLESS LIE"

Some lies merely oil the bearings of social relationships. We use them to reduce the friction in our rubbing against other people. They smooth the wrinkles in our social fabric.

1. *Polite lies*. A woman is invited to a party she does not want to attend. She responds: "I'd love to come, but I am engaged on the 15th." A crude guest leaves after an insufferable visit; his hostess says to him: "We do look forward to seeing you again." A person begins a letter to a man he despises, "Dear Ralph," and ends it, "Cordially yours." All of this deception is well meant, not to deceive a neighbor, but only to keep unpleasantness from becoming impolite.

2. *Euphemisms*. In a world of rough-edged reality, we like to soften the corners with words that do not cut so easily into the flesh. We "terminate a pregnancy" instead of "kill a fetus." We have "meaningful relationships" instead of "commit adultery." Pornographers cover up the ugliness of their business by calling their shops "adult bookstores." And, of course, the ultimate euphemism was calling the Nazi killing of six million Jews "the final solution." One could argue that euphemisms are not really lies but, as Mary Poppins sang, the "spoonful of sugar" that "helps the medicine go down."

3. *Exaggerations*. We often inflate our words, not to hurt anybody, but to make them feel better and, maybe, to spice up

our own conversation. An average woman becomes a "beautiful person." An ordinary sermon becomes an "inspiration." Someone tries rather hard and he is credited with an "incredible effort." We sprinkle compliments to our friends with "Sensational!" and "Fantastic!" to describe what are only passable performances. Anything less than "terrific" has these days become a failure. I once returned from a vacation and was asked if I had enjoyed myself. Yes, I said, I had a pretty good time. My inquirer responded: "What went wrong?"

4. *Glosses.* When we put a little phony luster on an ugly reality, or pull a false cover over a wretched fact, we are glossing. Uncle Joe is a lush; but Father tells the children: "Uncle Joe is lonely and once in a while he drinks too much." The company has suffered disastrous losses; but the president tells the stockholders: "The company is in good shape after some seasonal reverses." A child is being told she was adopted; her mother tells her, "You are special, because you are a chosen child." We make life a little easier for the people we deal with by making believe, for a moment, that the walls are off-white when, in fact, they are sad grey.[15]

The harm of "harmless lies"

Are "white lies" really harmless? Are they *as a class*, spread through our communication, lies that do not hurt anyone? And, if they might hurt somebody, is the total harm they do to the human community less than the harm that the plain truth would do? We must judge the "white lie" in terms of its tendency, its cumulative impact on people, not just in terms of a single lie. Let us see if we can get a sense of the trade-off involved. Here are some possible negative factors to consider when we try to justify the harmless lie.

1. *Erosion of our "sense of truthfulness."* The person who uses the harmless lie as an escape route from every uncomfortable conversation can soon become addicted to lying. If you always try to make people around you feel good by exaggerated praise, if you always soothe anger by glossing over whatever it was that made you angry, if you always rescue yourself from socially tight situations by lying about your feelings, you are likely to develop a habit and you risk losing your feel for being truthful, your sense of the claim truthfulness has on you. Your conscience will be "sicklied o'er" with the "pale cast" of harmless lies.

2. *Evasion of reality*. The "white lie" is to communication what Valium is to stress. Used in emergencies, they might be detours around trouble we are not equipped to cope with today. But as a habit, they both become patterns of evasion. We use them, not to give us time to catch our breath so that we can confront trouble tomorrow, but to live as though trouble did not trouble us. The habitual white liar is a person who "cops out" of risk and unpleasantness; he deals with interrelational pain by freezing persons into the numbness of habitual hypocrisy.

3. *Moral handcuffing*. The "white lie" ties the deceived person down to the lie and prevents him from a free response to reality. Preventing a small pain for now, the "white lie" often causes more pain later on. A writer gets a manuscript back from a publisher with the gentle lie: "Your work is too sophisticated for our readers." The "white lie" is just enough of a bromide to discourage the writer from the painful job of rewriting a boring book. A husband passes through twenty years of secret misery in his marriage, afraid to share the truth of his discontent with his wife. Finally he leaves her, never having allowed her the freedom of painful encounter with the truth about herself. "White lies" that start out as social crutches tend to become shackles.

4. *Nurture of cynicism*. The white lie as a way of life gradually creates cynicism in both liar and deceived. Gradually nobody trusts the other to tell the truth. When we have told "white lies" often enough we assume that others do the same to us. The game of life, we assume, calls for both people in a conversation to be gentle liars. But does it stop there? Once you assume that I lie in polite circles, can you trust me in business or politics?

Not that every white lie is an evil thing. But the burden of proof in justifying the "harmless lie" is on the one telling the lie, who must show that "white lies" are—as a class of lie—justifiable. I think the effort is doomed to fail. In the long run, truthfulness in social intercourse, occasionally painful as it may be, is better than the evils that heap up from our perpetual festival of the "white lie." The craziness of life may sometimes make them necessary; an overdose may be fatal to the human community.

B. LIES FOR OTHER PEOPLE'S GOOD

Sizing up a bald-faced lie, Joseph Fletcher looks at the motive behind it and says: "Love made it good."[16] Can this be? Does love make any lie good?

228   Let us look at various sorts of loving lies. I take only a
few typical examples from life, but they may suffice to help us
evaluate the argument that a lie told to help people, a loving lie,
is a good lie.
      1. *Lies to protect our equals*. An incompetent colleague, profes-
sionally marginal but a fine character, would not be promoted
if we told our supervisor what we knew about him. So we lie
for him, not grandly, just enough to get him by. A physician
does needless spinal surgery, and botches it. He is sued; his
colleagues on the staff cover for him by repairing his damage
with follow-up surgery, and they lie for him on the stand. A
minister is playing sexual games with admiring women in his
congregation. A few parishioners are getting suspicious and one
or two of his colleagues know for sure; but when the presbytery
investigates, the colleagues lie to give the man of God another
chance. A trial lawyer defends his rich client with a barrage of
lying legalese. After all, we have to stick together and protect
our own. A little lying may be the least we can do for our brothers and sisters in the trade.
      2. *Lies to protect our lessers*. People in power often think that
ordinary people cannot cope with the truth. So they lie in order
to protect us. They act as our parents who decide when their
children are ready for the truth about life. Most of us get a
chance to be patronizing liars once in a while. But what happens
when national leaders act like parents who lie a little to protect
their children?
      Political leaders tell lies for the good of multitudes. They
"know" that the little people cannot be trusted with the truth.
Sissela Bok recalls the great lie of 1964. Lyndon Johnson "knew"
that his own election was for the supreme good of the nation.
One way to secure it was to portray his opponent, Barry Gold-
water, as a man who would expand the war in Vietnam and
himself as the man of peace and restraint. So he promised to
restrict the US role in the war, all the while planning behind the
scenes for massive bombing of North Vietnam. The President
lied for the "good" of his children, the people.[17]
      Leaders are often high-minded people. Indeed, the more
high-minded they are, the more they assume they "know" what
is good for people. We may suppose that Franklin Roosevelt felt
that he was gently nurturing his national family when he promised he would never send their sons to foreign wars. We may

guess that Richard Nixon had a patronizing motive when he lied to cover his tracks through Watergate to "save the Presidency." "Noble lies" seem at the time to be absolutely necessary for the good of the little folk. But, high-minded as they are, lying leaders are deciding for the rest of us when we may know the truth.

Religious leaders, too, are tempted to lie for the good of the flock. The stakes are high here, as high as heaven. What if the pastor's private life and secret thoughts would cause a scandal? Surely a little lie is small price to protect the people of God. If the preacher does not share his congregation's literal belief in this or that article of the faith, let him keep his private interpretation to himself. If the people in the pew need instant support for their faith, let the preacher launch a cheap polemic against disbelief which grossly misrepresents the skeptic's real point of view. What does it matter if the people are deceived so long as their faith is made stronger? Evangelists need to seem like saintly paragons; so they act out a winsome model of flawless sanctity. Finally, the preacher needs compelling anecdotes to tell. In a day when personal sharing is confused with honesty, the anecdote is best if the preacher is the leading person in it. Hence, if you hear a good story, put yourself in it as the leading character—a small lie for a generous payoff in greater "authenticity."

3. *Lies to protect the suffering.* Few people enjoy the superiority over people that a doctor does over his patient. Doctors take an oath to relieve suffering; surely, any doctor may guess, obeying the oath comes before petty scruples about truthfulness. So the physician decides whether the sick and dying patient will be told the truth about his condition. Reasons for lying to the sick and dying are reasons of compassion, of course. They arise from the weakness of the people whom the doctors serve. Sick people often need protection from truthfulness. Why?

First, it is said, the truth will hurt them. The truth hurts sick and dying people in almost every conceivable way. It hurts just because it is the truth about painful reality. If you are dying of leukemia, it may hurt more to hear about it than it does to die of it. It hurts a woman with cancer to be told that her days are numbered, because the information may take away her will to live. A doctor cannot know for sure how a patient will react to bad news. How can he be certain that the man who is told he is soon going to die a painful death will not go berserk and jump out the window or fall into a depression? Truthfulness can be a

230   dangerous weapon. Sometimes it may be better to put it in a
drawer and use a tender lie instead. There are, it seems, tender
reasons for deceiving people.

A second reason is that the truth is too hard to tell. For one
thing, the truth about illness is very complex, and it can be told
accurately only in technical medical jargon. No doctor can make
it all understandable. Besides, there is so little time; there are
other patients waiting. How can a busy physician take time to
explain everything? To make it harder, many patients are very
limited. In large cities many patients may comprehend very little
English. The truth about a doctor's fees is simple; we can put
that on a computerized invoice. But telling a person the truth
about the one thing that touches him most—whether he will live
or die—is often too hard even for a graduate of medical school.
Every doctor knows, however, that truthfulness is not the same
as truth. Truthfulness requires honesty—even when it cannot
deliver clarity and completeness. We are talking here about lying
as deception—which is different from inability to make everything clear. The question is whether it is good to deceive whenever it is hard to explain.

Third, the truth may be unwanted. Physicians may assume
that patients do not want ugly and painful truthfulness. After all,
who wants pain? Perhaps it is only healthy people who are certain that they would want to know the truth if they were fatally
ill. In the time of their own illness these same persons may be
comforted by a lie. From this philosophical observation, many
doctors conclude that most people who face terrible news about
their illness would really rather be lied to than given the truth.
In any case, the physician decides whether or not any specific
sick person wants the truth; no doctor *asks* a patient whether he
wants to be lied to.

All the lies we have been reviewing in this section are told
for other people's good. Are such lies, *by reason of their loving
purpose*, right to tell?

The answer depends to some extent on whether, on balance,
loving lies are really helpful—more helpful, anyway, than harmful—over the long term. The commandment pushes us into the
field with a bias against lying on the ground that truthfulness is
of the essence for a human community. In order to overcome
this bias, the champion of the loving lie must show that benevolent lies save us from needless evil while causing, at worst, only

"minimal harm." It is not enough to claim that a loving lie helps the individual being lied to; we need to be shown that the *practice* of loving lies is not harmful to the community. So, let us examine the "minimal harm" of benevolent lying.

The damage done by benevolent lies

1. *Benevolent lying demeans the people deceived.* First, it casts the deceived in infantile roles. Somebody else is deciding for them when they are strong enough to bear up under the truth and when they ought to be deceived.

Second, benevolent lying robs the deceived of their right to truth. Someone else has decided that people who are mere citizens or patients do not have an intrinsic right to trust people to speak truthfully to them.

Third, lying to help someone robs the deceived of freedom. No one can be free who is forced to make decisions on the basis of false or misleading information. People who are lied to for their own political or physical good are, by that lie, being held in bondage. They cannot make their own response to the bad news about their own reality.

Fourth, such lies rob a person of his very touch with reality. It would seem to be important for a human being to be in contact with the reality of himself and his environment. To lose contact with reality is, in some measure, to lose orientation, to lose rationality, and to lose a dimension of one's self. A person who lives with falsehood is living in an unreal world, and to force someone into that world by benevolent lies is to demean him.

2. *Benevolent lying corrodes the character of the liar.* Few people in our sinful condition can long resist the corrosive effects of patronizing lying. The sheer arrogance of assuming that you have a right to decide when other people should be lied to is morally destructive. No one can play this godlike role for long without thinking that he personally matches the role. The loving liar who begins by lying only in an emergency for the other person's good soon comes to believe that he really has the wisdom to know when anyone deserves the truth. Furthermore, people in power have a hard time keeping clear the line between what is good for the public and what is good for the liar. The patronizing politician becomes a liar whenever he needs to lie to cover his own flanks. The patronizing medic begins to tell lies whenever lying helps him escape a painful encounter with his own medical

232 failure. Benevolent lies, habitually told, corrode the character of the patronizing liar.

3. *Benevolent lying breaks community.* Patronizing lies tend, in the long run, to erode the trust people need for common life. Lies told by politicians for the public good eventually create a cynicism about government which pulls people out of participation in democracy. Lies told to help incompetent colleagues survive tend to erode the community's confidence in professional people. Lies told to protect the suffering undermine the trust a community has a right to have in the healing professions. On the liar's side, benevolent lying becomes a tool for manipulating people. The liar destroys communication because he uses it as a tool to get what he needs from the weak. No community can exist as a community of rational and caring people in an atmosphere of patronizing deceit.

4. *The good achieved by lying tends to be short-range good.* We lie to spare people pain today; our lying may prevent them from doing something about the cause of pain in the future. We lie to protect our colleagues and friends; but we do not give them a chance to correct their faults, and we foist them instead on unsuspecting victims of their incompetence. Lies are almost always told for today's good without due regard for those who must pick up the pieces tomorrow.

We are in a position now, I think, to make a judgment on benevolent lying. We began with a strong moral bias that lying will usually be wrong. If someone poses a kind of lie that might be right, in spite of the law of respect for truthfulness, he is obligated to make a case for it. What he proposes is that lies of this particular *class* are justifiable lies. But are *all* lies told for other people's good clearly justifiable? The answer must be that they are not. The evils that attend a general practice of benevolent lying outweigh the short-term good that loving lying might manage to promote. In some special cases, a benevolent lie is probably justified. But it must be justified by something more than the fact that—in the mind of the liar—it was told for somebody's good. In any case, we can hardly set forth as a general rule that lies told for other people's good are good lies.

C. LIES TOLD TO BAD PEOPLE

The great Dutch jurist Hugo Grotius taught that some people do not have a right to the truth from us. Anyone who has ever had an enemy is comforted by Grotius' version of the just lie. Did Hitler have a right to know the truth about the Allies' plan to invade Europe? No, we say, we must lie to the great liars of the world in order to protect the truth. Or, as Churchill remarked at Yalta, "in wartime . . . truth is so precious that she should always be attended by a bodyguard of lies."[18] Does the Devil, the prince of lies, have a right to our truth? Do those people who do the Devil's work? Tell a lie, then, to any person who has lost his right to truth and you tell a justifiable lie. Does this test work?

Were all the lies told to save the Anne Franks of Europe justified on grounds that the Nazis did not deserve the truth? Possibly so. But if you agree, you must face up to some hard questions before you conclude that *all* lies told to unworthy people are justifiable lies. One is this: Who has the right to judge when another person has lost his right to truth? Grotius, for example, believed that children and mentally retarded people had no right to truthfulness. How did he decide that these innocent people should be cut off from the community of truth? What prevents the genius, on the same premise, from deciding that all inferior people lose their right to truth? What prevents a business person from assuming that all tough competitors lose the right to truth? Responsible societies do not trust an elite to separate people who deserve the truth from those who do not. The society that tolerates a lying elite is a society fast turning to a jungle in which no person can act on the inexpendable premise of a human community—the premise that people can trust each other to communicate in truthfulness.

Hitlers do arise on the surface of the earth's scum, to be sure, and lies may be necessary to drown them. But when we justify such lies, we must have more to go on than the sheer fact that bad people do not deserve our truth. We cannot live with an ethic that invests every man with the right to decide when the people around him are good enough to deserve truthfulness.

D. LIES TO SAVE LIVES
We finally come down to the issue of lie versus life. This may be a workable test: if I can save another person's life only by telling a lie, I am justified in lying. And, by the law of self-defense, if I may lie to save a neighbor's life, I should be allowed to lie to save my own. In short, when a human life is pitted

234   against truthfulness, let life have the day. Is this a guideline we can trust with everyone, without worry for loss of truthfulness in our world?

We feel confident about lying to save life because we have an undeniable intuition that destroying a human life is far worse than lying. Most of us simply feel that when it comes to life, we may lie boldly and grandly, and without qualms. We do not need an argument; we rely on our primitive sense for what counts.

Lying to save a life, however, is often a gamble. We are not dealing with legal contracts, as a rule, as if your life can be guaranteed by my lie. Situations in which a person lies to save a life are not always cut and dried. The Gestapo is at the door; you have two Jews in your attic and the Nazis are hunting them. You lie, because you *know* that if the Gestapo finds them, the Jews are dead. But consider an armed man trapped in a bank. He takes everyone in the bank hostage and threatens to kill them all. You tell him that he will be allowed to go free if he puts down his gun and surrenders. You lie; you know he will be arrested. You lie with only a hope that your lie will save a life. You do not even have favorable odds—yet human life is so much more important than truthful words that even a reasonable chance of saving a life would seem to justify the lie.

Are we going to quibble about odds when life may be at stake? Would we not calculate that, if lying had a 51% chance of saving human lives, we would lie—on the ground that the odds in favor of life were good enough to outweigh the evil of lying? The value of a person's life, then, is so overwhelming that we should lie when lying has a reasonable chance of actually saving the life. Have we, then, found a safe test for justified lying? I think so. It all depends, of course, on whether our feeling about the priority of life is true. In a world bent out of shape, we must sometimes—though not often—choose; and when we must, we are right to choose life even if it requires a lie.

E. LOVING LIES OF SILENCE

There is, as a wise man said, a "time to keep silence and a time to speak" (Eccl. 3:7). But is there a time for a silence that tells a lie?

You are in a group when boring old Harry asks, "Is anyone driving to Pasadena?" and you keep your mouth shut even though you plan to take off to Pasadena in five minutes. Your silence is a bald-faced lie. Is it right? Or must we always speak out and say, "Yes, Harry, I'm driving, but I prefer to drive alone"?

We are not morally bound to tell the truth whenever we have a chance to blurt it out. I do not need to tell a friend that my son has made Phi Beta Kappa when I know his son just dropped out of college. No mother needs to tell her daughter she is ugly. And no student is obligated to tell a retiring professor that his lectures were platitudinous harangues. Silence can be golden.

We get into murky moral waters, however, when we ask whether we ever ought to tell silent lies to people who do have a normal right to our truthfulness. Some of our relationships depend on open truthfulness; we make covenants that are kept alive by truth and are broken by deceit. Marriage is a covenant like this. Yet—in life's brokenness—may it ever be necessary to deceive precisely for the sake of keeping the covenant?

Elsa Echtbreek is a married woman with a strong belief in the permanence of marriage coupled with a great need for passion. She has just ended a passionate love affair with another man; and she is now determined to rescue her marriage. She intends to turn it, if she can, into a loving, as well as permanent, relationship. She is certain that her husband Tony would leave her and call the marriage quits if he ever found out about her affair. So, torn between her dedication to marriage and shame at being a silent liar, Elsa chooses a policy of loving silence. Is she right?

Elsa believes that she is lying about the past to honor a duty of the present. The important duty of the present is this: she ought to save her marriage. The truth about her affair is a truth about a past infidelity; she is now practicing a living truth for the sake of future fidelity. Her duty to her lasting covenant overtakes her duty to the facts about an affair that is over.

Elsa acts out a weak sort of lie; keeping one's mouth shut does not have the same sort of moral wallop that bald-faced lies do. But weak as it is, her silent deceit puts the same shackles on Tony that a "robust lie" would. He is being kept from making his own free response to important facts that have invaded his life. He is being denied his right to truthfulness. True enough. But Elsa is sure that he will use his right to truthfulness to prevent her from having a second chance to save their marriage.

236 So she opts for the strong value of marriage and pays for it with the price of a weak sin.

Elsa's decision is made within a welter of uncertainties. She can only make a good guess about most of the factors in her situation. Would she surely destroy her marriage if she told Tony the truth? Maybe Tony would be forced to face up to his own responsibility for Elsa's affair; he has been a clumsy and inconsiderate husband, after all. Maybe he will change when he sees what came of his bungling. Maybe Tony will find out in spite of her cover-up. If he does, will he not be even more likely to throw her out? And even if she manages the deception, can she be sure it will save her marriage? There are question all over Elsa's situation, yet she has to decide.

The stakes were high. So she took the safest odds she could get. She gambled on the silent lie as the way to take the decision out of Tony's court. She bought time. Was she justified?

The situation is laced with an irony that afflicts a lot of morality in a fallen life. Marriage is a kind of relationship that needs truthfulness as its essence. Can deception save a covenant that depends on trust? To ask the question seriously is to swallow irony as part of our diet in a world haunted by moral failure. We sinners turn life into a crazy place sometimes. Our own sins make it necessary to compromise with truthfulness in order to keep life from getting even crazier.

Would it be right for Elsa to ask God to help her get away with her lie? Some people would tell her that she should simply obey the divine commandment and leave her marriage to divine grace. Others might support her decision to go for the high value of marriage on grounds that silent lies are not all that bad. Still others may be opposed to her lie because the odds are it won't do the job. I do not think we know enough to be sure. But it seems to me that her marriage is important enough, and silent lying is different enough from explicit lying, that she may well be justified in her quiet deception.

Have we found a way to test for silent lying? If Elsa's silence was golden, can we endorse every roving spouse's cover-up? Could this formula be a test: Silent lying is justified whenever the lying person feels that lying will help save his marriage? I do not think so. As a test, it is too flabby. It would turn adultery itself into its own justification for lying. Since adultery always threatens to destroy a marriage, lying about it is almost always required to save the marriage. So the offense itself guarantees the "right to lie." The irony is too great.

The most we can say is that there may be times when, in our mixed-up lives, it is better to lie by silence than to risk losing something extremely precious. The fact that we admit this points, not to a weak spot in divine law, but to the ambiguity that our fallen ways bring to our lives. How do we know the time for a silent lie when it comes? I doubt that we can ever know for sure beforehand. Our style must be to walk into every situation with a heart bent on being truthful, telling the truth whenever it is appropriate to speak, and praying for discernment to sense when the situation commends silence.

God knows that truthfulness almost always serves our neighbor and our community. He also knows that "due to the hardness of our hearts," discreet deceit sometimes seems the better route. And he knows that it is desperately hard to know when the moment for a discreet deception has come upon us. So he is present in our lives with a threefold relevance: as lawgiver to direct our paths toward truthfulness; as the "spirit of understanding" to awaken our powers of discernment; and as gracious Father to forgive us when we fail the truth through our own self-deceit.

*   *   *

Truthfulness is one more invisible fiber that holds people together in humane community. When we cannot assume that people communicating with us are truthful, we cannot live with them in trust that they will respect our right to freedom to respond to reality. If we cannot trust each other to respect this basic right, we have lost our chance to be human together in God's manner.

Therefore, when God sounds the trumpet for truthfulness, he summons us to live humanly; he provides a survival guideline for community. This makes his command an intrinsically reasonable one. Life in a broken world would no doubt be very difficult if we absolutized this rule. Surely, there are emergencies that require a white lie or sometimes a falsehood. But we must keep these in the emergency rooms of life. The bias needs to move us toward truthfulness in every situation we enter. Generalized formulas for just lies seldom work; the only one that comes close is the formula of life vs. lie—lying in defense of human life.

238   Exceptions must be dealt with in the actual situation that requires them. We will know only as we discern what is going on whether the price of truthfulness is too high to pay.

In another time, perhaps, people could be more flexible and less stringent. In our age when deceit threatens every area of our society, the last word must be: Speak the truth, be the truth, for your truth sets others free.

QUESTIONS FOR DISCUSSION

1. Do you agree that self-deception can be a form of lying?

2. Do you agree that we ought to be perfectly open to others about what we are really like—warts and all?

3. Do you believe that the demands of love may conflict with the rigors of truthfulness when truthfulness can hurt people unfairly? And do you believe there are times when a bold-faced lie is justified?

4. What do you think human society would be like if no one trusted other people to keep their promises?

5. What would Christ think of Immanuel Kant's opinion that our duty to tell the truth is absolute, unconditional, allowing no exceptions?

6. Do you agree that a lie to save a life would be morally right? How do you know?

7. If you admit that a lie might sometimes be justified, are you watering down the will of God for truthfulness?

8. Why do you think Jesus considered hypocrisy one of the worst forms of lying?

9. Do you think "silent lies" are sometimes a good way to avoid trouble? Under what conditions may a "silent lie" be justified?

OBEDIENCE AND GRACE

SUMMING IT UP

The best way to end our long journey may be to take one last look down the main avenues we have traveled. Our point of departure was the ancient biblical commandments. One way to know what God expects all of us to do, we assumed, was to consult his commands. But this assumption only gave us the material for asking the three questions that dominated this book: What do the commandments actually tell us to do? Why do they command this? How can they be understood and obeyed within our real worlds of conflict and change?

Expecting that a few commandments embedded in an ancient religious document can tell us all what to do in our modern world requires fundamental assumptions about God and ourselves. For one thing, we need to assume that there is indeed a God out there who is interested in how we shape our lives—whose will is what morality is ultimately all about. If there is a God like that, he could reasonably be expected to have given some signals as to how he wanted us to live, at least in broad strokes. If, besides, this same God came into human history to save us from our failure to live up to his expectations, we might expect him still to point us, once saved and enabled by grace, back to his original design and early directives. I frankly assumed that these things about God were true when, in search of moral guidance, I went back to the commandments of the Bible. I did not try to make a case for God's reality or for the belief that it was really he who gave the commandments. I only wanted to ask what those commandments actually tell *us* to do in our times and places.

If my assumptions are right, we are not stuck with having to improvise new solutions to every moral problem we encounter. There is a pattern that we can have in our heads beforehand. Nor do we have to keep our ears cupped constantly for the latest word from heaven. God has already delivered his basic directions.

We have a road map at our disposal. It shows only the main roads, to be sure. The commandments do not tell us everything we need to know as we face concrete decisions. But they provide direction and they give us a bias. They lay out some of the most important *sorts* of things we ought to do in some of the most

239

240   important zones of human life. The specifics are not always included in the map. Whatever extra help we get—sound reason, intuition, or hints from the Spirit—can be tested by using the main thoroughfares as reference points.

I was obviously selective in my choice of biblical commandments. Not every "Thou shalt" in the Bible gives us direction for moral choices today. I suggested earlier a rough way of testing for universal moral commands; here it is enough to say that I chose only those commandments which the Judaeo-Christian morality has always discerned as guidelines for survival as a human community—justice, love, and the moral half of the decalogue.

Justice and love are the two absolute moral commandments. They cover every conceivable human situation. There is no nook or cranny in our lives together in which we may ignore the demands of justice and love. Everything we do must be fair; if it is not fair, it is not right. And everything we do must be helpful, or at least not hurtful; if we mean it to hurt and not help people, it is not right. Justice and love form a kind of moral counterpoint in life. Justice holds us back in respect; it tells us to let people be what they are and have what they have. Love pushes us toward people in care; it tells us to get into people's lives so that we can help them be what they ought to be and get what they ought to have. Justice tends to urge us to keep the rules, especially the "Thou shalt not's." Love translates the negative commands into positive invitations to creative helpfulness. Justice and love are the absolutes of life to which the other commandments point; the other commands are valid because they direct us to embody justice and love in the complex realities of human life.

The first question I asked of every commandment was what it asked us to do, or asked us not to do. We asked what the commandment itself said and how people in biblical times understood it. But we also asked what it required of everyone beyond the boundaries of the biblical people who first heard it. In order to grasp the scope of each command, we had to ask about both its negative and positive thrust. What did it ask of us as a rule of justice; that is, what right of our neighbor did it forbid us to violate? And what did it ask of us as a rule of love; that is, what did it require us to do as a way of being helpful to our neighbor in his quest for a humane existence?

I also asked *why* the commandment required what it did. We expect the Creator to tailor his expectations to what he has made. God's commands should be congenial to his creation. Perhaps this betrays my Calvinistic Thomism of sorts; both men believed that the moral commandments pointed from outside of us to the sort of life toward which our true natures pushed from within. If we are in tune with ourselves, we will be disposed to do what God commanded. Hence, there ought to be reasons for what God requires, and we should be able to recognize them.

Of course, anyone could tell that I sought the reasons with the eyes of faith. I did not use data from social sciences to explain why God should have commanded what he did. For instance, I did not try to explain why children have to honor their parents by making a sociological study of the family. Nor did I discover the reasons for sexual fidelity in clinical researches on human sexual behavior. On the other hand, I did not extract the reasons for the commandments straight from a reading of biblical texts. They came as the end product of what I think is a biblical or Christian discernment of life. In the light of what I believe, I found structures in life that matched the commandments which applied to them.

How do I know that human beings really do have rights simply because they are human? How do I know that all people, even sinful people, are worthy to be loved? Is it not because I *believe* it to be so? How do I know that parents are called to be the teachers and guides of their children in all that is deeply important about living, and that they therefore deserve to be honored by their children? I think I know it because I believe it. Again, how do I know that every person is sacred and therefore, morally speaking, may not be killed? Basically, I think I know it because I believe there is a God and that every person is like God, loved by God, and allowed by God to be a person in community with others. My search for reasons has been carried on in a circle of faith. Faith constantly merges into reason, and we can never be sure where one ends and the other begins. I *am* sure that I intend faith to inform reason and that I intend reason to interpret faith.

Faith, in any case, supported what seemed to be reasonable explanations for God's commands. The reasons were at least not bizarre; any reasonable person would have to admit that the commandments and life (as construed in the light of faith) fit together. Besides, the reasons for each commandment add a rational motive for obeying it. For if the commandments fit life, determined disavowal of them will eventually break life apart. Patterns of obedience tend to make life humane in the land which the Lord our God gives us.

I went from *why* to the question of *how*. How can we understand and obey the commandments in our changing and broken world? A commandment is a clear shaft of light until it invades the real world in which we must apply it. We see it in all its simple clarity and then, turning to the conflicting data of life, we sweat out daring acts of obedience with fearful and trembling doubts.

We have no ideal world in which to find out what God expects us to do; we have only this changing and broken one. Life changes, and obedience to unchanging commands must adjust to changing conditions. Take the honoring of parents, for instance. All children everywhere ought to honor their parents. But each generation has to find its own ways, appropriate to its own culture, for honoring its parents.

Life is also broken. In a broken world, it is necessary sometimes to break a commandment. It may be necessary to lie to save a person. It may be necessary to kill a person to save a cause. But the exceptions need to be carefully guarded; they must underscore and not undermine the rule. We have in these chapters tested many commonplace guidelines for breaking commandments. Most of these guidelines failed, because if they were generalized the human community would be jeopardized. Guidelines for breaking the commandments tend to be too loose. They allow too much. Turn an exception into a general permission, and you open the gates to trouble in the human family. Commandment-breaking must be an exceptional event. Single and exceptional acts of breaking cannot be used to justify other breaking as a rule. The word for everyone in general remains: Do not lie! Do not steal! Do not kill! Obey the commands!

The final word for a book like this must be a word of grace. If anything is clear after a searching look at what God expects even of ordinary people, it is that the moral standard for human beings remains an ideal. After learning what God expects of us we must face up to our private and public history of failure. Only a complacent soul enjoys a feeling of success when he thinks deeply about mere morality. What needs to be said to this human situation is simply that the God who commands is also the God who forgives.

The gospel of grace releases us from the guilt of failure and opens new possibilities for a new effort. Moreover, it offers a new relationship with the Commander. He who pointed us to his design for living at Mount Sinai embraces us with his love at Mount Calvary. He who pins us down with demands at every nook and cranny of life frees us from any and all condemnation.

What God expects of ordinary people is obedience born of gratitude; what God gives ordinary people is forgiveness born of grace. Once forgiven, we hear his commands, not as a burden, but as an invitation to enjoy our humanity, and in our joy to glorify our Creator.

NOTES

NOTES TO CHAPTER ONE

1. For a summary of scholarly opinions about the origin of the decalogue as we have it see J. J. Stamm and M. D. Andrews, *The Ten Commandments in Recent Research* (London: SCM Press, 1967), pp. 22-35.

2. The most powerful way the Bible speaks to the moral life is in its panoramic vision of life as a whole. The Bible first of all lets us "see" life through a new set of glasses. The vision is important to morality because the way we see life is usually the way we live it. The Bible provides a perspective on where we came from, what we are, and where we are needed. And by letting us see ourselves, it helps us see our duty.

The vision of our origin. The Bible tells us that we are creatures. If we see ourselves as such, we are open to two powerful moral influences—one more rational, the other more emotional. The former has to do with how we *think* about life with a Creator; the latter affects how we *feel* toward the Creator.

If we see life as created by a rational God, we are likely to look for and find purpose in it. We assume that the world has been created with plan and purpose for its rational inhabitants and tend to think of our life as a calling to conformity with the Creator's design. We also tend to believe that the divine commandments will match the divine design. On that basis, to believe in creation is to believe that the call to be moral is nothing more than the call to be human.

To *feel* life as a creature is to sense one's dependence. Life around us and in us, every tender relationship with another person, every outstretched hand, each deep breath, every ray of beauty, every experience of love, is received as an instant-by-instant gift of the Creator who intends our welfare and wills our joy. The experience of being created is the same as the feeling of gratitude. To a person who experiences life as a creation, it will seem natural and appropriate that he ought to do what the Creator expects him to do. No wonder, then, that the Heidelberg Catechism says we should obey the law so "that with our whole life we may show ourselves thankful to God for his benefits" (Lord's Day 33).

The vision of our fallenness. The second perspective the Bible opens on our humanity is its fallenness. The Bible is not about sin, but about redemption from sin. But we hear the story of redemption well only in context. What this means for morality is that we do not take our final cue from how people generally manage their affairs. Social research is not the last word on how life ought to be lived. Customs are too often corrupt and people too generally obstinate for moral direction to come from our collective human habits. This is why humanists often label the commandments "heteronomy"—an outsider's

246   law. But God's commandments are alien only to fallen inclinations, not to creation's designs. For fallen life is not typically human; it is a loss of humanness.

The vision of our future. The biblical story of salvation also opens up broad moral perspectives. To begin with, it makes clear that we do not need to be morally good in order to be accepted by the Creator and Judge of humanity. We are saved, not by morality, but by divine love. Second, it tells us that while we cannot be saved by morality, we are saved for morality. We are engaged by the Creator Spirit so that we can be human again, brought to our true selves within a genuinely humane community of loving people. Accepted by God in the cross of Christ, we are given Christ's Spirit so that "the just requirements of the law can be fulfilled in us" (Rom. 8:4). Third, we are born into a hope that all phases of human life will be recast in the form of justice (2 Pet. 2:13). Obedience to God's commands therefore brings about at least some fragments of what God in Christ promises for his saved creation.

Interpretative keys. One way to prepare for a biblical morality is to lift one motif from the redemptive story and let it be the interpretative key for God's moral will. For instance, the *Exodus* of the people of God has become the symbol for a theology of liberation from evil systems of oppression. *Eschatology,* God's ultimate vindication of his justice on earth, may be a motif that interprets God's will in terms of what he is doing in history now to bring in fragments of justice that correspond to the perfect justice of his kingdom. The *incarnation* of the Son of God tells us that discipleship must lead us to identification with needy people, just as God fully identified himself with us as a "man for others." The *cross* of Christ may be a call to a life of suffering, to a willingness to bear the burden of loving nonviolence as the redemptive answer to all injustice. Finally, the vision of *human beings as stewards,* caretakers of God's limited resources, may be the interpretative key for an ethic of an ecological stewardship for our fellow earth-dwellers today and in the future.

The Bible's guidance for the moral life is a symphony, not a single lyric. We may be sure that every shaft of light which truly illumines our moral choices is of God. Allowing one of the interpretative keys we have mentioned to dominate the moral view of life frees one from everyday moral questions like the ones we are asking in this book. The grand *leitmotifs* provide a splendid overview of the moral landscape, but they do not much illuminate decisions ordinary people must make about ordinary dilemmas of ordinary life. For these, the commandments probably have more to say.

3. How do we distinguish the abiding and universal laws in the Bible from the temporary, specific commands? In a learned 19th-century book on biblical moral law Thomas Fairbairn argued that if we just put our mind to it we can always get behind the peculiarities of any biblical commandment to see what "is essential and . . . properly of no age or time"—which is to say, *for every* age and time. But Fairbairn added one escape clause: we would recognize the universal

law in a command "insofar as it is . . . not unsuited to my position and circumstance"; *The Revelation of Law in Scriptures* (repr. Grand Rapids: Zondervan, 1957, p. 348). The "insofar as" was Fairbairn's Catch-22; he did not explain how we would recognize whether or not a command was suited to our position and circumstance. Thomas Aquinas was sure that the abiding law in any command would be recognized by any average intelligence—except for some hard ones which would be clear "only to the wise" (*Summa Theologica,* 1a, 2ae, quest. 100, art. 11). Calvin was sure that the commandments speak a universal moral language, and ask nothing more than what "all reasonable men will know the rightness" of (*Institutes,* II. viii.11).

Yet no one has ever worked out an easy and reliable way to tell the commandments meant for everyone from those meant only for people living when they were spoken. It obviously does not work to assume that the Old Testament commands are obsolete, while all of the New Testament commands are God's will for everyone. Some Old Testament commands are clearly universal; some New Testament commands are clearly not. The believing community looking for God's will in the Bible has attempted to allow the clearest revelation of God's will in the large and redemptive areas and its own experience of life to shed light on whether a particular commandment is meant for everyone who reads it. We decided that Moses' command forbidding interest (Exod. 22:25) was not an enduring indictment of the banking business after we discovered that modern life would be extremely difficult without credit and that credit would not be available unless people who lent money could charge interest for it. Similarly with Paul's command of obedience to slaves. We decided these things not so much because a scholar told us how to exegete the texts as from our own growing sense of what God really wants in the light of his commands for justice and love.

Separating temporary commands from abiding ones becomes more difficult as the commands become more concrete. Maybe there is a parallel here between rules for playing games and rules for the moral life. Game-playing could give us a hint for a moral hermeneutic.

First, there are *rules of the game.* Some rules control the essence of the game; change the rules and you change the game. Take baseball. If you give up the rule that a batter is out when a fielder catches a ball he hits, you will have altered the basics of the game. Some of the Bible's rules are rules of the game. In marriage, you would change the essence if you gave up the rule of fidelity. Take communication; you would change the nature of human dialogue if you gave up the rule of truthfulness. Rules of the game? The best known set is in the decalogue.

Second, there are *rules of strategy.* Take baseball again. There is a rule that you never purposely walk the potentially winning run. But this rule only tells you the best way to play the game. Any manager can walk the potentially winning run without tampering with the essence of the game. The Bible has rules of strategy too. Moses' rule against charging interest on loans was a strategy for helping poor

248 people keep their farms (Exod. 22:25). Maybe Paul's rule for slaves to obey their masters was a bit of strategy for letting the Christian mission procede without an oppressive response from slave owners (2 Tim. 6:1). Strategy, yes. Rule for the game of life, no.

Third, there are *rules of propriety.* Baseball again. There are rules against swearing at umpires, or kicking sand at their pant legs. Important rules, especially if you are an umpire. But the angry player does not assault the game of baseball by kicking a little dust at a myopic umpire. The Bible has many rules of propriety too. Paul's rule (1 Cor. 11:4f.) that women wear veils when they pray in public is one of them. Flaunting a bare female face in church hardly upsets the moral scales. And when feelings about the female face changed, the rule was seen for what it is, not a rule of the game of life, but a rule that said: be sensitive to the feelings of people. When feelings change, the rules change.

Clearly, only rules of the game are morally binding on all people who play the game of life.

These distinctions will not settle which biblical commands are directions for all people, but I suspect it is pretty much how believers read the Bible's commands. And I think it reflects what was really going on in the mind of the Commander.

4. When situation ethics was fashionable, such a caricature was popular. Joesph Fletcher talks of people with an "apparatus of pre-fabricated principles, precepts, and rules," who force every "life situation to fit procrusteanly the 'relevant' rule"; *Moral Responsibility* (Philadelphia: Westminster, 1967), p. 73.

5. In his seductively brilliant work on Christian freedom, Jacques Ellul lures us into these false options—a totally static world, alien to freedom, and a wondrously mobile world, hospitable to Christian freedom. In the static world we "set up lists of what is pure and permissible." In the world of movement we "affirm the full freedom in Christ"; *The Ethics of Freedom* (Grand Rapids: Eerdmans, 1975), p. 193. In a world of order, morality takes over; love is put to flight and the Christian person is handcuffed by "total and absolute law" (p. 348). But Ellul's antithesis between loveless order and loving freedom is a false one, if it is true that we are most free when we respect the order that a Creator designed to match our deepest inclinations.

6. Karl Barth, *Ethics* (New York: Seabury, 1981), p. 209. *Ethics* is a series of lectures Barth delivered in 1928 and 1930.

7. It is easier to give examples of a moral law ("It is not permissible to take the life of a human being") than to define the general category. We can indicate some characteristics of moral laws in general.

For one thing, a moral law is a statement that tells us all what we ought or ought not to do (Kant). It is also, for that reason, a measure or standard by which we can tell whether we did what we ought not to have done (Aquinas).

Second, as a statement, a moral law is intelligible to reasonable persons. We can share it with others and expect them to understand it. A moral law, then, is not like a private feeling; it informs the mind. As a statement, it is as rational as other laws are. "The energy of the universe cannot be destroyed, but only converted to other forms" is a rational statement about a physical law. "Everyone ought to keep his promises" is an equally understandable rational statement of a moral law.

Third, as a statement of what we ought to do, a moral law informs us of what free people are obligated to do but are able not to do if they choose. A moral law does not describe how people *will* act, but prescribes how they *ought* to act. It is a law of necessity which says that if Ted hits Jane in the face with his fist, she will feel pain. It is a moral law which says that Ted ought not cause Jane needless pain.

In the fourth place, as a statement of what everyone ought to do, a moral law reflects an enduring design for and tendency within human life. The statement is a law only because people are the sorts of creatures who were intended by their Creator to do the sorts of things the moral laws command. If it is a moral law that people ought to honor their marriage covenants, there must be an ingredient set in human sexual life which inclines us normally toward committed and exclusive partnerships. Law fits life.

Fifth, as a statement that tells all people what they ought to do, a moral law is rooted in ultimate reality. In biblical faith, the ultimate source of moral law is the mind of God. Moral law only expresses the personal will of an intelligent and loving Creator who alone is ultimate.

These are some properties of the idea of moral law. They do not tell us anything about the content of moral laws or whether the statements that I believe are moral laws really are moral laws.

8. K. Barth, *Church Dogmatics* (hereafter *CD*), II/2 (Edinburgh: T. & T. Clark, 1957), 663f.

9. Emil Brunner, *The Divine Imperative* (London: Lutterworth, 1937), p. 111.

10. Dietrich Bonhoeffer, *Ethics* (New York: Macmillan, 1955), p. 245. Bonhoeffer echoes Barth: the commandment "thus requires no interpretation to come into force. . . . To the last and smallest detail, it is self-interpreted" (*CD*, III/4, 11).

11. *CD*, III/4, 9. Sometimes Barth gives the impression that everyone in the world learns what God expects of him only by waiting alone for God to whisper (or shout) the message in his ear. Barth guards himself against this caricature by warning us not to expect a "chaos of individual conflicting intimations to individual men in individual situations" (*CD*, II/2, 711). When God speaks, he is always in harmony with his primary command of the gospel—"Be free in Christ." And, being the reliable God he is, he will stay in tune with his other biblical commands. So the speaking God is not likely to shift moral ground whimsically, nor is he turning the moral life into an individualistic waiting game. Yet, the question remains, how does one hear the clear command, and how do we hear it together?

12. Barth probably had three pastoral motives for denying moral law. (1) Moral laws would tie God down to abstract principles; the living God must be free to speak to men and women in new and sometimes surprising ways. (2) Moral laws get between the believer

and God. Instead of listening for the direct Word, the believer consults an abstract ancient law; besides, the finite person is tempted to believe that his deductions from the law are as divine as the law itself. (3) Moral laws discourage people from keeping their hearts open to new adventures with God. The basic problem with these understandable objections is that they are aimed at a Kantian notion of moral law which turns law into an ultimate rational principle. This is as unfortunate as it would be to reject the Barthian view of command on grounds that it is a form of irrational existentialism.

13. A study of *Church Dogmatics*, III/4, will, I think, confirm that Barth did not follow to the end his ethic of commands. The same is true of Bonhoeffer who, when he spoke to moral issues like suicide, abortion, and war, appealed to what looks very much like natural law (cf. *Ethics*, p. 151).

14. C. S. Lewis, *Christian Reflections* (Grand Rapids: Eerdmans, 1967), pp. 46f. Calvin inclines toward this position. Pessimist that he was about the human moral condition, Calvin, on reading the commandments, would say: "nature itself teaches us this." Or "all reasonable men will know the rightness of this" (*Institutes,* II.viii.11). Or, again, the decalogue "prescribes nothing which nature does not itself dictate to be most certain and most just"; *Commentaries on the Last Four Books of Moses* (Grand Rapids: Eerdmans, 1950), III, 193.

15. Helmut Thielicke represents this "morality of the gap"; he talks of "an infinite qualitative distinction between man's original state and the fall"; *Theological Ethics: Foundations* (Philadelphia: Fortress, 1966), p. 419. Thielicke is not talking merely about what we can know; he is talking about the state of our natures, of what we are as well as what we know. Thielicke's pessimism is in contrast to the Calvinist creed according to which the Creator is still manifest in creation as in "a most elegant book wherein all creatures, great and small, are as so many characters leading us to see clearly the invisible being of God" (Belgic Confession, Art. 2).

16. *Institutes,* II.ii.15.

17. Calvin, who so often conceded that the decalogue's commands were recognizable to the natural reason, also perceived the gap between knowing and doing: "In reply to the general question, every man will affirm that murder is evil. But he who is plotting the death of an enemy contemplates murder as something good. The adulterer will privately flatter himself in his own adultery. Herein is man's ignorance: when he comes to a particular case, he forgets the general principle he has just laid down" (*Institutes,* II.xi.23). The trouble is not the intellectual move from general principle to concrete cases, but the "evil desires that gently tickle the mind" of a person with "the most excellent disposition," leading him to snuff out the light of reason when he walks in the darkness of his own desires.

18. To say that basic biblical morality is common knowledge is to affirm the intention behind the classic doctrine of natural law. The problem with talking about natural law is that it suggests that something called "nature" teaches us what God's law is, but there are three

reasons why "nature" alone is not able to tell us what God expects us to do.

First, "nature" is no longer our guide; we are nature's guide. Nature does not tell us what to do; we tell it what to do. We put our order—or inflict our chaos—on nature. We decide how people can be born and when they should die; we decide what genetic inheritance a child should have and whether he should be conceived at all.

Second, mere "nature" cannot do justice to the personal dimensions of life. Nature, in classic natural law, teaches us through how subhuman nature works. Paul was certain that "nature itself teaches" certain moral truths, for example, that homosexual behavior is against God's will. But nature did not tell Paul that homosexual people may be splendid people caught in a sexual channel they never chose for themselves. The Vatican is confident that nature teaches us that sexual intercourse is for the sake of conception; but watching animals copulate does not tell us anything about the personal union and the personal love expressed in human sexual intercourse. So the goodness or badness of sex is not simply a matter of whether it is "natural," unless nature is enlarged to include our soul's yearning to stretch and soar toward another to satisfy our deepest personal longings in sexual intimacy.

Finally, natural law assumes that conscience is an unshakable moral bloodhound, inerrantly sniffing out the rights and wrongs of life. Actually, conscience is easily led astray; it is like a computer that can be fed false data and print out elaborate tissues of lies. Conscience can make us feel horrible when we are as innocent as babes or splendid when we are as guilty as Beelzebub. Conscience is by no means worthless; but left to its own devices, it is likely to pull the wool over our moral eyes.

For a sympathetic but trenchant criticism of natural law by a Catholic ethicist, see Charles Curran, *Themes in Fundamental Moral Theology* (Notre Dame: Univ. of Notre Dame Press, 1977), pp. 35ff.

19. Jesus' attitude toward the moral commandments has been variously interpreted as follows:

Jesus was against the moral commandments. Laws and rules stifle our freedom. Jesus had only one command: be free. Hence, Jesus "opposes the view that the fulfillment of the law is the fulfillment of the will of God." This is the existentialist view of Rudolf Bultmann, *Jesus and the Word* (New York: Scribners, 1958), p. 92.

Jesus replaced the old commandments with his own new ones. Some people believe he made new rules for the few months left for the world before the kingdom came (an ethic only for the interim). This was the view of Albert Schweitzer, *The Quest for the Historical Jesus* (New York: Macmillan, 1948). Others believe he issued new rules for the life of the kingdom itself. The commandments Jesus gave were not for this ordinary life, nor for that brief time left until the kingdom came, but for the perfect life within the kingdom once it came. This is the view of the dispensationalist Louis Sperry Chafer, *Systematic Theology* (Wheaton: Van Kampen), V, 97ff.

252   *Jesus complemented the old commandments with his own special words.*
He topped off the moral rules for ordinary people with directions for
moral heroes. This is a common view within older Catholic moral
theology, at least on a popular level (cf. Curran, *op. cit.,* pp. 12-13).

Jesus exposed the true and positive meaning of the old commandments.
He neither replaced nor added to the moral teachings of the law, but
told us instead what the old law really always asked of us. This was
the view of Calvin; cf. *Institutes,* II.ix.4, where he says that the gospel
differs from the old law "only in clarity of manifestation."

20. Paul's attitude toward the rules which overly spiritual people
were drawing up to discipline other Christians in piety was of a piece
with his contempt for turning God's commandments into a ladder for
climbing to God's favor. He had two criticisms of the rules: (1) They
violated Christian freedom (Col. 2:20)—they subjected Christianity
to the judgment of stupid rule-keepers (cf. Col. 2:16); and (2) they
did not help check "the indulgence of the flesh"; passions are never
tamed by rules against them (Col. 2:23).

21. K. Barth, *The Christian Life* (Grand Rapids: Eerdmans, 1981),
p. 36.

22. K. Barth, *Ethics,* p. 264.

23. *Institutes,* II.vii.12. To Calvin the Ten Commandments were
"like a whip to an idle and balky ass, to arouse it to work" (*Institutes,*
II.viii.12).

24. I am using the word absolute in a limited sense. I mean here
that if a commandment is absolute, it allows for no exceptions. "Absolute" is different from "universal." A command may be universal—
that is, it may obligate everyone on earth—and yet allow for exceptions. Some writers in ethics, however, use the word "absolute" for
any law that is universal; one is the Jesuit moralist Joseph Fuchs, "The
Absoluteness of Moral Terms," in *Moral Norms and Catholic Tradition*
(New York: Paulist Press, 1979), pp. 94ff.

25. *Summa Theologica,* 1a, 2ae, quest. 94, art. 4.

NOTES TO CHAPTER TWO

1. While "justice" points to rights that people have, the word is
also used in a larger and a smaller sense. In the larger sense, justice
points to the wholly good and wholly perfect person or society. When
a person is benevolent, honest, temperate, humble, courageous, and
the like, he is called a "just" person, by way of indicating this whole
package of virtues. And when everyone in a society stays in his or
her proper place, doing his or her proper task, and where life is
therewith well ordered, healthy, prosperous, and at peace, that society
is called a just society. Justice, then, is a word for complete excellence,
everything splendid in itself and everything in right relationship with
others. The wholistic idea of justice may be a secular hint of what the
Bible means by the righteousness of the kingdom of God. Plato provides a model of the well-ordered society, and calls that perfect state
by the name "justice"; cf. *The Republic,* VI, 508b-510b.

A narrower notion of justice relates to the laws of the land. Justice is done, it is sometimes said, when a person is tried and convicted according to the letter of the law. A "just" judge delivers judgments according to a strict understanding of the law; a just person is one who obeys the laws strictly. The Old Testament sometimes speaks of justice in this way; cf. Deut. 1:16, 16:18; Prov. 11:4, 19, 12:28. But to speak of justice as compliance with laws assumes that the laws themselves are just. No one on looking back will say it was just to be condemned according to Nazi racial laws, or that black people were treated justly when arrested for breaking segregation laws in the United States. To speak properly of justice, we need more than laws; we need a standard above laws by which the laws themselves are judged.

2. Thomas Aquinas sums up the common sense of justice: "It is generally agreed that it is for justice to pay what is due." Justice "renders an exact due"—no less, but no more, than what the claimant has a right to get. Cf. *Summa Theologica,* 1a, 2ar, quest. 60, art. 3.

3. What we call *civil* rights are the rights that a society has legally decided that individuals have; civil rights are rights that we have legislated. They may or may not make for justice. In Nazi Germany, a Jew had practically no civil rights, even though he had human rights, and the fact that a Jew could be burned in an oven without violating his civil rights had nothing at all to do with justice. It is the task of justice to bring our civil rights into harmony with our human rights.

4. Cf. G. von Rad: "It is all important not to read [the prophets'] message as if it consisted of timeless ideas, but to understand it as the particular word relevant to a particular hour in his time, which therefore cannot be replaced by any other word"; *Old Testament Theology,* II (New York: Harper, 1965), 129.

5. E. Brunner, *Justice and the Social Order* (New York: Harper, 1945), p. 104.

6. Cf. Isa. 26:9; Jer. 22:3; Pss. 72:1-4; 82:3, 4. The Hebrew word usually translated "justice" is *mishpat,* and the word usually translated "righteousness" is *tsedek.* But while these are two different words, we are hard put to separate their meanings. In the New Testament we have just one Greek word, *dikaiosune* and its variations, for both ideas—a hint that for the Bible justice and righteousness are not clearly distinct from each other.

7. Paul Ramsey, *Basic Christian Ethics* (New York: Scribner, 1953), p. 16. Ramsey insists that biblical righteousness is the measure of human obligation in our world, that we are called to fulfil, not mere human justice, but the righteousness of God. He means to keep us from being content with bare rational justice, constantly rearranging the human furniture to keep a balance between our competing claims; he means to prod us to strive for the fuller biblical picture under the Lordship of Christ. The whole will of God for righteousness is a judgment on the inadequacy of human justice.

8. The predator view of justice was argued by Plato's friend

Thrasymachus (cf. Plato's *Republic*); it has enjoyed revivals in every generation since.

9. John Rawls' view of "justice as fairness" is developed in what is probably the most important book on the theory of justice written in several decades; John Rawls, *A Theory of Justice* (Cambridge: Harvard U. P., 1971).

10. J. Pieper, *The Cardinal Virtues* (Notre Dame, 1966), p. 54.

11. H. Stob, *Ethical Reflections* (Grand Rapids: Eerdmans, 1977), p. 125.

12. William Frankena, *Perspectives on Morality* (Notre Dame: Notre Dame U. P., 1976), p. 97.

13. John Rawls lumps the natural gifts people have by birth into the pool of his society's wealth. What we have as a result of chance, he claims, is not ours by private right, but belongs in the same category as rivers and air. We do not really deserve our natural gifts, nor is it unfair for us to have them. The "natural distribution [of talents] is neither just nor unjust. . . . These are simply natural facts. What is just or unjust is the way social institutions deal with these facts" (*op. cit.,* p. 102).

NOTES TO CHAPTER THREE

1. The "great commandment" appears three times in the gospels. In Matthew, Jesus gives the command to an unfriendly lawyer who had challenged his loyalty to the law. Mark reports that Jesus gave it to a friendly lawyer; here, it is the "most important" commandment instead of the "great" one (Mark 12:31). Luke uses the commandment to introduce the story of the Good Samaritan and has the lawyer speaking it to Jesus, rather than Jesus speaking it to the lawyer (Luke 10:28). Others besides Jesus fixed all human duty on love: "Owe no man anything," said Paul, "except to love one another" (Rom. 13:8). Even the loving apostle, John, felt a need to set love in the frame of obligation as well as gift and power, saying that, in view of God's gift, "we also ought to love one another" (1 John 4:11). And—if only to remind ourselves that love was not a New Testament novelty—we may recall the early words to Israel about loving the stranger: "You shall love him as yourself, for you were strangers in the land of Egypt . . ." (Lev. 19:34).

2. "Assuming what is impossible," wrote Thomas, "that God were not man's good, there would be no reason to love"; *Summa Theologica,* 2, quest. 36, art. 13, ad 3.

3. "Morality was made for man, not man for morality. . . . In other words, all of our duties, even that of justice, presuppose the principle of benevolence. . . . To this extent, and only to this extent, is the old dictum that love is what underlies and unifies the rules of morality correct"; W. Frankena, *Ethics* (Englewood Cliffs: Prentice Hall, 1963), p. 37. Donagan sums up all natural law as a requirement that we "act so that the fundamental human goods, whether in your own person

or that of another, are promoted as may be possible, and under no circumstances violated"; *The Theory of Morality* (Chicago: Univ. of Chicago Press, 1974), p. 81.

4. Kant, "The Doctrine of Virtue," Part II of *The Metaphysics of Morals* (New York: Harper, 1964), p. 120.

5. *Ibid.*, p. 121. To overcome the subtle ways in which eros infects our gift-love with selfish motives, Kant contrived a few tests for genuine selfless love. (1) We must help our neighbor in a way that makes him feel as if we are only paying a debt we owe him. (2) We must help him secretly, so that he nor anyone else knows who it was who lent him a hand. (3) We must help him sacrificially, so that what we give will always be more than he can repay. It is hard to imagine a more relentless zeal for selfless love. We are tempted to flee to the gospel for a gentler law of love.

6. E. Fromm, *The Art of Loving* (New York: Harper, 1956), p. 20.

7. *Ibid.*, pp. 22-25.

8. Dag Hammarskjöld, *Markings* (New York: Knopf, 1964), p. 69.

9. *Agape and Eros* (New York: Harper, 1953). A few sentences from Nygren can show the decisiveness of his antithesis. "There cannot be any doubt that Eros and Agape belong originally to two entirely separate spiritual worlds between which no communication is possible" (p. 31). "Christianity does not recognize self-love as a legitimate form of love" (p. 217). "So far from self-love being a natural ordinance of God in nature, it is a devilish perversion" (p. 740). "When Paul sets self-love and neighbor-love in opposition to each other, he is not merely condemning a lower self-love . . . but all self-love whatever, even in its most highly spiritual state" (p. 131).

10. *Institutes*, I.i.1.

11. *CD*, IV/3, 375.

12. J. Gustafson, *Can Ethics Be Christian?* (Chicago: Univ. of Chicago Press, 1975), p. 165.

13. It may well be that my friend is filling a high-level need of his own. Perhaps he is—at one level of his mind—doing what he wants to do. And he has no doubt been paid dividends of good feeling at being the sort of person he is. But I believe that this does not account for his sense of obligation, nor does it explain why people believe that we ought to care for needy people even if we do not feel like it.

14. Kant articulated this view very clearly: "[The] maxim of . . . beneficence toward the needy is a universal duty of men, and indeed for this reason: that men are to be considered fellow-men—that is, rational beings with needs, united by nature in one dwelling place for the purpose of helping one another"; *The Doctrine of Virtue*, p. 121. Kant means that the reality behind the law of benevolence is the fact that needy people are rational creatures. The believer says that the deepest reality which grounds the law of love is God as the loving Lord and Savior. In short, the gospel's agape is rooted in God as love; rational benevolence is rooted in man as rational.

15. *Institutes*, II.ii.13-15.

256

16. Alan Donagan, *The Theory of Morality,* p. 209.

17. Cf. Paul Ramsey, *Basic Christian Ethics,* p. 151: "The old Calvinist test for candidates for the ministry, 'Are you willing to be damned for the glory of God?' is, of course, totally unacceptable. . . . [But] whoever is willing to be damned for the glory of God is truly saved—for his neighbor. Whoever willingly lets go of his own supreme interest in eternity presumably among lesser values in this life seeks not his own but acts always for the glory of God . . . and obediently in love for his neighbor."

18. The most devout commentators tend to shave the edge off the pure motive Paul appears to ask for. Calvin writes: "The apostle does not expressly forbid individuals to consult their own advantage, but he requires that they should not be so devoted to their own interests, as not to be prepared to forgo part of their right, as often as their brothers' needs should require it" (*Comm., ad loc.*). If Calvin is right, he must be getting his information from somewhere other than the text. It is common sense that tells him that Paul simply could not be asking for so much more than any of us can manage.

19. Cf. B. Gert, *The Moral Rules* (New York: Harper, 1973): "Morality does not require that you regard the good and evil of another as of equal weight with your own. . . . Even the moral ideals do not encourage you to take as much interest in the good of your neighbor as you take in your own" (p. 148). But what of Kant's humanistic demand for the pure motive of selfless love? Was this "rational benevolence" not as selfless as Christian love? I think not. What really concerned Kant was the purity of the lover's will, the excellence of his virtue. Christian love, by contrast, is far more interested in the neighbor's needs.

20. Nygren opposes agapic love and justice in this way, just as he opposed agape and eros (*op. cit.*, pp. 88ff.). Emil Brunner also supports this dichotomy; cf. *Justice and the Social Order,* p. 126.

21. Joseph Fletcher sees the relationship in this way. "Justice is Christian love using its head, calculating its duties, obligations, opportunities, resources"; *Situation Ethics,* p. 95.

22. Cf. Calvin: "I do not deny that the more closely any person is united to us, the greater claim he has to the assistance of our kind offices" (*Institutes,* II.xvii.45).

23. The questions here come down to what James Gustafson asks in the title of his book *Can Ethics Be Christian?* (Chicago: Univ. of Chicago Press, 1976). Gustafson does not believe the Christian command of love is a moral requirement for everyone: "It is unreasonable to assume that those who do not share the 'believing' should be obligated to follow the principles that are . . . distinctive to that [Christian] community" (p. 178). My own belief is that Christian discipline is basically a human way of living, though sometimes unusual conditions (like the presence of enemies) summon unusual loving. What God expects of believers, therefore, he wants of all people. This does not mean that he anticipates that unbelievers will accept Christian obligations. Nor, of course, does it follow that, since everyone is

morally obligated, they may be politically forced to obey. My point is not so much directed to what others are likely to do; it aims at a belief that what God asks of us as Christians he asks of us as human beings, renewed to our humanity.

24. *Op. cit.*, p. 91; cf. p. 77: "It is only when all thought of worthiness of the object is abandoned that we can understand what agape is."

25. Nygren says that the only reason God has for loving us is that it is "his nature to love" (*ibid.*, p. 75).

26. T. Merton, *Contemplative Prayer* (New York: Image Books, 1971), p. 70.

27. Calvin, without peer at putting sinners in their humble station, has a better feel than Nygren had for the ambivalence in God's love. God loves the sinner, he confesses, because "he wills not to lose what is his in us; out of his kindness he still finds something to love." Something good, he adds, because we are, after all, still his creatures. And he adds a word from Augustine in the same vein: "God manages to hate in each of us what we had made and to love what he has made" (*Institutes*, II.xix.3).

28. Outka's definitive study of the ethics of love selects "equal regard" as the essence of gift-love; all true love includes regard for the loved one, but what makes agapic love special is its "equal regard" for all persons. To have regard is to have respect, to recognize worth. Thus, agape is equal regard for everyone's "irreducible value." Gene Outka, *Agape: An Ethical Analysis* (New Haven: Yale U. P., 1972), p. 13.

29. R. Niebuhr, *Love and Justice*, p. 53. Niebuhr's phrase coincides with St. Thomas's confidence that, while charity is a supernatural virtue, it leads those for whom it is given to their true destinies as human beings (cf. *Summa Theologica*, 1a, 2al, 65, 3).

30. T. P. McDonell (ed.), *A Thomas Merton Reader* (New York: Harcourt, Brace and World, 1961), p. 314.

31. If agape is native to our humanity, love and law belong together. The law of God tells us how to live humanly with each other, nothing more. Love is the fulfilment of the law. Love tells us what the law is really for. In this sense, then, love uses law to lead us home to our humanity.

32. T. Merton, *New Seeds of Contemplation* (New York: New Directions, 1961), p. 5.

33. Nygren, *op. cit.*, p. 735.

34. Augustine's famous rule for conduct, "Love and do what you will," is debatable in two senses. First, exactly what Augustine meant by it is debatable. Second, taken as it stands, what it might mean as a guide is debatable. It is true that if our hearts were right, we would will only what was good. It is false that if we now *feel* loving we can be trusted to will what is good.

35. The phrase is from H. Stob, *Ethical Reflections*, p. 145.

36. *Institutes*, II.viii.54.

37. Perhaps the best discussion of how love may work as a moral

guide is still William Frankena's essay, "Love and Principle in Christian Ethics," in *Faith and Philosophy,* ed. Alvin Plantinga (Grand Rapids: Eerdmans, 1964), pp. 203-25. Paul Ramsey's book, *Deeds and Rules in Christian Ethics* (New York: Scribner, 1967), clearly defines the difference between what he calls "in-principled love"—which is roughly my view—and situation ethics.

38. Christian liberty in things that do not matter morally was very important to Calvin. It was a life or death issue for him because it touched the conscience. If a person once allows his life to be governed wholly by rules, he has no way to free himself; he will forever be tantalized by the fear of being condemned. "If any man should consider daintier food unlawful, in the end he will not be at peace before God when he eats either black bread or common victuals. . . . If he boggles at sweet wine, he will not with clear conscience drink even flat wine, and finally he will not dare touch water if sweeter and cleaner than other water" (*Institutes,* III.xix.7). We are free from rules about things that do not touch on the moral will of God. But the Christian has freedom "in outward matters" in order that "he may be the more ready for all the duties of love" (III.xix.12).

NOTES TO CHAPTER FOUR

1. A promise of long life is added to this commandment: Honor your father and mother *so that* your days may be many in the land. The promise provides a special *motive* for obeying the command: honoring parents results in value added. But the motive for obedience differs from the reason for the command. The reason for the command lies in the structure of family life. If there is a divine design for family life, it is reasonable to suppose that respect for it will enhance, if not extend, life in the long run. But it would be wrong to suppose that the command was given only because things tend to work out well for those who obey it.

The presence of the promise, however, does raise other questions. Why is a promise fixed only to this command? In Deut. 6:2, the same promise is a prediction of long life for obedience to all the commands. Possibly, the promise comes after the Fifth Commandment because it is the climax to the preceding religious commands. To honor one's father and mother, then, is a guarantee that one will obey the commands relating to God. If this is a true reading, then the commandment to honor parents is really about life with God; it is the conclusion of the first table, not the beginning of the second table of the law. It would not summon Israel's children to God's will for family life so much as it would summon them to believe and practice what their parents taught them about God.

Such speculation, however, is too insecure a basis for eliminating the Fifth Commandment from the moral sphere of life. The command has a great moral meaning and has traditionally been read as one of the moral rules.

Another question is this: What is promised, long life for individual children or a long future for the nation or society? The latter interpretation views the command as coming to the people of Israel with a promise of stable national life if it is obeyed. Stability could be seen, then, not as a special reward, but as a predictable outflow of respect for parents. Comparative histories of societies may add support to the promise. To individualize the promise, on the other hand, is to make it sound like magic, as if honoring parents wards off disease and accident. Hence, there is good reason for supposing that the promise is social, not individual.

2. C. Lasch, *Haven in a Heartless World* (New York: Basic Books, 1977), p. 140. Richard Sennett, in his brilliant analysis of authority and its corruptions, observes: "We have come to fear the influence of authority as a threat to our liberties, in the family and in society at large"; *Authority* (New York: Knopf, 1980), p. 15. Summerhill confirms Sennett's observation by his pre-emptory strike against authority: "I believe that to impose *anything* by authority is wrong"; A. S. Neal, *Summerhill: A Radical Approach to Child Rearing* (New York: Holt, 1960), p. 114 (italics mine). Thomas Gordon lends credence to Lasch's lament with these words: "The stubborn persistence of the idea that parents must and should use authority in dealing with children has, in my opinion, prevented for centuries any significant change or improvement in the way children are raised by parents and treated by adults"; *Parent Effectiveness Training* (New York: New American Library, 1975), p. 154.

3. T. W. Adorno, *The Authoritarian Personality* (New York: Harper, 1950).

4. Erich Fromm, *Crisis of Psychoanalysis,* p. 126.

5. Erich Fromm, *Escape from Freedom,* p. 191.

6. Kenneth Kenniston, *All Our Children: The American Family Under Pressure* (New York: Harcourt, Brace, Jovanovich, 1977), p. 17.

7. Stanley Hauerwas, *The Community of Character* (Notre Dame: Univ. of Notre Dame Press, 1981), p. 164. I regret that this valuable book was published too late for me to profit from it more extensively.

8. Durkheim was convinced that the despair at the root of the suicides of young people could be partly explained by their sense of *anomie,* a lawlessness that leaves one dangling without support from strong families; *Suicide* (London: Routledge and Vegas, 1952).

9. I. Boszormenyi-Nagy and G. M. Spark, *Invisible Loyalties* (New York: Harper, 1973), p. 40.

10. P. Berger and R. Neuhaus, *To Empower People* (Washington: American Enterprise for Public Policy Research, 1977), p. 20.

11. Some useful works on the general subject of authority, in addition to Sennett's and Adorno's already cited (notes 2 and 3 above), are F. Adelmann, *Authority* (The Hague: Nijhoff, 1974); C. Friedrich (ed.), *Authority* (Cambridge: Harvard U. P., 1958); R. Nisbet, *Twilight of Authority* (New York: Oxford, 1975); W. W. Meissner, *The Assault on Authority* (Maryknoll: Orbis, 1971).

12. Cf. Sennett, *op. cit.*, pp. 20ff. The various sources of authority

relate roughly to the *kinds* of authority we know in life. There are at least three different kinds of authority: (1) coercive, (2) scientific, and (3) moral.

Coercive authority we concede, for the most part, to governments. It is the legitimate power to force all people within a political state to do what is necessary for a just and orderly society.

Scientific authority is the power experts have to persuade people to listen to them with a bent toward believing them. We recognize scientists' authority when they persuade us that their methods of getting at the truth are valid and because their track record of accuracy is impressive. Obviously, scientific authority is quite different from coercive authority; no scientist can punish you for disagreeing with his findings. Yet both are authorities in the sense that we concede to them a legitimate power to influence us.

Moral authority is the power to move people to feel, believe, and act in obedience to a spiritual vision. We recognize people who are able to persuade us to change our lives and follow purer goals, and we concede their right to use their power with us.

Living with others is often a balancing act among the different kinds of authority. Imagine a government that claimed the right to coerce us to subscribe to the theory of evolution or the doctrine of the Holy Trinity. Or a scientist who worked out a method of cloning people and claimed on the basis of his scientific prowess the right to decide who among us were good enough to be cloned. Or a preacher who, on the ground that he had received the Holy Spirit, ordered his congregation to vote a straight Democratic ticket. Authority is as diverse as it is real, and one of the most important moral tasks of any human society is keeping straight *who* has authority to do *what* to influence people.

13. The subtle interplay between legitimacy and power emerged when some friends of a paralyzed lad brought him to Jesus for healing. Jesus sensed that the boy's friends believed in him. So, "when Jesus saw their faith, he said to the paralytic, 'Take heart, my son; your sins are forgiven' " (Matt. 9:2). We should not suppose that Jesus forgave the boy's sins as a reward for his friends' faith; in some way, their faith made it possible for him to forgive. But forgiving sins is not verifiable; how could anyone know that it had actually happened? The only thing people could know empirically was that Jesus *claimed* the right and the power to forgive. So he was challenged, and he responded by showing his verifiable power to heal: "But that you might know that the Son of Man has authority on earth to forgive sins," he said to the paralytic, "Rise, take up your bed and go home" (Matt. 9:8). This time his power to heal persuaded people that he was legitimate, that he had power from God and not from demons. He demonstrated that he had the authority all along; yet the people's faith was a needed means for its exercise.

14. Sennett, *op. cit.*, p. 197.

15. Erikson writes: "Mothers create a sense of trust in their children by that kind of administration which in its quality combines

sensitive care of the baby's individual needs and a firm sense of personal trustworthiness within the trusted framework of their culture's life style"; E. H. Erikson, *Childhood and Society* (New York: Norton, 1963), p. 249.

16. This is the underlying premise of Ivan Boszormenyi-Nagy and Geraldine Spark in their profound study of the family: "Loyalty commitments are like invisible but strong fibers which hold together complex pieces of relationship 'behavior' in families as well as in the larger society" (*op. cit.*, p. 39).

17. "God did not leave man alone in an unchartered, unstructured world; rather, he so structured the world by his creative word that man could know how to live. As a human community, the family is structurally anchored in the law-order of God and takes its place as one of the central 'rooms' in the creation"; James Olthuis, *I Pledge You My Troth* (New York: Harper, 1975), p. 78. This expresses a Protestant belief that God set within humanity a tendency to arrange life in certain orderly patterns, and that in these patterns there is a built-in hierarchy of authority. Readers of Bonhoeffer are sometimes surprised to discover that he strongly shared this belief, even though he disliked the notion that the tendency to order life was built into creation. The commandment of God, which was free and unpredictable in its concreteness, entered human life already arranged in its orders: "The commandment of God wishes to find man always in an earthly relation of authority, in a clearly defined order of superiority and inferiority" (Bonhoeffer, *Ethics,* p. 289). Calvin, of course, believed in the created order of family life: "nature itself" teaches us, he wrote, that there are "degrees of pre-eminence" in human communities, that "someone has been placed over us by the Lord's ordination . . ." (*Institutes,* II.viii.35). The upshot is that, in Protestant faith, there is a stubborn tendency to affirm that the family order is a product of divine intention for his creation, that the order is one in which parents are authorities over their children, and that this order can be recognized and respected by all people because it is embedded in their very nature. Karl Barth's fear that this belief is a compromise with Roman Catholic natural law is rather beside the point. It is more likely, in any case, that Protestant theologians cannot shake this belief because it makes as good sense to them as it has to Catholics.

18. Hauerwas, *The Community of Character,* p. 166.

19. *Ibid.*

20. Meissner writes: "The family is the matrix of authority out of which the roots of all authority spring. The psychological sense of this is basic. The child comes to the adult world with its more highly evolved and elaborate authority structure with a residue of attitudes and dispositions toward authorities which were acquired and honed in his childhood existence" (*op. cit.*, p. 82).

21. Nearly 40 years ago the U.S. Supreme Court said that "the right to practice religion freely does not include the liberty to expose . . . a child . . . to ill health or death. Parents may be free to become

martyrs themselves. But it does not follow they are free, in identical circumstances, to make martyrs of their children before they have reached the age of full and legal discretion when they can make that choice for themselves" (*Prince vs. Massachusetts,* 321 US 1944). In short, children's rights sometimes outweigh their obligation to follow their parents' leading, and sometimes society is justified in protecting their rights over against their parents' normal rights to use authority over their children. The court limited this to situations in which the child's health or life is jeopardized by the parents. The definition of "health" is not at all specific, and it may be that so indefinite a ground for injecting the state into family life provides government with a dangerously broad warrant for interfering with parental authority.

22. Barth argues that the sayings of Jesus "refer to specific situations in which there must be a clear and unconditional decision for Him and for the kingdom in the tension between the relationship to parents and relationship for himself" (*CD,* III/4, 262).

23. *Institutes,* II.viii.38.

24. In addition to studies already mentioned, the following are some contemporary studies of the family. Not all of them support my point of view, but all are helpful for an understanding of the modern family crisis: D. Blitsten, *The World of the Family* (New York: Random House, 1963); D. Cooper, *The Death of the Family* (New York: Pantheon, 1970); P. H. Glasser and Lois N. Glasser, *Families in Crisis* (New York: Harper, 1970); J. Piaget, *The Moral Development of the Child* (Glencoe, Ill.: Free Press, 1932); T. K. Rabb and R. I. Rotberg (eds.), *The Family in History* (New York: Harper, 1971); E. Shorter, *The Making of the Modern Family* (New York: Basic Books, 1975); L. Young, *Wednesday's Children: A Study of Child Neglect and Abuse* (New York: McGraw-Hill, 1964).

NOTES TO CHAPTER FIVE

1. Brevard Childs gives a handy survey of the textual arguments; *The Book of Exodus* (Philadelphia: Westminster, 1974), pp. 419ff. When you consider the textual arguments for "kill" or "murder," the case for "neither of them is completely beyond doubt," says Stamm, concluding that the matter is basically one for Christian ethics to resolve; *The Ten Commandments in Recent Research,* pp. 98ff.

2. The Sixth Commandment, Calvin writes, requires that "if we find anything of use to us in serving our neighbors' lives, faithfully to employ it; if there is anything that makes for their peace, to see to it; if anything harmful, to ward it off; if they are in danger, to lend a hand" (*Institutes,* II.viii.37). It was common sense which taught Calvin that the sparse negative implied this rich affirmative. If the command forbids A, it must require the opposite of A; and since helping someone live is the opposite of causing them to die, the command against killing must require that we help people live. It is the logic in Jesus' word that the whole law "hangs on" love.

3. Since a person's sacred right to live without assault from his neighbor is most deeply embedded in a relationship with God, we must face up to three issues. Here we can do little more than point to the tip of the theological iceberg.

If a person's sacredness depends on a relationship with God, what of these who do not believe in God? To put it as crudely as possible: do the damned have as much right to life as the saved? The answer to this must be clear: persons are in the image of God because God made them so, not because they *admit* to being God's image. Persons are sacred not because they love God but because God loves them. The universal human right to life derives not from belief that God is the Creator, but from the fact that God is Creator. Hence, the personhood of every man and woman, boy and girl, is sacred because God is related to every person on earth and all bear within them the reason why God forbids killing people. It is as wrong to kill an infidel as it is to kill a saint.

The second question is much more difficult, both to state and to answer it. Perhaps we can put it this way: is there something sacred about a person, as he lives and breathes in the company of men and women? Or is he sacred *only* in that God's love is set on him? Is a person's sacredness built-in or is his sacredness a kind of add-on because he walks in God's presence? A man married to a brilliant and famous woman could feel that he gets his own worth as a shadow trailing at the heels of his illustrious wife; but she loves him, so he swallows his pride and enjoys his borrowed dignity. Worried that mere human beings would claim a sacredness all their own, some theologians have allowed them only a borrowed dignity, what Helmut Thielicke calls an "alien dignity," not theirs at all, but God's, lent to them because he loves them. The image of God, writes Thielicke, "is not an attribute of man himself . . . but an attribute of the relationship in which he stands" (*Theological Ethics,* I, 180).

The notion of "alien dignity" raises doubts about what God actually made when he created human beings. Did he create real persons who were truly his image or not? When he looked on his male and female images and called them very good, was he seeing only a mirror of himself, or did he see real persons before him, different from himself, yet endowed with features that were (and are) God-like in their glory? It seems clear that God relates to human beings as he does because they are splendid creatures to be in relationship with. It is not as though they get only a borrowed splendor as shadows of God. God relates to a real being, the person walking and talking on earth, a little lower than the angels (Psalm 8), a marvelous creation, superb even in his fallen misery.

Of course, we exist as persons only through the love of God. And there is no way for any person to exist except in a relationship with God. We are always God-related beings, whether we enjoy the relationship or despise and deny it. So we do get our sacredness, in the deepest sense, from our being God's loved ones. But the fact is that God relates to a somebody, not a shadow; he loves someone

264 wonderful whom his love created. The Jesuit Josef Fuchs comes closer to truth than evangelical personalism does: "God's love creates its object—man. He is truly and in himself . . . the image of God's glory which God embraces in his love"; *Natural Law* (New York: Sheed and Ward, 1965), p. 63. On this basis, the Lord God declares to all human neighbors: You shall not kill this splendid personal creature of mine, my fallen image, my estranged partner, the one for whom my Son died.

The third question is this: if a person's holy right to live is finally rooted in God, can atheists recognize that right? Is the deepest reason for the commandment against killing hidden from the eyes of unbelievers? The issue here is not whether the track record of believers on respect for life has been noticeably better than that of unbelievers, but whether the person who denies God can share the believer's *reasons* for respecting human life.

One experience we all seem to have is a deep sense of our own right to life. I need no theological argument to bolster my belief that my neighbor ought not shoot me in cold blood; my unbelieving neighbor has the same strong sense about his own right to live. And ordinary unbelievers are usually ready to grant me a right to be left alone with my throat uncut. What, then, is the difference between my unbelieving friend's respect for my life and my respect for his? I suspect that the unbeliever sees signals of sacredness in every person; he has a feel for the mystery of a person, even though he does not have the faith to see its ground in God. "It is believed to be sacred not because . . . of a transcendent creator from whom life comes: It is believed to be sacred because it is life"; Edward Shills, cited by Daniel Callahan in *Abortion: Law, Choice, and Morality* (New York: Macmillan, 1970), p. 313. Thanks to the grace of God which has kept human life from losing all its self-evident sacredness, the unbeliever can share the believer's respect for persons' right to life. The unbeliever has, at least, a strong hunch that an ordinary person's life is sacred. The wonder is not so much that believers and unbelievers can share a respect; the wonder is that all of us violate it as often as we do.

4. *Institutes,* II.viii.37.

5. James Gustafson, *Theology and Christian Ethics* (Philadelphia: Pilgrim Press, 1974), p. 170.

6. These are Aquinas' summary judgments on the wrong of suicide (*Summa Theologica,* 2a, 2ae, quest. 64, art. 5). No one since has summed up the arguments any better. Karl Barth stressed that life is only ours on loan from God and that, for this reason, "He who takes what does not belong to him, in this case, only to throw it away, does not merely kill; he murders" (*CD,* III/4, 404). G. K. Chesterton probably used the harshest words anyone can speak against suicide: "Not only is suicide a sin, it is *the* sin. It is the ultimate and absolute evil, the refusal to take an interest in existence; the refusal to take an oath of loyalty to life"; *Orthodoxy* (New York: John Lane, 1908), pp. 131f. Immanuel Kant's objection to suicide left God out of the picture, and

focused on the person as a moral subject. Each of us is a creature of duty; to destroy the center of moral duty is to attack morality itself. And this is the sin of suicide. "To destroy the subject of morality in one's own person is to root out the existence of morality itself from the world . . ." (*The Doctrine of Virtue,* p. 85).

7. The Bible is remarkably indulgent with people who commit suicide. There are at least six stories of suicide, and the Bible writers judge none of them harshly: Abimelech (Judg. 9:50-54), Samson (Judg. 16:23-33), Saul (1 Sam. 31:2-5), Ahithophel (2 Sam. 17:23), Zimri (1 Kings 16:18f.), and Judas (Matt. 27:3-5). Perhaps we can read into these stories the underlying conviction that honor is more important morally than life itself. More likely, the Bible writer merely excuses the suicides because of extenuating circumstances.

8. F. Dostoevski, *The Possessed* (tr. by Constance Garnett) (New York: Modern Library, 1936), p. 628.

9. "Suicide is the ultimate and extreme self-justification of man as man . . . a man's attempt to give a final human meaning to life which has become humanly meaningless" (*Ethics,* p. 167).

10. The Heidelberg Catechism (Lord's Day 40), asking what the Sixth Commandment requires, says: "to show patience, peace, meekness, mercy, and all kindness toward [our neighbor], and prevent his hurt as much as in us lies." This surely applies to our suicidal neighbor as well.

11. *CD,* III/4, 375.

12. *Ibid.,* p. 378.

13. Some useful sources for further study of suicide are Doman Lum, *Responding to Suicidal Crisis* (Grand Rapids: Eerdmans, 1974); James Hillman, *Suicide and the Soul* (New York: Harper, 1965); Paul W. Pretzel, *Understanding and Counseling the Suicidal Person* (Nashville: Abingdon, 1972); Jacques Choron, *Suicide* (New York: Scribners, 1972); Earl A. Grollman, *Suicide* (Boston: Beacon, 1971).

14. People who advocate killing killers also argue that murderers should be destroyed precisely because of the law of the sanctity of life. The commandment against killing is, in effect, a commandment to kill killers. John Murray writes: "It is the sanctity of life that validates the death penalty for the crime of murder. . . . The deeper our regard for life the firmer will be our hold upon the penal sanction which the violation of that sanctity merits"; *Principles of Conduct* (Grand Rapids: Eerdmans, 1957), p. 122. Gordon Clark goes further: "Abolition of the death penalty presupposes the falsity of Christian principles." Clark believes that only an anti-Christian view of life can lead anyone to be against capital punishment; "Capital Punishment," in *Dictionary of Christian Ethics* (ed. Carl Henry) (Grand Rapids: Baker, 1973), p. 84. My starting point is obviously different. I begin with the same prejudice that the commandment compels Karl Barth to adopt when he writes: "On the basis of the command, capital punishment must always be rejected and opposed as the legally established institution of a stable and peaceful state" (*CD,* III/4, 437f.). We must begin by believing that the commandment is for life; capital punish-

ment is for death. Therefore, we must not *assume* that God permits it.

15. Christian teachers have tended to stress a government's duty to keep the lid on disorder. With some exceptions, like Lactantius and Tertullian, the Church Fathers tended to think that the government's calling included killing very disorderly people. Thomas Aquinas argued that "the common good is of greater value than the particular good of an individual." So if anyone was extremely "pestiferous" and "hinder[ed] the concord of human society" he was fair game for execution. Thomas never made it clear how "pestiferous" a person had to be in order to merit death, and he left his commentators to guess about it. What is clear is that Thomas did not think "Thou shalt not kill" was addressed to the executioners. Cf. Aquinas, *Summa Contra Gentiles,* III, c. 146, nn. 4, 5.

Luther and Calvin accepted capital punishment. Luther argued that killing killers was God's way of honoring the Sixth Commandment; he punished violators with his left arm, the state, and thereby showed how awful it was to kill people. Calvin was just a little more reluctant. God did give the sword to governments, and so he must have meant it to be used. On the other hand, the sort of situation that might call for execution seemed pretty wild; he talks about capital punishment for "abandoned men" wickedly ranging about "with slaughter and massacre" (*Institutes,* IV.xx.10)—which suggests that it was not meant to be a regular feature of society.

The Anabaptists were an exception to the prevailing view at the time of the Reformation. Suffering the deadly stings of official intolerance themselves, they saw the whole thing as an instance of governmental demonism. Some were only against killing Christian people, but most were against killing anyone at all. Cf. Ronald Knox, *Enthusiasm* (Oxford: Oxford U. P., 1950), p. 131.

16. According to Koestler, "the last recorded case [of capital punishment for animals] was the trial and execution of a dog for having participated in a robbery and murder in Delerent, Switzerland, 1906"; *Reflections on Hanging* (New York: Macmillan, 1957), pp. 65f.

17. Cf. E. B. Block, *And May God Have Mercy* (San Francisco: Fearon Press, 1962), pp. 18ff.

18. Koestler (*op. cit.,* p. 30) quotes from Sir Edward Coke (1552-1634), who defended the practice of drawing and quartering the condemned. Since God has condemned him, wrote the great jurist, and "since God made his head declining downward, and lying so near the ground as may be, being thought unfit to take the benefit of the common air. For which cause also he shall be strangled . . . between heaven and earth, as deemed unworthy of both. . . . Then he is to be cut down alive, and to have his privy parts cut off and burnt before his face as being . . . unfit to leave any generation after him. . . ."

19. The argument for self-defense is not quite the same as the argument for deterrence. We defend ourselves against sure or almost sure attack; our purpose is not to kill, but to defend ourselves. The

deterrence argument is that killing murderers will persuade others not to kill. We propose to kill the criminal as an object lesson. No one, to my knowledge, has ever shown conclusively that capital punishment is a deterrent, that fewer people are killed where the death sentence for murder is the rule. This is why I have not discussed deterrence here. Since the burden of proof is on anyone who intends to violate the commandment, it seems to me we need very persuasive evidence that capital punishment cuts the crime of murder down. We do not seem to have persuasive evidence; "statistical findings and case studies converge to disprove the claim that the death penalty has any special deterrent value"; Karl F. Schuessler, "The Deterrent Influence of the Death Penalty," *The Annals of the American Academy of Political and Social Science,* Vol. 284 (Nov. 1952), p. 62; cf. also John Pritchard, *A History of Capital Punishment* (New York: Citadel Press, 1960); David Bedau, *The Death Penalty in America* (Chicago: Aldine Publishing Company, 1969).

20. Pro-life crusaders always call the fetus a child or a baby; but these words stack the deck and eliminate all serious discussion of the issue. Others invent neutral words; Callahan calls it a "conceptus" and Nathanson calls it "Alpha." We could try to keep the technical distinction between the zygote (the single-celled fertile egg), the blastocyst (the organism of divided cells during the first two weeks), and the embryo (the sac of many cells, plus the amniotic covering). When the embryo begins to look like a human body, almost everybody calls it a fetus. Here I shall use the word "fetus" throughout, though once in a while, to point to its very early age, I use "zygote."

21. The staggering number of abortions worldwide (legal and illegal) was set at from 30 to 35 million in 1968 by K. H. Mehlan, "Die Abortsituation im Weltmaszstab," *Arzt und Familienplanung* (Berlin: VEB Verlag Volk und Gesundheit, 1968), p. 69. I am taking the reference from Daniel Callahan, *Abortion: Law, Choice and Morality,* p. 298.

22. We need not define personhood here. I mean only to appeal to the intuition that an individual human being is more than the biological support system that provides the conditions of life for him or her. It is the person, not the biological organism, that makes a claim on society for protection of its existence. We may not kill the biological organism as long as it is the base of individual personal life. The law protects the person. Jesus Christ died for the person. No matter how we finally describe the essential ingredients which lift a life into personhood, we must distinguish living person from bodily life. If we do not make this distinction, we run into conflict with both Christian piety and medical ethics.

23. Since "all that makes up the adult is present as the ovum and sperm are united," Schaeffer and Koop seem to take the view that abortion after conception is equivalent to infanticide; Francis Schaeffer and C. Everett Koop, *Whatever Happened to the Human Race?* (Old Tappan, N. J.: Revell, 1979), p. 41.

24. Paul Ramsey concludes from the genetics data: "Thus it might

be said that in all its essential respects the individual is whoever he is going to be from the moment of impregnation. He already is this while not knowing this or anything else. Thereafter, his subsequent development . . . can only be described as a process . . . of becoming the one he already is"; in John T. Noonan, Jr. (ed.), *The Morality of Abortion: Legal and Historical Perspectives* (Cambridge: Harvard U. P., 1970), pp. 66f.

25. Analytic philosopher Baruch Brody, an anti-abortionist, rejects the argument from genetics: "What the fetus has is the chromosomal mechanism by which the [individual's] properties are finally produced. . . . It does not follow that the fetus out of which A will develop is identical with A and, like A, is a human being. The argument from genetics will not do"; *Abortion and the Sanctity of Human Life* (Cambridge: MIT Press, 1975), p. 89. Daniel Callahan calls the genetic argument a "prohibitive jump" (*op. cit.*, p. 383).

26. Quoted by Callahan, *op. cit.*, p. 379.

27. Bernard Nathanson defends this point of view: "Biochemically, this is when alpha announces its presence as part of the human community by means of its hormonal messages, which we now have the technology to receive"; B. Nathanson and Richard Ostling, *Aborting America* (New York: Doubleday, 1979), p. 216.

28. *Ibid.*, p. 281.

29. Brody takes the position that the "property of having a functioning brain . . . is one that every human being must have because it is essential for its being human; by the time that an entity acquires that property, it has all the other properties that are essential for being human. . . . Therefore, when the fetus acquires that property it becomes a human being" (*op. cit.*, pp. 108f.).

30. I am not sure that any serious pro-abortionist expressly subscribes to the view that a fetus is not a person until birth, but the view follows necessarily from the position that abortion is a morally neutral affair.

31. A. Donagan, *The Theory of Morality,* p. 171.

32. *Ethics,* p. 176.

33. Daniel Callahan finally decides for a socially permissive position on abortion on the ground that we ought not outlaw practices which do not cause serious harm to society. So, "despite all the possible moral obligations to abortion, the social harm of permissive abortion laws has not been shown; there exists, then, no grounds for society to forbid abortion to those women who want them" (*op. cit.*, p. 478). Yet all the medical data that Callahan cites as to the status of a fetus at, say, six months, seem to clamor for attention as grounds for legal control of abortion at that stage.

34. For a more philosophical critique of the logic of the main freedom of abortion arguments, see Brody, *op. cit.,* pp. 42ff.

35. In the text I lump together several ways of causing people to die, but they are not all in fact the same. For instance, helping people to die and abandoning people to die are not quite the same as actually killing someone. You help someone to die when he wants to die and

cannot manage it by himself. Helping makes you a co-conspirator; you are like the lookout at a bank robbery. You do not do it, but it could not be done without you. A husband helps a very sick wife die if he buys the poison, puts it within her reach, and leaves the room. He causes her to die if he persuades her to take it or if he feeds it to her. The difference between causing and helping is so fluid that, for the time being, we can pit them together against merely letting someone die when you have the tools to keep him or her alive.

Is letting people die different from abandoning people? In times of scarcity, some Eskimo groups have abandoned their elderly people to the cruelties of subarctic cold. Other peoples have abandoned their baby girls to die. The so-called lifeboat ethic in which a rich civilization decides not to feed poor people lest we overload and sink earth's boat, is a form of mass abandonment. If we abandon people to die we leave them without normal protections against nature's abnormal cruelty; we force people to die before their time seems ripe. If we permit someone to die we let nature win its normal victory over mortal life. So there seems to be a crucial difference between abandoning people to die and letting people die and a crucial similarity between abandoning people and causing them to die.

36. Father Gerald Kelly offers this useful way of stating the difference between ordinary and extraordinary means: "Ordinary means are all medicines, treatments, and operations, which offer a reasonable hope of benefit, and which can be obtained and used without excessive expense, pain, or other inconvenience. Extraordinary means are all medicines, treatments, and operations, which cannot be obtained or used without excessive expense, pain, or other inconvenience, or which, if used, would not offer a reasonable hope of benefit"; "The Duty to Preserve Life," *Theological Studies* (Dec. 1951), p. 550; quoted by James Chaldress, *Priorities in Biomedical Ethics* (Philadelphia: Westminster, 1981), p. 41.

37. Richard A. McCormick, S.J., "To Save or Let Die: The Dilemma of Modern Medicine," *Journal of the American Medical Association,* Vol. 229, No. 2 (July 8, 1974), 172-76.

38. In stressing the patient's right to decide, I differ from Paul Ramsey, who believes that the weight of decision should rest with the pro-life-committed physician lest we lapse into an individualism that would leave every man to do whatever is right in his own eyes; *Ethics at the Edges of Life: Medical and Legal Intersections* (New Haven: Yale U. P., 1978), pp. 157ff. I agree with Robert Veatch who supports a patient-first viewpoint; *Death, Dying, and the Biological Revolution: Our Last Quest for Responsibility* (New Haven: Yale U. P., 1976), pp. 103ff.

39. The importance of trust to the healing community is made forcefully by James F. Chaldress, *op. cit.*

40. I did not think it possible in this chapter adequately to discuss the most crucial life and death moral issue of our day—nuclear war and nuclear armament. To mention only one reason: the argument against nuclear war is simple morality, while the question of nuclear

270   armaments is complex strategy. The moral argument against all-out nuclear war, it seems to me, is clear and unanswerable. The only justification for killing a human being is some immensely important benefit to other human beings. All-out nuclear war would leave precious few people to benefit, and nothing for them to benefit from. So, total nuclear war is clearly unjustifiable if only for this one reason. God will not approve of pushing the nuclear button, no matter who pushes it or for what reason.

But the second half of the issue is not as simple: What is the most promising strategy for making the holocaust least likely to happen? Where do the fewest risks lie? Is nuclear deterrence, with full intention to retaliate in kind, the best way to prevent anyone else from pushing the button? What is there to say for the nuclear bluff, the pretense of a deterrence that we resolve never, under any circumstances, to use? Or should we quit the arms race by ourselves, dismantle all our nuclear weapons and build no more, leaving others to decide for themselves whether to take advantage of our weakness? Or, should we combine the full intention to fire the shot—first shot or second, it does not matter, since we all die anyway—with a fanatic dedication to disarmament agreements with the Soviet Union? The question comes down to which strategy has the best odds for avoiding the ultimate showdown.

NOTES TO CHAPTER SIX

1. Cf. Stamm and Andrews, *op. cit.*, p. 110; G. von Rad, *Deuteronomy* (Philadelphia: Westminster, 1963), p. 59; R. Gordis, *Love and Sex: A Modern Jewish Perspective* (New York: Farrar, Straus, and Giroux, 1978), p. 179; J. L. Koole, *De Tien Geboden* (Baarn: Bosch & Keuning, 1964), p. 107.

2. Contrary to common opinion, the abused husband did not merely suffer property damage when his wife committed adultery. Abuse of a man's property rights may have been part of the picture, as G. von Rad notes in *Genesis* (Philadelphia: Westminster, 1949), p. 360; but if adultery involved only theft it could be compensated for by financial remuneration. What was probably more deeply involved was a husband's honor as lord of the family, and the wound he suffered was more like personal shame than property loss. As time went on, however, and mercy grew, a prophet named Hosea reached out in tender love to a wife who betrayed and shamed him. Flying in the face of his tradition, Hosea acted in "steadfast love" toward his errant wife, and stuck with her in reconciling devotion. As we learn, he was acting out an object lesson of Yahweh's own committed love for his adulterous people: "I will betroth thee unto me in faithfulness, and thou shalt know the Lord (Hos. 2:20).

3. Calvin, *Institutes,* II.viii.41.

4. The material in this section is borrowed heavily from my book, *Sex for Christians* (Grand Rapids: Eerdmans, 1975), Chapter 8.

5. Immanuel Kant, *The Doctrine of Virtue,* Part 1, Art. 2: "The

ground of proof, of course, is that man surrenders his personality (throwing it away) by using himself merely as a means to satisfy his animal instincts."

6. Aquinas, *Summa Theologica,* 11, 154, art. 11, ad 3.

7. If I understand him well, Joseph Fletcher's view of adultery is that it is usually wrong because, as much as we can tell, it tends to hurt people; but if it does not hurt anyone, it is not wrong. Cf. Fletcher, *Moral Responsibility* (Philadelphia: Westminster, 1967), pp. 125ff.

8. For a good discussion of the covenantal view of marriage, see James Olthuis, *I Pledge You My Troth,* pp. 19ff.

9. Dwight Small is right, I think: "Two human beings who have shared the sex act can no longer act toward one another as if they had not done so"; *Christians Celebrate Your Sexuality* (Old Tappan, N.J.: Revell, 1974), p. 175.

10. Paul Ramsey rightly refuses to cut the tie between sex and children: "To put radically asunder what God joined together in making love procreative . . . or to attempt to establish a relation of sexual love beyond the sphere of marriage means a refusal of the image of God's creation in our own"; "A Christian Approach to the Question of Sexual Relations Outside of Marriage," *The Journal of Religion,* XV:2 (Apr. 1965). Cf. *Sex for Christians,* pp. 219f.

11. Stanley Hauerwas talks provocatively about the "political significance" of sex and marriage. Sex is (among other things) meant to play a role in the ongoing history of the church as the people of God. Thus, he says, "the issue is . . . whether we have lived in a manner that allows us to bring a history with us that contributes to the common history we may be called upon to develop with one another" (*op. cit.,* p. 195). Hauerwas wants us to see our sexual lives within the setting of God's purpose for his family, the church, and for us as participants in this history.

12. There is no doubt that contemporary attitudes toward marriage are changing. Much of the mood today contradicts the covenantal view of marriage. But the crucial issue for us is whether these changing attitudes require a changed norm, whether feelings about marriage change the fundamental design for marriage. As titillating books like Gay Talese's *Thy Neighbor's Wife* (New York: Doubleday, 1980) tell us in endless detail, some people want to have marriages with open doors to many people's bedrooms. But the fact that contemporary culture can digest open marriages is no proof that marriages are meant to be sexually open. There is strong cultural evidence, in fact, that most people in all cultures still think of marriage—whether monogamous or polygamous—as stable and firm in this single point: there is a covenant between the partners to keep sex within the bonds of the partnership. Cf. Clellan S. Ford and Frank A. Beach, *Patterns of Sexual Behavior* (New York: Harper, 1951), p. 123. For a view that marriage has no ideal form and can become anything we want it to be, see Jessie Bernard, *The Future of Marriage* (New York: Bantam, 1973), pp. 301ff.

13. D. Bonhoeffer, *Ethics,* p. 281.

14. J. Fletcher, *Situation Ethics,* pp. 164ff.

15. Carl Rogers, *Becoming Partners* (New York: Delta, 1972), p. 214.

16. Nena O'Neil and George O'Neil, *Open Marriage* (New York: Avon, 1972), p. 253.

17. Gay Talese, *Thy Neighbor's Wife,* p. 352.

18. Cf. Robert S. Weiss, *Marital Separation* (New York: Harper, 1975), pp. 31-33.

19. It is utterly unlike Jesus to be so technical and, let it be said, unrealistic as to declare that adultery has such power that it can break a marriage in a single blow or that the non-adulterer is so innocent that only he or she may marry again without the guilt of adultery. In the grace of God, biblical scholars recognize other ways of interpreting Jesus' words in Matt. 19:9. Cf. David Atkinson, *To Have and to Hold* (Grand Rapids: Eerdmans, 1981), pp. 114ff.

20. To say that a marriage is created by two human wills is not a secular way to exile God from marriage. "What God hath joined . . ." is not a magic formula that makes God the sole creator of every single marriage. What an easy escape route from a miserable marriage this would be: "We are not really married because God did not 'join' us." The statement simply means that God ordained marriage and intends it always to be permanent.

21. A convincing exegetical argument for this interpretation is given by Atkinson, *op. cit.,* pp. 99ff.

22. Jesus' words about divorce and adultery are not the only biblical words that apply to remarriage. Paul too spoke directly and indirectly to the question. In his expectation of Jesus' return, he advised *all* single people to stay single for the time being, and this no doubt included divorced people (1 Cor. 7:7-9). He also told divorced people to stay single in case they might be reconciled to each other (1 Cor. 7:10b, 11a). But, in spite of his advice, he granted formerly married people permission to remarry: "Are you free from a wife? Do not seek remarriage. But if you marry, you do not sin, and if a girl marries she does not sin" (1 Cor. 7:27, 28).

NOTES TO CHAPTER SEVEN

1. "It is today regarded as certain that the prohibition of stealing referred originally to the kidnapping of a free person"; G. von Rad, *Deuteronomy,* p. 59.

2. Th. C. Vriezen, *Old Testament Theology,* p. 300.

3. If the "covet" commandment *is* the rule against stealing, it offers a special insight into the Old Testament sense of property. Among the "things" people ought not to covet were a neighbor's wife or servant. Wives and servants as property? The idea offends. Yet it may also suggest a deep sense of what property is. Consider this: property is what is proper to you. It is an extension of yourself. The

Old Testament herdsman saw his wife—as he saw his place, his land, his herd, and his people—as part of himself. He belonged to his animals and his land as truly as they belonged to him, and in this way he belonged to his wife. She was proper to him; he belonged to her and only thus was she his property.

4. For a survey of scholarly opinion on the Eighth and Tenth Commandments, see J. J. Stamm and M. E. Andrews, *The Ten Commandments in Recent Research,* pp. 101ff.

5. People do take vows of poverty, shedding things they need so that their spirits can be free. A monk does not diminish his humanity when he sacrifices his right to property. But we cannot think of the monk as a model of how to live with things—any more than we can take him as a paradigm of how the rest of us should deal with our sexuality. The monk had warm cassocks covering his body, plenty to eat, and roof over his head—for a lifetime, secure in the bosom of the church. He must not be compared with the unemployed man who cannot pay a month's rent, let alone scrape enough together for a down payment on a house of his own. Besides, the monk made a free choice to give up one dimension of his humanity, the easier to reach for a higher one. His vow of poverty is not a signal that property is an expendable luxury any more than his celibacy is a sign that sex doesn't matter much. He reminds us that making things our own is a partial dimension of personhood, and that the person who tries to find his wholeness only in things to own shrinks his soul. But the poverty that a monk freely chooses is the exception underscoring the rule that people need to own things precisely because they depend on them.

6. Gert thinks that stealing is wrong because, and only because, it violates the law. I have tried to find the reasons in a more humane setting. Cf. B. Gert, *The Moral Rules,* pp. 113, 114.

7. In Karachi, we are told, cities have "unauthorized zones." "Unauthorized" means that the city does not recognize the existence of people in that zone. As many as 400,000 poor people live in an unauthorized zone; but officially, not one of them exists. They are given none of the services that the city provides to others. They are cast out of the community—a tragic instance of how we are able to pretend that the poor do not exist.

8. Calvin, *Institutes,* II.viii.45. Calvin's theology of property never justified having whatever you happened to possess. What it came to was this: since you owe God for everything you have, you had better be generous to his children, the poor. "Let those, then, that have riches, whether they have been left by inheritance or procured by industry and efforts, consider that their abundance was not intended to be laid out in intemperance or excess, but in relieving the necessities of the brethren" (*Comm.* on 2 Cor. 8:15).

9. Aquinas, *Summa Theologica,* II-II, 66, 2 ad 1.

10. A man has owned his house for thirty years; it is almost paid for. He is poor, illiterate, and easily persuaded. A salesman comes to his door with an offer to improve his house with aluminum siding for

274 low monthly payments. The poor man signs a contract he cannot read; he takes its promises and demands on the word of the salesman. The contract stipulates that if the owner fails to make payments on time, the entire house becomes the possession of the contractor. But the contractor sells the contract to a third party who is unknown to the owner. The payments are late for two months. The poor man receives notice that his house is now owned by the stranger who bought the contract. The contract is legal. The new owner has legal title. But his moral right to the property is as suspect as the social conscience of the Mafia.

11. John Locke championed the thesis that if a person made a thing his own by working at it, reshaping it, putting his vision on it, he had a right to what he had made; *Two Treatises on Government* (Cambridge, 1967), p. 315. In his encyclical *Rerum Novarum,* Pope Leo XIII eloquently made creation a basis for ownership when he said man "makes his own that portion of nature's field which he cultivates—the portion on which he leaves . . . the impress of his individuality; and it cannot but be just that he should possess that portion as his very own, and have a right to hold it without anyone . . . violating that right."

12. Adam Smith, *The Wealth of Nations* (New York: Modern Library, 1937), pp. 699ff.

13. In the late 19th century, Abraham Kuyper surprised his contemporaries with this vision of turning owners into co-responsible owners; cf. *Christianity and the Class Struggle* (Grand Rapids: Eerdmans, 1950; originally published in 1891). See also Michael Fogarty, *Christian Democracy in Western Europe* (Notre Dame: Univ. of Notre Dame Press, 1957); P.C.J.M. Steenkamp, *De Gedachte der bedrijfsorganisatie in protestants-christelijke kring* (Kampen: Kok, 1951); John P. Windemuller, *Labor Relations in the Netherlands* (Ithaca: Cornell U. P., 1969).

14. A society may be viewed as an interlacing network of mini-communities, smaller circles of loyalty in which individuals are enabled to live and work together. Examples are the family, the school, the church, the labor union, and the factory, or commerce. A number of terms have been used to describe these mini-communities: classical Lutheran theologians spoke of "orders"; Kuyper called them social "spheres"; Peter Berger and Richard Neuhaus later coined the phrase "mediating structures." Whatever they are called, the mini-communities remind us that a society is more than just a collection of individuals; it is an organic combination of small communities.

15. From R. Meyer, "The Story of Michael," *Los Angeles Times,* Aug. 10, 1980.

NOTES TO CHAPTER EIGHT

1. Cambridge Survey Research, cited by Sissela Bok, *Lying* (New York: Vintage, 1979), p. xviii.

2. "The very stress on individualism, on competition, on achieving material success which so marks our society also generates intense pressure to cut corners. To win an election, to increase one's income, to outsell competitors—such motives impel many to participate in forms of duplicity they might otherwise resist" (*ibid.*, p. 258).

3. According to Stamm and Andrews, "It is quite clear to everyone who is acquainted with the original text that the ninth commandment refers exclusively to witness in the court of law, and not to lying in general as well. . . . The extension of the commandment to the sphere of lying must take place only secondarily. But here it may be done in good conscience . . . because false witness is an extreme particular case of lying" (*op. cit.*, p. 109); cf. G. von Rad, *Deuteronomy*, p. 59.

4. That superb actor Sir Laurence Olivier calls acting "a long game of pretense," so that "it's hard for a person like me to know if he's being honest. . . . When you think about it, what is acting but lying?" Quoted in the *Los Angeles Times*, Sunday, October 1980. The answer must be that acting is not lying, since it does not pretend to be anything other than pretense.

5. Immanuel Kant, "On a Supposed Right to Lie from Benevolent Motives," *The Critique of Practical Reason* (Chicago: Univ. of Chicago Press, 1949), pp. 346-50.

6. Augustine, "On Lying," *Treatises on Various Subjects,* XIV (New York: Catholic Univ. of America Press, 1952), 66.

7. Thomas Aquinas, *Summa Theologica,* 2, 2, quest. 110, art. 2.

8. *Comm.* on Josh. 2:4.

9. John Murray, *Principles of Conduct* (Grand Rapids: Eerdmans, 1957), pp. 142ff.

10. The notion that God cannot lie (Titus 1:2) seems to mean, for the neighbor, "You can trust him." In Heb. 6:13ff., the writer says that God (who cannot lie) actually took an oath, publicly, to signify his seriousness. The result? You can count on him, trust him, hope in him.

11. Hugo Grotius, the father of the modern just war theory, saw the chief evil of lying as its denial of the neighbor's right to "liberty of judgment." We owe people this liberty, the great jurist said, because without it they live with mirages instead of reality. Hugo Grotius, *On the Law of War and Peace* (New York: Bobbs-Merrill, 1925), Book 3, Chapter 1, xi.

12. In a letter in Max Lenz (ed.), *Briefwechsel mit Bucer,* Vol. 1, cited by Sissela Bok, *op. cit,*, p. 50.

13. Henry Sidgwick, *The Methods of Ethics* (London: Macmillan, 1970), p. 316.

14. *Ethics,* p. 367.

15. I am not counting game-playing deceits under harmless lies. In many games we must deceive in order to play. Every decent poker player wants to be deceived—within limits, of course. The game is ruined by too much honesty. What would happen to a football game if neither team tried to deceive the other into expecting an end run

276   when the pass was called for, or to baseball if the third base coach
never gave off false signals? Even flirtations need deceit; the two
persons giving signals must trust that neither means it if they are to
have a safe adventure. But games keep deception within the bounds
created by the rules of the game; no poker player is allowed an extra
ace.

16. J. Fletcher, *Situation Ethics,* p. 65.

17. Bok, *op. cit.*, p. 182.

18. Winston Churchill, *The Second World War: Closing the Ring*
(Boston: Houghton Mifflin, 1951), p. 383.

Subject Index

277

Name Index

Scripture Index